HAIKU

HAIKU

BY

R. H. BLYTH

IN FOUR VOLUMES

VOL. I

EASTERN CULTURE

HOKUSEIDO
1952

GRATEFULLY

DEDICATED

TO

SAKUO HASHIMOTO

THROUGH WHOSE PATRIOTIC GENEROSITY

THE PUBLICATION OF THESE VOLUMES

WAS MADE POSSIBLE

PREFACE

The history of mankind, as a history of the human spirit, may be thought of as consisting of two elements: an escape from this world to another; and a return to it. Chronologically speaking, these two movements, the rise and fall, represent the whole of human history; and the two take place microcosmically many times in peoples and nations. But they may be thought of as taking place simultaneously or rather, beyond time, and then they form an ontological description of human nature.

There seems to me no necessity, however, to make a Spenglerian attempt to show from historical examples how there has been a movement towards ideas, ideals, abstractions; and a corresponding revulsion fom them. In our own individual lives, and in the larger movements of the human spirit these two contradictory tendencies are more or less visible always, everywhere. There is a quite noticeable flow towards religion in the early world, and in the early life of almost every person,—and a later ebb from it, using the word "religion" here in the sense of a means of escape from this life.

The Japanese, by an accident of geography, and because of something in their national character, took part in the developments of this "return to nature," which in the Far East began (to give them a local habitation and a name)

i

with Enô, the 6th Chinese Patriarch of Zen, 637–713 A.D. The Chinese, again because of their geography perhaps, have always had a strong tendency in poetry and philosophy towards the vast and vague, the general and sententious. It was left, therefore, to the Japanese to undertake this " return to things " in haiku, but it must be clearly understood that what we return to is never the same as what we once left, for we have ourselves changed in the meantime. So we go back to the old savage animism, and superstition, and common life of man and spirits and trees and stones,—and yet there is a difference. Things have taken on something of the tenuous nature of the abstractions they turned into. Again, spring and autumn, for example, non-existant, arbitrary distinctions, have attained a body and palpability they never before had. We also, we are the things,—and yet we are ourselves, in a perpetual limbo of heaven and hell.

It was necessary for us to prostrate ourselves before the Buddha, to spend nine long years wall-gazing, to be born in the Western Paradise. But now, no more. Now we have to come back from Nirvana to this world, the only one. We have to live, not with Christ in glory, but with Jesus and his mother and father and brothers and sisters. We return to the friends of our childhood, the rain on the window-pane; the long silent roads of night; the waves of the shore that never cease to fall; the moon, so near and yet so far; all the sensations of texture, timbre, weight and shape, those precious treasures and inexhaustible riches of every-day life.

Haiku may well seem at first sight a poor substitute for the glowing visions of Heaven and Paradise seen of pale-lipped asceties. As Arnold says:

Long fed on boundless hopes, O race of man,
How angrily thou spurn'st all simpler fare!

Haiku have a simplicity that is deceptive both with regard
to their depth of content and to their origins, and it is the
aim of this and succeeding volumes to show that haiku require
our purest and most profound spiritual appreciation, for they
represent a whole world, the Eastern World, of religious and
poetic experience. Haiku is the final flower of all Eastern
culture; it is also a way of living.

Haiku are to be understood from the Zen point of view.
What this is may be gathered more of less directly from this
volume, and perfectly because indirectly from the verses
themselves.

We should mention that the word "Zen" is used in two
different ways and the reader must decide for himself which
is intended. Usually, throughout these volumes, it means
that state of mind in which we are not separated from other
things, are indeed identical with them, and yet retain our own
individuality and personal peculiarities. Occasionally, as in
the diagram on page 3, and in Part 2 of the first Section, it
means a body of experience and practice begun by Daruma,
(who came to China 520 A.D.) as the practical application to
living of Mahayana doctrines, and continued to the present day
in Zen temples and Zen books of instruction. "Haiku" also is
used in two different senses:—in the plural, meaning the poems
themselves; in the singular, signifying the poetical attitude of
mind of the haiku poets, their way of life, their "religion."

In Archer's *Faiths Men Live By*, there is a description
of the Polynesian *mana*, which has some approximation to
Zen its relation to poetry:

Mana is everywhere, intangible and all-pervasive as the ether. All things have it; rather, each separate thing is manaized, for *mana* is not a spiritual entity in a physical body; it is a dynamism which permeates, tones and colours the whole object. It is, for example, *of* the arrow, *of* the poison on the arrow-head; and that which kills is *not* the poison, the arrow, but *mana*. *Mana*, however, is not a universal something, a portion of which imbues each object,—for the primitive has not risen high enough to generalize a prime and universal reality. He acts in response to immediate, concrete situations and things—to objects *mana*-saturated, whether stream, stone, mountain, cloud, plant or animal. Furthermore, *mana* itself has no moral quality; rather, it may be good or bad, favourable or dangerous, according to the time or place; it may do good or evil, according to the agent's will. It is seen in operation when a man, attempting the strange and " impossible," succeeds.

Here we feel something of the intangibility, indefinability, non-thing-ness, non-abstractness, non-morality and non-rationality of Zen.

Yet we may say outright that haiku is haiku, with its own unwritten laws and standards, its aims and achievements. It has little or nothing to do with poetry, so-called, or Zen, or anything else. It belongs to a tradition of looking at things, a way of living, a certain tenderness and smallness of mind that avoids the magnificent, the infinite and the eternal. Its faults are a tendency towards weakness and sentiment. but it avoids lyricism and mind-colouring both instinctively and consciously.

If we say then that haiku is a form of Zen, we must not assert that haiku belongs to Zen, but that Zen belongs to haiku. In other words, our notions of Zen must be changed to fit haiku, not vice-versa. We may have a hard time showing how the ancient code of the samurai, the beatings of Zen masters, the absence of words, the philosophy of the *Kegon Sutra* are at bottom one with haiku; but it can be done.

The meaning of haiku, their directness, simplicity and unintellectuality, are not to be twisted in any way. I do not forget, then, Arnold's words in *Human Life:*

> Ah! let us make no claim
> On life's incognizable sea
> To too exact a steering of our way!

I understand Zen and poetry to be practically synonyms, but as I said before, if there is ever imagined to be any conflict between Zen and the poetry of haiku, the Zen goes overboard; poetry is the ultimate standard.

The life of haiku, the mood in which they are written and in which they are to be read, is the same as that of Rôshi, the same as that of the *Diamond Sutra* and the verses of the *Hekiganroku*. The difference is in the concreteness and abstractness respectively of their vision of reality. In haiku the intellectual element is absent, or is so completely fused with the intuitive-poetical that no analysis can separate them. To express it in other words, the Chinese philosophers stimulate through their intellectual "form" that "serene and blessed mood" which haiku poets arouse through their representation of the things of nature. These two groups correspond to the theoretical and practical aspects of the same nameless thing we call Life. They are not, however, consciously connected in the minds of the Japanese, to whom the comments on the poems in this book would seem not merely superfluous, but an attempt to separate inseparable elements, a dragging out into the light of reason of an organism that can live only in its own profound darkness,—indeed, a negation of the whole spirit of haiku.

We may say that to understand, to read properly a single haiku requires years of unconscious absorption of all the culture of India, China and Japan that comes to fulfilment in these small verses. To assist the non-Japanese reader, there is given this lengthy introduction with numerous quotations, and a commentary on each haiku in the succeeding volumes. But the average Japanese has not read the works of Rôshi, S shi, or the Zen masters. He would find the commentary stiff, over-intellectual, worse than unnecessary. He understands haiku without effort, by instinct, by the inherited intuition of centuries. In other words, the whole of the introduction and the commentaries should be in the memory, in the unconscious mind, not standing on the printed page between the reader and the verse.

There are, however, two excuses that can be made for the interpretations and quotations. The first is implied above, the difference of cultural background, of *weltanschauung*. The second is that haiku is not only poetry, that is, a representation in words of the real world; it is a way of life, a mode of living all day long; it is religion, and as such, has its bearings upon social life, politics, war, all our business and bosoms. Poetry, culture, religion, are a *manner* of living, and this manner, like ordinary manners, is to a certain extent a matter of education, of thought and ideas, of habit and imitation.·

Every haiku, then, in so far as it is representative of a way of life, manner of living daily, is unwittingly didactic, teaches us above our will. The great danger is mistaking the explanation for the poetry, the pointing finger for the moon, the sermon for reality. The aim of the explanation, like that of the pointing finger and the scriptures, is to make itself unnecessary. Once more we come to a fact through a paradox, that the indispensable must be got rid of in order that the truth may emerge.

Haiku record what Wordsworth calls those "spots of time," those moments which for some quite mysterious reason have a peculiar significance. There is a unique quality about the poet's state of feeling on these occasions; it may be very deep, it may be rather shallow, but there is a "something" about the external things, a "something" about the inner mind which is unmistakable. Where haiku poets excel all others is in recognizing this "something" in the most unlikely places and at the most unexpected times. It belongs to what Pater calls, in speaking of Wordsworth,

the quiet habitual observation of inanimate or imperfectly animate existence.

Haiku is a kind of *satori*, or enlightenment, in which we see into the life of things.

We grasp the inexpressible meaning of some quite ordinary thing or fact hitherto entirely overlooked. Haiku is the apprehension of a thing by a realization of our own orginal and

essential unity with it, the word "realization" having the
literal meaning here of "making real" in ourselves. The
thing perceives itself in us; we perceive it by simple self-
consciousness. The joy of the (apparent) re-union of ourselves
with things, with all things, is thus the happiness of being
our true selves. It is with "all things" because, as Dr.
Suzuki explains in his works on Zen, when one thing is taken
up, all things are taken up with it. One flower is the
spring; a falling leaf has the whole of autumn, of every
autumn, of the eternal, the timeless autumn of each thing and
of all things.

Haiku is the creation of things that already exist in their
own right, but need the poet so that they may "come to the
full stature of a man." These "things" may be in the form
of moonlight, with a no-stone and a barking dog included in it;

犬を打つ石のさてなし冬の月   太 祇

Not a single stone
To throw at the dog, ,—
The wintry moon!   Taigi

It may be the chirping of a cicada and the silence that
interpenetrates the sound, as the sound does the rock:

閑さや岩にしみ入る蟬の聲   芭 蕉

The silence!
The voice of the cicada
Penetrates the rocks.   Bashô

It may be the shortness of a night or the length of a day:

砂濱に足跡長き春の日かな   子 規

On the sandy beach,
Footprints:
Long is the spring day.   Shiki

Historically speaking, haiku is the flower of all the pre-Buddhist religious speculation, Mahayana Buddhism, Chinese and Japanese Zen, Taoism and Confucianism. The Upanishads say,

> That from whence these things are born, that by which when born, they live, that into which at their death they re-enter, try to know that. That is Brahman.   *Taitt. Up.* 111. i.

Mahayana Buddhism says,

差別即平等、平等即差別。

Difference is identity; identity is difference.

Taoism has,

故有之以爲利無之以爲用。   孝子、十一。

Therefore from what exists we have profit, and from what does not exist, utility.

Zen says,

儞有柱杖子我與儞柱杖子、
儞無柱杖子我奪儞柱杖子。   無門關、四十四。

If you have a stick, I will give you it.
If you have no stick, I will take it away from you.

Tôju Nakae, 藤樹中江, 1608–1648, the famous Japanese Confucianist, the first to teach the philosophy of Oyômei, 王陽明, said,

> Heaven and earth and all things exist in my mind ……There is no difference between life and death, being and non-being……The real nature of man's mind is delight.

Bashô, born four years before the death of Tôju Nakae, received all this, adding to it the poetry of the Tang and

Sung. Blending Indian spirituality, Chinese practicality, with Japanese simplicity, we get:

落ざまに水こぼしけり花椿　　　芭蕉

> A flower of the camellia-tree
>
> Fell,
>
> Spilling its water.　　　Bashô

曙や麥の葉末の春の霜　　　鬼貫

> The dawn of day:
>
> On the tip of the barley-leaf
>
> The frost of spring.　　　Onitsura

牛もうもうもうと霧から出たりけり

　　　一茶

> The cow comes
>
> Moo! Moo!
>
> Out of the mist.　　　Issa

Haiku does not, like waka, aim at beauty. Like the music of Bach, it aims at significance, and some special kind of beauty is found hovering near. The real nature of each thing, and more so, of all things, is a poetical one. It is because Christ was a poet that men followed and still follow him, not Socrates. Socrates showed us our ignorance. Haiku shows us what we knew all the time, but did not know we knew: it shows us that we are poets in so far as we live at all. Here again is the connection between Zen and haiku, Zen which says,

平常心是道。　　　無門關、十九。

> Your ordinary mind, —that is the Way!

The essential simplicity of haiku and Zen must never be forgotten. The sun shines, snow falls, mountains rise and

valleys sink, night deepens and pales into day, but it is only
very seldom that we attend to such things.

繪草紙に鎮置く店の春の風   几 董

In the shop,
The paper-weights on the picture-books:
The spring wind !   Kitô

When we are grasping the inexpressible meaning of these
things, this is life, this is living. To do this twenty-four hours
a day is the Way of Haiku. It is having life more abundantly.

We may note in passing that Japanese readers will all
have slightly different translations and meanings to give
most of these verses. This is both the power and the weakness of haiku. It is a weakness in that we are not quite
sure of the meaning of the writer. It is a power in that
haiku demand the *free* poetic life of the reader in parallel
with that of the poet. This "freedom" is not that of wild
irresponsibility and arbitrary interpretation, but that of
the creation of a similar poetic experience to which the
haiku points. It corresponds very much in English poetry
to the different, the very different way in which people read
the same poem. In the interpretation of music, conductors
vary greatly in emphasis and tempo. There are cases on
record where a conductor has for example greatly increased
the tempo of a movment, with the astonished approval of
the composer (Beethoven).

It may be interesting in this connection to compare two
different translations and commentaries on the same verse,
made by the author at an interval of a few months. Even
to the spelling of the word veranda(h), everything is seen

differently. The second is perhaps better than the first, in that there is less psychology and more poetry in it.

(i)　二文なげて寺の椽かる涼みかな　　子 規

> Throwing in a halfpenny,
> I borrowed the temple veranda,
> In the evening cool.　　　Shiki

This kind of verse comes from Issa. It has his innocence, and delicacy of feeling, combined with a faint self-mockery. Shiki goes to the temple (Sumadera), throws in two copper coins, bows, then sits on the temple veranda and enjoys the evening breeze.

Sensitive people, that is, morally sensitive people, know that they have no rights, no right to anything at all, even to life itself. And it is human nature to require some kind of justification for our possession or use of things. This justification, a kind of psychological " rationalization," it seen in the two coins that Shiki throws into the money-box of the temple. After that, he sits on the veranda with some kind of complacency, feeling that he has done something, however little, to earn the pleasure of the cool evening breeze in such a calm and holy place.

(ii)　二文なげて寺の椽かる涼み哉　　子 規

> Throwing in a couple of coins,
> I cooled myself
> On the temple verandah.　　　Shiki

This was written at the Temple of Sumadera, 須磨寺. The interesting thing in this verse is to perceive the secret poetic life that lives in such a commonplace. The poetry is in the words of the verse; not in something implied, not in associations or overtones of meaning. The poet climbs the steps of the temple, takes out two copper coins from his purse, and throws them into the offertory box. He bows before the Buddha, and his devotions thus finished, sits on the long, broad, shining verandah. But the rattle of the coins, the smell of the incense, the remote calm of the Buddhas is still with him as he sits in the cool, shady breeze. The poetry is in the sphere where the tinkling of the metal on the wood of the great box, and the coolness of the gusty wind, are perceived by the same spiritual organ.

In addition to the haiku described above, we must note also that some poets have availed themselves of the haiku form to express thoughts and ideas of predominantly intellectual import. We have in English much didactic poetry that has great value; this value is not a poetical one, but indirectly it may give assistance to our poetical understanding of life, by removing errors of thought that come from custom, self-interest, or excessive abstraction.

Haiku, and not haiku alone, but the whole of Japanese art and literature are aimed at the same infinity as that of the western world of the last five centuries, but not through space, not through the horizon. It is the infinite grasped in the hand, before the eyes, in the hammering of a nail, the touch of cold water, the smell of chrysanthemums, the smell of *this* chrysanthemum. Haiku are thus an expression of the union of those two forms of living which Spengler regarded as irreconcilable and mutually ununderstandable, the Classical feeling of the present moment, of restricted space, and the Modern European feeling of eternity, infinity. It is this latter which Matthew Arnold perhaps refers to when he says,

> In many respects, the ancients are far above us, and yet there is something that we demand which they can never give.

Those who are interested in the subject should read Miyamori's *An Anthology of Haiku, Ancient and Modern,* and better still, Henderson's *The Bamboo Broom, An Introduction to Japanese Haiku.*

Of the great number of Japanese books that I referred to while writing this and the succeeding volumes, hardly any escaped the air-raids, but from memory or from new buyings, I give a list in Appendix 1.

A Romanized version of the haiku contained in this volume is given in Appendix 2. In the other volumes, the Romanised version will be given immediately under each haiku.

The illustrations in this volume, all explained in Section I, page 81 ff., have been chosen to show how the Japanese poets and artists gradually " toned down " the mysticism and realism of the Chinese artists to the delicate humour and tender crudeness of haiga.

R. H. Blyth,

Tôkyô,

January 1947.

CONTENTS

TABLE OF ILLUSTRATIONS

xvii

TABLE OF ILLUSTRATIONS

SECTION I

THE SPIRITUAL ORIGINS
OF HAIKU

To be explained in the present volume, is the historical development of the Zen state of mind into the creation of haiku by Bashô and his followers. We can trace it from its origins in pre-buddhistic thought in India, through Chinese culture, into the Japanese world-view and the poetic expression of it.

The aim of this first section is to give what may be called the background of all oriental culture; but this theatrical or pictorial metaphor is misleading, because mechanical. In haiku, all those deep thoughts and experiences of the Indian, Chinese, and Japanese races, rooted in the dark backward and abysm of time, here show their small, tender, flower-like faces with that faint, secret smile that instantly attests their heavenly origin and nature. We ourselves are to pass through all those phases once more until we can say of these verses, with Masefield,

> Spring in my heart agen
> That I may flower to men.

We do not wish to insist upon the thought that Zen is that alone which is common to haiku, the poetry of English literature, the mysticism of Sôshi (Chuang Tse), the lofty moral flights of Confucius; for when we do this, even within our own breast arises the feeling that things are after all not the same; each thing is itself and nothing else.

二もとの梅に遅速を愛す哉　　　蕪 村

> The two plum trees;
> I love their blooming,
> One early, one later.   Buson

And when we assert the separateness of things, the mind swings back insensibly but inevitably to the other extreme of identity and sameness. This law is the profoundest realm of our mental universe. It belongs to the inherent, original, *intrinsic* inexplicability of everything.

The accompanying diagram represents the various streams of thought-feeling. The relation of oriental thought to haiku will be treated under these.

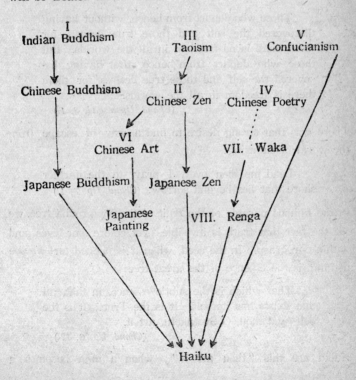

I
Buddhism

We must go back to pre-buddhistic Indian thought if we are to see the beginnings (as far as they are known) of what ultimately became the simple directness and instantaneous perception of haiku.

In the earliest times there was a realization that the secret of life is in the understanding of what the self is:

> Those who depart from hence, without having discovered the self and those true desires, for them there is no freedom in all the worlds. But those who depart from hence, after having discovered the self and those true desires, for them there is freedom in all the worlds.
>
> *(Chand. Upanishad, 8, 1.)*

There was that strong desire to find a way of escape from the world of suffering:

> Lead me then over, I pray, to the farther shore that lies beyond sorrow. *(Chand. Up. 7, 1.)*

In the famous parable of the fruit of the Nyagrodha tree, we see the fact that truth is invisible,—yet before our eyes and within our grasp. In the seed, when it is opened and we see nothing, is the essence of the great tree:

> That which is the subtle essence, in that, all that exists has its self. It is the True. It is the Self, and thou, O Svetaketu, art it.
>
> *(Chand. Up. 6, 12.)*

Haiku are this "thou art it"; when a man becomes a

Plate 1

Dainichi Nyorai   (Kamakura Period)

bamboo grove swaying in the windy rain, a cicada crying itself and its life away, then he is " it ".

> That from whence these things are born, that by which when born, they live, that into which at death they re-enter try to know that. That is Brahman. *(Taitt. Up. 3, 1.)*

The effect of Indian-Chinese-Japanese Buddhism of a general kind upon the life and thought of the Japanese people, and therefore upon haiku, may be treated of under two headings: (a) Popular ideas (b) Philosophical ideas.

(a) Life is sorrow and suffering. There is more than a tinge of this in Bashô and Issa; but Buson and Shiki, in their objectivity, feel the meaningfulness of things more deeply than their evanescence. The morning-dew nature of all things, even of the universe itself, may arouse grief; it may also be seen, or overlooked, as the inevitable element in all change and variety. In Buddhism, ignorance is the great evil of the world, rather than moral wickedness. The great problem of practical, everyday life is thus to see things properly, not to valuate them in some hard and fast moral scale of virtue and vice, use and uselessness, but to take them without sentimental or intellectual prejudice.

The polytheism of the ordinary Japanese, like that of the Greeks, had a great effect upon their mode of poetical life. The gods are many: Amaterasu, Miroku, Hachiman, Jizô, Amida, Dainichi Nyorai, Tenjin, Kwannon, Emma O, Shaka-muni, Benten, and a hundred others.

But these gods are not far from us, either in place or in rank. There is also no clear-cut distinctinction between human and sub-human. The scale of beings in the Buddhist

universe puts man midway. The primitive animistic ideas of
the Japanese fall in with the Buddhist system, and all are
united by the theory of transmigration. The result is (or is
it the cause?) that our sympathies are widened in both
directions:

留守の間にあれたる神の落葉かな　　芭蕉

> The god is absent;
> Dead leaves are piling
> And all is deserted.　　Bashô

さまづけに育てられたる蠶かな　　一茶

> Bringing up the silkworms,
> They call them
> " Mister."[1]　　Issa

(b) The Mahayana doctrine of the identity of difference,
or indifference of opposites, is one that sets apart Buddhism
and Christianity as nothing else does. This distinction explains how deeply connected Buddhist experience and Oriental
poetry are, and why Christianity has been inimical or indifferent to such poets (as poets) as Wordsworth, Coleridge,
Chaucer, Blake, Shelley. Paradox is the soul of religion, as
it is of poetry, but where it is not recognized, or where it is
anathematized, religion and poetry dwindle into dogma and
sentimentality respectively.

Again, the Mahayana teaching of the equivalence of the
phenomenal and the noumenal worlds offers to the Oriental
mind that strange fusion of spirituality and practicality which
is the most striking characteristic of Chinese art and Japanese
haiku. It is this world, yet it is not this world. It does not

---

[1] The word *sama* implies not only respect, but a gentle, pious
feeling towards the silkworms.

hint at another world than this, an absolute; it is this everyday world seen for the first time as it really is, a playground of Buddhas.

Buddhism is in a sense pantheistic, especially in the teaching of the Tendai and Shingon Sects, but the all which is one is not thought of as a person but, as something which is neither personal nor impersonal. The same is true of Amida in the Shin and Jôdô sects. Amida is only personalized for the sake of speech or conception; in actual fact he represents some ultimate. In the literal sense of the words, "God is love."

The doctrine that all things, even the inanimate, have the Buddha-nature, has far-reaching consequences. While the no-soul teaching of primitive Buddhism tends to efface the idea of a water-tight separate individuality of things, including ourselves, the belief that everything will one day attain Buddhahood gives value (gives equal value) to the most trivial objects, and lays a foundation for a spiritual and practical democracy that Christianity as such could never afford.

"Are ye not of greater value than many sparrows?"

The answer is "No".

The following are verses by Bashô in which the Buddhistic element is obvious:

白魚や黒き眼をあく法の網

The whitebait
Opens its black eyes
In the net of the Law.

たこ壺やはかなき夢を夏の月

> The octopuses in the jars:
> Transient dreams
> Under the summer moon.

もろもろの心柳にまかすべし

> Yield to the willow
> All the loathing, all the desire
> Of your heart.

蓮池や折らでそのまゝ玉まつり

> The lotuses in the pond,
> Just as they are, unplucked:
> The Festival of the Dead.

秋のいろ糠味噌壺もなかりけり

> Signs of autumn;
> I have no pot
> Of rice-bran mash.

We may mention here one of Bashô's pupils, Sonojo, 園女, 1649–1723. She earned her living as an eye-doctor. After her husband died, she went to Edo, where she is buried. In later life she shaved her head and studied Buddhism. In a letter to the priest Unko, 雲虎, she writes:

不求眞不求妄は大道の根源.....柳は綠花は紅ぬ
唯其儘にして常に句を云ひ歌を綴て遊び申候事
に候.....我平日の行は念佛と句と歌となり。極
樂へ行くはよし、地獄へ落るは目出たし。

> Not to seek for the Truth, not to seek error,—
> this is the fundamental of the Great Way......The
> willow is green, the flower is red; just as things
> are, haiku and waka must be composed....... My
> days are passed in the saying of the Nenbutsu,

the making of haiku and waka. Going to Paradise is good, and to fall into Hell also is a matter of congratulation.

誰か見ん誰か知るべき有にもあらず
　　　無きにもあらぬ法のともしび

Who can see it?
Who can have knowledge of it?
　　It is not in " that which is ",
Nor " that which is not ",—
This Light of the Law!

Her death verse, a waka, is in the true Buddhist, and one may say, Japanese spirit:

秋の月春の曙みし空は
　　　夢かうつゝか南無阿彌陀佛

The skies seen in the dawn of spring,
　　　Seen with the moon of autumn,—
Were they real? Were they a dream?
Namuamidabutsu!

All that is, all that seems to be, the past and the present and the future, the discovered and the created worlds,—we are to live in them and by them and for them, self-less, with desireless desire. This is Namuamidabutsu, and the reality or unreality of it all is to be the least of our concerns. It may be a dream from which we never wake; perhaps life is real, life is earnest; but the answer to every question must always be, " Namuamidabutsu! "

II
Zen

Zen is the putting into practice, the realizing (making real) of Mahayana Buddhism in daily life. A learned monk must show his "learning" when a robber threatens him, when he is being cheered by ten thousand people, when he is caught in a sudden downpour of rain, when he has to wait hours for a bus. At the same time, in the same action, and in the same state of mind, there is no robber, no rain, no waiting; nothing is shown, and there is no one to show anything. That is to say, on the one hand Zen is severely practical, on the other hand wildly idealistic and suprarational; and yet it is only a man writing words on paper, or a mother giving her child the breast.

And what has this to do with haiku? We shall see. In the next few pages, some of the short passages collected in the *Zenrinkushu* are translated. This anthology was compiled by Eichô, 東陽英朝, who died in 1574, a disciple of 雪江, Seccô of Myôshinji. The items are what are known as agyo, 下語, or chakugo, 著語, collected by Eichô from about two hundred books, including various Zen writings, e.g. *The Hekiganroku, Mumonkan, Shinjinmei;* the Sutras; *The Analects, The Great Learning, The Doctrine of the Mean; Mencius; The Odes; Laotse, Chuangtse;* the poetry of Kanzan, Tôenmei, Tôhô, Ritaihaku, Hakurakuten; the *Tôshisen.*

They were used, and still are, by monks studying Zen in the monasteries, who select the passage which seems to them to solve the problem they are given by the master. A glance at the following will show a deep relation between them and haiku. In particular we may note:

破鏡不重照
落花難上枝

The broken mirror will not again reflect;
Fallen flowers will hardly rise up to the branch.

Compare this to Moritake's verse:

落花枝に歸ると見れば胡蝶かな

A fallen flower
Returning to the branch?
It was a butterfly.

Moritake, 1472–1549, was a high priest of the Great Ise Shrine; it is quite probable that his verse was for him an original one. Take again the following:

春來遊寺客
花落閉門僧

When spring comes. many visiters enjoy themselves at the temple;
When the flowers fall, only the monk who shuts
the gate is left.

The origin of this is unknown, but we may compare it with the following verses;

花散つて又しづかなり圓城寺　　　　鬼 貫

The cherry blossoms having fallen,
Enjôji Temple
Is quiet once more.　　　　Onitsura[1]

花散るや伽藍の樞落しゆく　　　　凡 兆

[1] *1660–1783.*

The flowers are falling;
He shuts the great temple gate,
And departs.　　　　　　　Bonchô[1]

花散りて木の間の寺となりにけり　　蕪村

The cherry blossoms having fallen,
The temple
　　　Through the branches.　　　Buson[2]

Compare also:

不知何處寺、風送鐘聲來

I know not from what temple
The wind brings the voice of the bell.

花の雲鐘は上野か淺草か　　　　　芭蕉

A cloud of cherry blossoms:
The bell,—is it Ueno?
Is it Asakusa?　　　　　　　Bashô

In the following selection, seventy three out of about four thousand, we can see the Zen view of the world on its way through poetry to haiku.

芭蕉葉上無愁雨
只是時人聽斷腸

The raindrops patter on the bashô leaf, but these are not tears of grief;
This is only the anguish of him who is listening to them.

溪聲便是廣長舌
山色豈非清淨身

The voice of the mountain torrent is from one great tongue;

[1] d. 1714.
[2] 1715-1783.

The lines of the hills, are they not the Pure Body
of Buddha?

如刀能割不自割
如眼能看不自看

It[1] is like a sword that wounds, but cannot wound
itself;
Like an eye that sees, but cannot see itself.

語不令人會
須得人譯之

Words do not make a man understand;
You must get the man, to understand them.

蹈破太虛空
鐵牛也汗出

To be able to trample upon the Great Void,
The iron cow must sweat.

似虎多雙角
如牛缺尾巴

It[2] is like a tiger, but with many horns;
Like a cow, but it has no tail.

相見呵呵笑
園林落葉多

Meeting, the two friends laugh aloud;
In the grove, fallen leaves are many.

黃昏雞報曉
半夜日頭明

The cock announces the dawn in the evening;
The sun is bright at midnight.

泉聲中夜後
山色夕陽時

[1] Life.
[2] Truth.

The voice of the fountain after midnight;
The colours of the hills at sunsetting.

樹密猿聲響
波澄雁影深

The cries of the monkeys echo through the dense
    forest;
In the clear water, the wild geese are mirrored
    deep.

木雞鳴子夜
芻狗吠天明

The wooden cock crows at midnight;
The straw dog barks at the clear sky.

山河並大地
全露法王身

Mountains and rivers, the whole earth,—
All manifest forth the essence of being.

風定花猶落
鳥鳴山更幽

The wind drops, but the flowers still fall;
A bird sings, and the mountain holds yet more
    mystery.

有水皆含月
無山不帶雲

All waters contain the moon;
Not a mountain but the clouds girdle it.

入林不動草
入水不立波

Entering the forest, he[1] does not disturb a blade
    of grass;
Entering the water he does not cause a ripple.

---

[1] The poet.

一句定乾坤
一劍平天下

One word[1] determines the whole world;
One sword pacifies heaven and earth.

梅瘦占春少
庭寬得月多

The plum tree, dwindling, contains less of the
spring;
But the garden is wider, and holds more of the
moon.

樹呈風體態
波弄月精神

The tree manifests the bodily power of the wind;
The wave exhibits the spiritual nature of the
moon.

出門逢釋迦
入門逢彌勒

Go out, and you meet Shakamuni;
Go home, and you meet Miroku Buddha.

古今無二路
達者共同途

From of old there were not two paths;
"Those who have arrived" all walked the same
road.

汲水疑山動
揚帆覺岸行

Draw water, and you think the mountains are
moving;
Raise the sail, and you think the cliffs are on the
run.

---

[1] For example, of Christ.

虛空無背面
鳥道絕束西

In the vast inane there is no back or front;
The path of the bird annihilates East and West.

只見錐頭利
不知鑿頭方

Only seeing the sharpness of the awl;
Not knowing the squareness of the stone-chisel.

佛此夜滅度
如薪盡火滅

This night the Buddha entered Nirvana;
It was like firewood burned utterly away.

一葉一釋迦
一鬚一彌勒

One leaf, a Shakamuni;
One hair, a Miroku.

護生須是殺
殺盡始安居

To preserve life, it must be destroyed;
When it is completely destroyed, for the first
　time there is rest.

雨中看果日
火裏酌清泉

Perceiving the sun in the midst of the rain;
Ladling out clear water from the depths of the
　fire.

懷洲牛喫禾
益州馬腸張

When a cow of Kaishû eats mulberry leaves,
The belly of a horse in Ekishû is distended.

袖中日月藏
掌內握乾坤

To have the sun and moon in one's sleeve;
To hold the universe in the palm of one's hand.

不向自己會
向什麼處會

If you do not get it from yourself,
Where will you go for it?

牛飲水成乳
蛇飲水成毒

The water a cow drinks turns to milk;
The water a snake drinks turns to poison.

叮嚀損君德
無言固有功

Many words injure virtue;
Wordlessness is essentially effective.

欄干雖共倚
山色看不同

Though we lean together upon the same balus-
trade,
The colours of the mountain are not the same.

善哉觀世音
全身入荒草

How good it is that the Whole Body
Of Kwannon enters into the wild grasses!

拈起一莖草
作丈六金身

Taking up one blade of grass,
Use it as a sixteen-foot golden Buddha.

青山自青山
白雲自白雲

The blue hills are of themselves blue hills;
The white clouds are of themselves white clouds.

不讀東魯書
爭會西來意

If you have not read the *Analects*,
How can you know the meaning of Zen?

移花兼蝶到
達磨道不知

Planting flowers to which the butterflies come,
Daruma says, "I know not."

火不待日熱
風不待月涼

Heat does not wait for the sun, to be hot,
Nor wind the moon, to be cool.

法法不穩藏
古今常顯露

Nothing whatever is hidden;
From of old, all is clear as daylight.

古松談般若
幽鳥弄眞如

The old pine-tree speaks divine wisdom;
The secret bird manifests eternal truth.

有眼不會見
有耳不會聞

Seeing, they see not;
Hearing, they hear not.

一點梅花蘂
三千世界香

Just one pistil of the plum flower,—
And the three thousand worlds are fragrant.

雲門棒頭短
藥山柺柄長

Unmon's' staff is too short;
Yakusan's[2] baton is too long.

人々脚痕下
有一坐具地

Every man has beneath his feet,
Ground enough to do Zazen on.

不是打殺人
被人打殺必

If you do not kill him,
You will be killed by him.

欲問花來處
東君亦不知

You may wish to ask where the flowers come
from,
But even Tokun[3] does not know.

路逢達道人
不將語默對

If you meet an enlightened man in the street,
Do not greet him with words, nor with silence.

是非交結處
聖亦不能知

Where the interplay of "is" and "is not" is
fixed,
Not even the sages can know.

---

[1] Died 996; famous for use of staff in teaching Zen.
[2] 751–834; also famous for use of stick.
[3] The god of spring.

前水復後水
古今相續流

The water before, and the water after,
Now and forever flowing, follow each other.

文章千古事
得失寸心知

What is written is of ages long ago,
But the heart knows all the gain and loss.

更無尋覓處
鳥跡印空中

There is no place to seek the mind;
It is like the footprints of the birds in the sky.

兀然無事坐
春來草自生

Sitting quietly doing nothing,
Spring comes, grass grows of itself.

上無瓦蓋頭
下無寸土立足

Above, not a piece of tile to cover the head;
Beneath, not an inch of earth to put one's foot on.

口欲談而辭喪
心欲緣而慮亡

The mouth desires to speak, but the words disappear;
The heart desires to associate itself, but the thoughts fade away.

要知山上路
須是去來人

If you wish to know the road up the mountain,
You must ask the man who goes back and forth
on it.

只可空諸所有
又莫實諸所無

Simply you must empty " is " of meaning,
And not take " is not " as real.

一塵飛而翳天
一芥墮而覆地

One mote flying up dims the sky;
One speck of dust covers the earth.

爭如著衣喫飲
此外更無佛祖

Is there anything to compare with wearing of
clothes and eating of food?
Beyond this there is no Buddha or Bodhisattva.

識得本心本性
正是宗門大病

To know the original Mind, the essential Nature,
This is the great disease of (our) religion.

如來正法眼藏
大似兩鏡相照

The Tathagata's True-Law Eye-Treasury,—
It is just like two mirrors reflecting each other.

不可以有心得
不可以無心求

It cannot be attained by mind;
It is not to be sought after through mindlessness.

不可以語言造
不可以寂默通

It cannot be created by speech;
It cannot be penetrated by silence.

雁無遺蹤之意
水無沉影之心

The geese do not wish to leave their reflection
  behind;
The water has no mind to retain their image.

落霞與孤鶩齋飛
秋水其長天一色

Falling mist flies together with the wild ducks;
The waters of autumn are of one colour with
  the sky.

老樹臥波寒影動
野烟浮草夕陽昏

The old tree leans over the waves, its cold image
  swaying;
Mist hovers above the grass, the evening sun
  fading.

不信只看八九月
紛紛黃葉滿山川

If you do not believe, look at September, look at
  October,
How the yellow leaves fall, and fill mountain and
  river.

落木千山天遠大
澄江一道月分明

Above the bare boughs of a thousand hills, a vast,
  distant sky;
Over the path of the river, a radiant moon.

拋出輪王三寸鐵
方知遍界是刀錎

When Buddha thrust out his three inches of iron[1],
Then for the first time were known the swords
   and spears of the world.

到得歸來無別事
廬山烟雨浙江潮

I went there and came back; it was nothing
   special[2]:
Mount Ro wreathed in mist; Sekkô at high tide.

Bashô and Zen

Before we speak of Bashô and Zen, we may refer to
the relation of renga[3] and Zen. Many of the masters of
renga were monks, some of them of the Zen sect. Among
them may be mentioned Musô Kokushi, 1271–1346, founder
of Tenryûji Temple, which became the headquarters of the
Rinzai branch of Zen. Several others were the pupils of
Ikkyû, 1394–1481; among them is said to have been Sôkan,
宗鑑, 1458–1546, one of the greatest masters of haikai. Sôin,
宗因, 1604–82, founder of Danrin School of haiku, also was
a student of Buddhism, and received the tonsure at the hands
of Houn Zenji of Fukushûji Temple, at the age of sixty four.

庭前に白く咲たる椿哉

In the garden
The camellia is blooming
Whitely.

---

[1] His tongue. Compare, " I came not to bring peace but a
   sword."
[2] Poetry, like Zen, is nothing out the way.
[3] The form of verse from which haiku developed. See page 130.

It is said that Onitsura, the great contemporary of Bashô, composed this in reply to a question of a Zen Master, Kudô, who asked what his haikai was. (空道和尚いかなる是汝が俳諧 といはれしに卽答). This is of course a kind of imitation of the 37th Case of the *Mumonkan:*

> 趙州因僧問
> 　　如何是祖師西來意。 州云、庭前柏樹子。

Jôshû was once asked by a monk,
　　"What is the meaning of Daruma's coming
　　　from the West?" (that is, the essence of Budd-
　　　hism).
Jôshû answered,
　　' The magnolia tree in the garden."

There seems to be other indirect but satisfactory evidence of Onitsura's concern with Zen.

Bashô's direct contact with Zen was through Bucchô, 佛頂, the abbot of Konponji Temple, 根本寺, and the best way for us to get an idea of the relation between disciple and master is to read what Bashô wrote, when he visited the temple after Bucchô's death, in *Oku no Hosomichi:*

> 木啄も庵はやぶらず夏木立
> 　　　　Even the woodpecker
> 　　Will not harm this hermitage
> 　　　　Among the summer trees.

Bucchô was one of Bashô's teachers of Zen when the former was residing in Edo. The above verse was composed at the temple of Unganji, 雲岸寺, which is near Kurobane, 黒羽. He afterwards became the chief monk of Konponji, in Kashima, 鹿島. The passage in *Oku no Hosomichi* in which the poem occurs is as follows:

當國雲岸寺のおくに佛頂和尚山居の跡あり。

　　たてよこの五尺にたらぬ草の庵
　　　　むすぶもくやし雨なかりせば

と松の炭して書付け侍るといつぞや聞へ給ふ。
其の跡見んと雲岸寺に杖を曳けば、人々すゝん
で共にいざなひ、若き人おほく道のほどうちさ
わぎて、おぼへず彼の麓にいたる。山は奥ある
けしきにて、谷道はるかに松杉黒く、苔したゝ
りて卯月の天今なほ寒し。十景盡くる所橋を渡
つて山門に入る。さてかの跡はいづくのほどに
やと、後の山によぢのぼれば、石上の小庵岩窟
に結びかけたり。妙禪師の死因、法雲法師の石
室を見るが如し。

　　木啄も庵は破らず夏木立

と、とりあへぬ一句を柱に残し侍りし。

　　In this region, behind Unganji Temple, deep
in the mountains, is to be found Buccho's hermitage.

> Less than five foot square,
> My thatched cottage;
> It is a nuisance
> To have to build even this,
> But the rain......

He told me once that he had written this here
with pine charcoal. Wishing to see the ruins, I
went to the temple. Some people, most of them
young men, came and offered to guide us. Making
a great noise, before we knew it we reached the
foot of the mountain, which was sequestered,
and the valley path distant among pine trees and
cryptomerias. Water dripping through the moss,
it was cold even now, in the Fourth Month,

After seeing the Ten Views, we crossed the bridge and entered the Great Gate of the temple. But where were the ruins of Bucchô's hermitage? Climbing up the mountain behind the temple, we found a small hut on a rock before a cave. I felt as if looking at Genmyô's[1] Death Gate or Hôun's[1] Stone Room. I wrote this verse on the spot, and left it on the pillar of the hut.

The verse is an expression of Bashô's own feeling of reverence for his dead teacher. Even the woodpecker has not harmed the wooden posts of the hut in this lonely spot, far from the haunts of men.

Some of Bashô's verses which have the " flavour of Zen," 禪味, to a noticeable degree:

咲きみだす桃の中より初櫻
> From among the peach-trees
> Blooming everywhere,
> The first cherry blossoms.

鐘消えて花の香は撞く夕べかな
> The sound fades,
> The scent of the flowers arises,—
> The bell struck in the evening.

原中や物にも着かず鳴くひばり
> In the midst of the plain
> Sings the skylark,
> Free of all things.

庭掃いて雪を忘るゝ箒かな

[1] Both Chinese monks.

Plate 2

Morning Glories   Bashô

Sweeping the garden,
The snow is forgotten
By the broom.

山も庭もうごき入るゝや夏ざしき

The mountains and garden also move;
The summer drawing-room
Includes them.

Bashô's disciples were naturally affected by the master's deep interest in Zen. It is said that when Kikaku was 13 years old, in 1674, he became a pupil of Bashô. He learned medicine, Confucianism, the *Book of Changes*, (from which he took his name) calligraphy, painting, Chinese poetry, haikai, and it seems he probably studied Zen to some extent, but it must be said that he had no idea of its real meaning. On the one hand he shows a kind of native freedom; he is not tied to any form of religious attitude. On the other hand, his depth is as it were accidental and fitful, and he easily degenerates into the puns and witticisms from which Bashô had delivered haiku.

Ransetsu, 嵐雪, studied Zen under Saiun, 濟雲, of Edo. His death poem is:

一葉ちる咄一はちるかぜの上

A paulownia leaf falls;
Totsu ! a single leaf falls,
Borne on the wind.

Totsu is a Zen exclamation, expressive of grumbling, of anger. It has the same meaning as *kwatsu*, 喝. This death-verse is worthy of a Zen adept. It is said that his name, Ransetsu, " Storm-Snow ", was taken from a Mondô, or question and answer, between himself and his teacher Saiun, who asked, "What is there when the snow covers a thousand mountains?"

雪千山を埋めて什麼

He answered "A single peak is not white."

孤峰不白

From this also is said to have come his name *Fuhakken*, "Not white eaves", 不白軒, but all this is highly doubtful.

The disciple of Bashô who had the deepest understanding of Zen was Jôsô, 丈草, 1661–1704. He studied under Gyokudô, 玉堂, of Senseiji Temple, of the Obaku branch of Zen, in his youth. He learned from him to write Chinese poems, and wrote a great number with a Zen meaning. His haiku also have the flavour that is imperceptibly unmistakable, for example:

水底の岩におちつく木の葉かな

> Leaves,
> Fallen on a rock
> Beneath the water.

野も山も雪にとられてなにもなし

> Fields and mountains,—
> All taken by the snow;
> Nothing remains.

水底を見て來た顔の小鴨かな

> The teal
> Looks as if to say,
> "I've been to the bottom!"

Ryôta, 蓼太, 1707–1787, a pupil of Ritô, 吏登, 1680–1754, also a pupil of Ransetsu, after interviewing Hakuin, visited

Tôrei, 東嶺, at Ryutakuji, 龍澤寺, who composed a haiku and
gave it to him:

飛込んだ力でうかぶ蛙かな

The frog
Rises up by the same force
With which it jumps in.

We have an example here of Zen (teaching) which is not
haiku. Haiku is in no sense of the word didactic. If it is,
like poetry, " a criticism of life," this word " criticism " must
itself be understood in a poetical and not philosophical or
psychological or analytic sense.

III
Taoism

Taoism, as represented by Laotse (Rôshi) and Chuangtse (Sôshi) reached Japan partly directly, and partly through Chinese poetry. Directly, perhaps, the influence was restricted, for Sôshi especially is very difficult in the original, though not in the English translation. The relation of Taoism to Zen is far from easy to make out. They may have originated together in the Chinese mind; Zen may be the practical application of Taoist ideals, grafted on to the Buddhist tree of religion. The orthodox history of Zen tells as that there was an unbroken succession of Zen patriarchs from Shakamuni through Daruma to the Chinese Zen masters. All this is of doubtful historicity, and somewhat improbable-sounding. However, the important thing for haiku is those ideas, those essays of the soul which have been conveyed to Japan from those old Chinese mystics. The following are characteristic passages from, first Rôshi, then Sôshi:

RÔSHI

道中而用之、或不盈。淵乎似萬物之宗。
　　　　　　　　　　　　　　　（第四章）

The Way is an unfillable emptiness, a bottom-less gulf, that is the origin of everything in the world.

天地不仁、以萬物爲芻狗。
聖人不仁、以百性爲芻狗。　　（第五章）

Heaven and Earth are ruthless; they deal with things as straw dogs. The sages are ruth-less; they deal with people as straw dogs.

上善若水。 水善利萬物而不爭。
處衆人所惡、 故幾於道。 (第八章)

The Great Good is like unto water, water that
serves all things without strife. It is where men
dislike to be (in the lowest place.) This is why
it is near the Way.

希言自然。 故飄風不終朝。 驟雨不終日。
孰爲此者。 天地。 天地尚不能久而況於人
乎。 (第二十三章)

To be of few words is to follow nature. A
tempest does not blow all the morning, neither
does a storm of rain fall the whole day. Who is
its cause? Heaven and Earth. And if Heaven and
Earth do not keep it up so long, much less should
man.

知人者智、 自知者明。 (第三十三章)

He who knows others has knowledge. He who
knows himself is illuminated.

反者道之動、 弱者道之用、 天地萬物生於
有、 有生於無。 (第四十章)

Returning (to Nature) is the activity of the
Way. Weakness is the using of the Way. All things
in Heaven and Earth spring from Existence, but
existence springs from Non-existence.

爲學日益、 爲道日損、 損之又損
以至於無、 無爲而無不爲。 (第四十八章)

Learning is adding something every day. Following the Way is taking something away every
day, taking away, taking away, until Inactivity
is reached, that Inactivity which is All-activity.

知者不言、 言者不知。 (第五十六章)

Those who know, speak not. Those who speak, know not.

聖人欲不欲、不貴難得之貨。(第六十四章)

The wise man wants things unwanted (by others); he does not prize things difficult to get.

信言不美、美言不信、善者不辯、
辯者不善、知者不博、博者不知。
(第八十一章)

Truth is not pleasant to hear. Pleasant-sounding words are not true. Good men do not argue. Argumentative men are not good. He who knows is not learned. The learned man does not know.

而後眼如耳、耳如鼻、鼻如口。

From now on, my eyes were one with my ears, my ears with my nose, my nose with my mouth.

Rishi, 2, 3.

Compare this with Rôshi, 56:

塞其戶、閉其門、挫其銳、解其紛、
和其光、同其塵、是謂玄同。

Shutting the door (of his mouth) closing the portals (of sight and sound), blunting sharpness, unraveling complications, tempering brightness, smoothing out the dust (of discrimination)—this is the mysterious levelling.

This is the region of such haiku as the following,—but **not** only of these:

海くれて鴨の聲ほのかにしろし　　　芭蕉

The sea darkens:
Voices of the wild ducks
Are faintly white.　　　　Bashô

SÔSHI

惠子謂、莊子曰、吾有大樹。人謂之樗其
大本擁腫、而不中繩墨、其小枝卷曲。而
不中規矩、立之塗。匠者不顧、今子之言。
大而無用。衆所同去也。莊子曰、……今子
有大樹、患其無用、何不樹之於無何有之
鄉、廣莫之野、彷徨乎無爲其側。逍遙乎
寢臥其下。不夭斤斧。物無害者。無所可
用。安所困苦哉。　　　　　(內篇逍遙遊第一)

Keishi said to Sôshi " I have a great tree called
' The Pride of India '. Its trunk is so twisted
and bulbous, a chalk-line[1] is useless. The branches
are so contorted that the compass and setsquare
can do nothing. It stands at the roadside, but
carpenters do not so much as glance at it. In
the same way, Sir, your words are big and useless, and people are indifferent to them." Sôshi
replied " ……Sir, you are grieved at the uselessness of your great tree; why not plant it in the
Region of Non-being, the Domain of the infinitely
Vast, wander beside it in a state of non-action,
slumber peacefully[2] reclined beneath its shade?
It would not then be hurt of the axe; nothing
could injure it. There being no way to use it,
how should it suffer harm?"

唯達者知通爲一。爲是不用、而寓諸庸。
　　　　　　　　　　　(齊物論第二)

Only " he who has arrived " knows and understands that all things are One. He does not take
himself as separate from things, but identifies

---

[1] For marking out lengths of timber.
[2] The title of the chapter, " Peaceful Pleasure ", comes from
this phrase.

himself with them in their essential activity.

夫大道不稱、大辯不言、大仁不仁、
大廉不嗛、大勇不忮。　　　　　　　（第二）

The great Way does not express itself; perfect
eloquence does not speak; absolute justice is not
disinterested; complete valour is not courageous.

注焉而不滿。酌焉而不竭。而不知其所由
來、此之謂葆光。　　　　　　　　　（第二）

However much we pour in, never to brim over;
to ladle out, never exhausting; moreover, not to
know the reason for it,—this is called the Hidden
Light.

上徵武士、則支離攘臂於其間。上有大役、
則支離以有常疾不受功、上與病者粟、則
受三鍾與十束薪、夫支離其形者、猶足以
養其身、終其天年、又況支離其德者乎。
　　　　　　　　　（內篇、人間性、第四）

When people were being called up by the au-
thorities, the hunchback stood swaggering among
them (taking 鬨＝間). When the order came for
public works, the hunchback, since he was a
hopeless cripple, was not set to work. When the
government distributed grain to the sick, he
received three *shô*, and ten bundles of firewood.
If then a hunchback, by reason of his bodily mal-
formation, is able to nourish himself and live to
the end of his allotted days, how much more
profitable is it to be a *moral* hunchback !

若然者、其心志、其容寂、其顙頯。淒然
似秋、煖然似春、喜怒通四時、與物有宜、
而莫知其極。故聖人之用兵也。亡國而不
失人心。利澤施乎萬世、不爲愛人。故樂
通物非聖人也。有親非仁也。　　（第六）

Such a man (a Real Man) is unaffected by circumstances, his demeanour is full of repose, his (facial) expression undemonstrative. His coolness is that of autumn, his warmth that of spring. His emotions follow their natural course like the round of the four seasons. His harmony with natural things is beyond all human estimate. So when the wise man uses the army in such a way as to ruin the country, he does not lose the love of that people. If he bestows his benevolence on this and succeeding generations, it is not for love of the people. Thus it is not the part of a sage to make other beings happy. Being fond of things,—this is not universal Love.

夫藏舟於壑、藏山於澤、謂之固矣。然而
夜半有力者負之而走。昧者不知也。藏小
大有宜、猶有所遯。若夫藏天下於天下、
而不得所遯。是恆物之大情也。　　(第六)

A boat hidden in a creek, or ("a hilly island hidden")[1] in a marsh,—these are called safe. Even so, something strong may bear them away at midnight. Men in their delusion do not realize this. The hiding of small things in large ones is all right, but they may be lost. If on the other hand you hide the universe in the universe itself, there is no place where it can be lost. This is the Great-Nature of all things.

俄而子來有病喘喘然將死、其妻子環而泣
之。子犁往問之曰、叱避。無怛化。倚其
戶與之語曰、偉哉造化。又將奚以汝爲、
將奚以汝適、以汝爲鼠肝乎。以汝爲蟲臂

---

[1] We may omit this altogether and take 有力者 as a man; or take 山 as a hill (island) and 有力者 as a force greater than man, i.e. Nature.

乎。子來曰、父母於子、東西南北唯之命
從、陰陽於人、不翅於父母、彼近吾死、
而我不聽、我則悍矣。彼何罪焉。夫大塊
載我以形、勞我以生佚我以老息我以死。

(第六)

Shirai became suddenly ill, gasping and on
the point of death. His wife and children stood
weeping around him. Shiri went there and called
out to them, "Shoo! be off with you; do not
thwart this change of his!" Then leaning against
the door (post) he said, "Wonderful indeed is the
Creator! What will he make of you now? Will
you be the liver of a rat, or the elbows of a
worm?" Shiri replied, "A child must go obedi-
ently East, West, South. North, according as his
parents tell him. In and Yô[1] are not merely a
man's mother and father. When they bring me
close to death, and I oppose them, I am rebellious
and unruly; they are blameless. Great Nature,
by bestowing upon me (human) form gives me
a place (in the world;) by life, enables me to
work; by old age, contentment; by death, cessation of existence."

孔子曰、魚相造乎水、人相造乎道。相造
乎水者穿池而養給、相造乎道者、無事而
生定。故曰、魚相忘乎江湖、人相忘乎道
術。

(第六)

Confucius said, "Fish are made for water,
men for the Way. Those who live in water, give
themselves wholly to ponds and are nourished
therein; those who live in the Way, live at rest,
a life of certitude. And so it is said, 'Fish are

---

[1] Ying and Yang, the negative and positive powers of Nature.

unconscious of rivers and lakes; men never think
of the Way, and how to walk in it'".

Before we speak of the influence of Rôshi and Sôshi upon
Bashô, we may mention what Sôin[1] wrote upon a portrait of
Sôshi; in part:

莊周が文章にならひ、
　　守武が餘風を仰がざらんや・

Do we not model ourselves upon the writings
of Sôshi, and revere the influence of Moritake?[2]

It ends with the verse:

世の中や蝶々とまれかくもあれ
The world
Is after all as the butterfly,
However it may be.

This of course refers to what is perhaps the best known
passage from Sôshi:

不知周之夢爲胡蝶與、胡蝶之夢爲周與。

Am I a man who dreamed of being a butterfly,
or am I a butterfly dreaming myself to be a man?

This was the origin of many haiku concerning butterflies, for
it involves their identification with the poet in that light and
dreamy way that is both part of the nature of the insect and
of the poet.

The poet who most strongly insisted on the fact that "the
writings of Sôshi are haikai", was Okanishi Ichû, 岡西惟中,
died 1692, a disciple of Sôin. In one of his works, 俳諧蒙求,
Haikai Môkyu, there occurs the following passage:

[1] Founder of the Danrin School of haiku; 1604–82.
[2] 1472–1549.

北の海に鯤と言魚有り、其の魚の大さ幾
千里と云ふ事をしらず、此鳥海の動く時
北より南の海へうつらんとす。水に羽う
つ事三千里、風に乗てのぼる事九萬里と
書けり、是則心の天遊變化自然の大自在
底なり。しかれば今する俳諧も、方寸の
胸中より顯れ出て、天地の外に打むかひ
自由變化の趣向をおもひめぐらし、有事
ない事とり合て活法自在の句體を誠の俳
諧と知るべし。
山にかけり野に遊びて、花をめで、紅葉
にあとがるゝ折ふしごとに、此心をもて
作する事是俳諧の直逍遊ならずや。

In the Northern Ocean there is a fish called
the Kon, I know not how many *ri* in size. When
the sea is moved, it prepares to depart to the
Southern Ocean. It flaps its wings on the water
for 3,000 *ri*. It ascends on a whirlwind 90,000 *ri*.[1]
This is the mind in its heavenly sporting, its
transformations and natural freedom. But haikai
also appearing out from a breast of a few inches
square and beholding what is beyond heaven and
earth, ponders over and forms its idea of free
change. Bringing together what is and what is
not, we get a verse of living freedom. This is
real haikai.

Wandering over the mountains, playing in the
fields, admiring the cherry blossoms, yearning
over the crimson leaves of autumn,—whenever
we do these things, is not our state of mind that
of "Enjoyment in Untroubled Ease"?

During the period covered by Bashô's life, Confucian studies

[1] These five lines are the beginning of Sôshi.

flourished greatly,[1] and Sôshi and Rôshi were read together with Confucius and Mencius as a matter of course, their books and commentaries on them being published during this time. It is said that Bashô himself studied the Chinese Classics, and especially Sôshi and Rôshi, under Tanaka Dôkô, 田中桐江, 1668–1742, but his dates hardly agree with those of Bashô, 1644–1694.

It should be mentioned that at this time it was common to apply the word *gugen*, 寓言, allegory, to Sôshi's thought, and to haikai also. This has a relation to the allegorizing of the Teitoku school of haikai.

Bashô's acquaintance with Sôshi is difficult to judge, but there is no doubt that the thought and mood of the Chinese "philospher" was extremely akin to his own character. The number of quotations and references to Sôshi is comparatively large. Those to Rôshi are few, partly because he is rather more political in application, and partly because he has not the lofty flights of fancy that characterize Sôshi.

In Kikaku's 田舍の句合, *Inaka no Kuawase*, 1680, it is said that Bashô took the name of 栩々齊, Kukusai. Previously he had assumed the pen name of Tôsei, 桃靑, Green Peach, in admiration of Ritaihaku, whose name means White Damson, 李白. The name Kukusai, "Flying about", is taken from the celebrated passage of Sôshi at the end of Chapter 2, *The Adjustment of Controversies*, alluded to before:

> 昔者莊周夢爲胡蝶。栩栩然胡蝶也。自喻
> 適志與不知周也。俄然覺、則蘧蘧然周也。
> 不知周之夢爲胡蝶與。胡蝶之夢爲周與。

[1] See page 66.

Formerly, I dreamed I was a butterfly *flying about* enjoying itself. I did not know I was Sôshi. Suddenly I awoke and was Sôshi again. I did not know whether it was Sôshi dreaming that he was a butterfly, or a butterfly now dreaming it was Sôshi.

In the same *Inaka no Kuawase* we find the following verses by Yajin, the comments being by Bashô:

壁の麥葎千年をわらふとかや　　野　人

壁に生る麥は朝薗の晦朔をしらす冥靈大
　　　椿を論ずるに似たり。

> The barley by the wall
> Laughs, it may be,
>   At the goose-grass's thousand years.

The barley by the wall is like the mushroom that knows nothing of the first of the month or the last day, like the tortoise that speaks of the Great Camellia Tree.

These two comparisons come from the first chapter of Sôshi.

凩となりぬ蝸牛の空せ貝　　　　野　人

> The storm has come:
> The empty shell
>   Of a snail.

蝸牛のうつせ貝もさびたり。されどもか
れが角の上にあらそはんときは、右いさ
ゝかまさりなんや。

This "empty shell of a snail" has *sabi*. But would it not be better to have them fight on the horns?

This comes from Sôshi, Chapter 25, in which Keishi introduces
Taishinjin to the king; Taishinjin tells him of the two horns
of a snail. On one horn there is a kingdom called Provocation,
and on the other a kingdom called Stupidity. These are
always fighting, causing misery and death among their inhabitants. Sôshi is of course pointing out the relativity of
things.

In addition to these examples of Bashô's comments on
haiku, we may give a few from Bashô's own compositions.
In the *Nozarashi Kikô*, 1684:

> 二上山當麻寺に詣で庭上の松を見るに凡
> そ千とせも經たるならん、大いさ牛を隱
> すとも云ふべけん。かれ非常といへども
> 佛緣にひかれて斧斤の罪をまぬかれたる
> ぞ幸にして尊とし

> 僧あさがほいく死にかへる法の松

I visited Tômaji Temple at Mt. Futakami.
In the garden I saw a pine tree; it must have
been about a thousand years old, big enough to
hide an ox, one may say. Insentient though it
was, by its karma relation to the Buddha, it had
avoided the sin of the axe, and this was both
fortunate and praiseworthy.

> The monk,—a morning-glory,
> Dying again and again;
> This pine-tree,—the Buddhist Law!

This reference to the ox comes from the fourth book of Sôshi:

> 匠石之齊至於曲轅見櫟社樹。
> 其大蔽牛。

A master-carpenter Seki, on his way to Sai,
came to Kyokuen, and saw a tree, sacred to the

spirits of the land. It was big enough to hide an
ox.

Sôshi is bent on showing the uselessness of this great
tree, from whose branches even a boat could be hollowed
out. Bashô is looking at it as a tree, lovingly and with awe,
but he also wishes to have Sôshi's peculiar flavour of spiritual
thought, the Chinese "local colour". He brings him in almost
as a habit. In the *Oi no Kobumi*, 1687, we read:

かの三月の糧をあつむるに力を入れず。

> I did not try very hard to collect provisions for
> those three months.

This comes from the first chapter of Sôshi:

適千里者三月聚糧

> He who goes a thousand *ri* will have to carry
> with him provisions for three months.

There are some haiku of Bashô which are connected in
some way with Sôshi, for example:

もろこしの俳諧とはん飛ぶ小蝶

> I will ask,
> Concerning the haikai of China,
> This fluttering butterfly.

This has the proscript 荘子畫贊, "Written on a picture of
Sôshi." The "butterfly" refers of course, to Sôshi's allegory
given above. The same relation is seen in:

君や蝶我や荘子の夢とゝろ

> You are the butterfly,
> And I the dreaming heart
> Of Sôshi?

起きよ起きよ我友にせんぬる胡蝶

Arise, arise,
And be my companion,
Sleeping butterfly!

Bashô says, in the *Genjuan Diary*, 幻住庵記:

畫はまれまれとぶらふ人々に心を動かし、
あるは宮守の翁、里のをのこども入り來
りて、ゐのしゝの稻くひあらし、兎の豆
畑に通ふなど我が聞きしらぬ農談、日旣
に山の端にかゝれば、夜座靜に月を待ち
ては影を伴ひ、燈を取りては岡兩に是非
をこらす。

In the day-time, my mind is once in a while
stimulated by people who call on me. Sometimes
the old shrine-keeper, sometimes the young men
of the village come in and tell how wild boars
devour and lay waste the rice plants, how rabbits
come often to the fields of peas, and such things,
speaking of farming matters that are new to me.
The sun is already behind the mountains, and I
sit quietly in the dusk with my shadow, waiting
for the moon. Lighting the lamp, I meditate on
the truth of the words of the Penumbra.

This last sentence is based on a passage from Sôshi:

岡兩問景曰、曩子行、今子止。曩子坐、
今子起。何其無特操與。景曰吾有待而然
者邪、吾所待、又有待而然者邪。吾待蛇
蚹蜩翼邪。惡識所以然。惡識所以不然。

(齋物論第二)

The Penumbra asked the Shadow, "You just
walked, and now you have stopped; you sat down
and now you are standing; why are you thus in-
constant?" The Shadow replied, "I await the

movement of something (form), and that (form)
I wait for, waits for the movement of something
else (the Creator). My waiting to move is like
the waiting of the scales[1] of the snake or the
wings of the *higurashi*[2]. How can I know why
I do this and why I don't do that?"

In *Oku no Hosomichi*, Bashô quotes a part of a waka by
Saigyô:

〔終夜嵐に波をはこばせて〕
月をたれたる汐越の松

(All night long, with the violent wind,)

> The pine trees of Shiogoshi,
> Hanging the moon in their branches,
> (Roll up the waves.)

此の一首にて數景盡きたり、若し一辭を
加ふるものは、無用の指を立つるがごと
し。

He then goes on,

> In this one verse, many scenes are expressed
> to the full. Adding another word would be " a
> useless finger."

This is a phrase that comes in the following passage from
Sôshi:

是故駢於足者連無用之肉也。枝於手者樹
無用之指也。　　　　　　（駢拇、第八）

> Therefore, adding to the foot is an addition of
> flesh; adding to the hand is planting there a use-
> less finger.

[1] On which it glides along.
[2] A kind of cicada.

IV
CHINESE POETRY

Chinese poetry affected haiku both through the Zen and the Taoism that infused it, and through its purely " poetical " merits of romance, nostalgia, world-weariness and evocations of glory. This last, which haiku has avoided, for some quite " Japanese " reason, may be illustrated by the following verse of Ritaihaku, (Li Tai Po):

GAZING AT THE WATERFALL ON MT. RO

The sun shines upon the peak of Kôro, making
the mist purple;
The cascade seen in the distance looks like a long
river
Rushing straight down three thousand feet:
Is it not the Milky Way falling from the Ninth
Heaven?

望盧山瀑布

日照香爐生紫煙
遙看瀑布桂前川
飛流直下三千尺
疑是銀河落九天

The older haiku poets at least hardly ever chose such subjects, nor did they treat them in such a vast way. There are big waterfalls in Japan, but there was an instinctive avoidance, almost a shrinking from such tremendous things. Compare the following verse by Bashô:

ほろほろと山吹ちるか瀧の音

> Petals of the mountain rose
> Fall now and then,
> To the sound of the waterfall?

How delicate and particular this is. The mind seems to grow more intense in the beauty and freshness of the scene. The next example is by Hakurakuten.

PLAYING THE LUTE IN THE COOL OF THE EVENING

The moon has arisen, the birds are all in their
　　nests;
I sit quietly among the trees, alone.
Now my heart is at rest,
And good it is to play the lute of white wood.
Cool-, clear-sounding, according to its nature,
Thin and quiet, it follows the human heart.
The mind is filled with the spirit of peace,
As it responds to the ancient mode of Seishi.
The sounds linger on, and trembling, cease.
The melody is finished, autumn night profound.
The True Sound echoes the Primal Changes;
Heaven and Earth deepen serene.

清 夜 琴 興

月出鳥栖盡寂然坐空林
是時心境閑可以彈素琴
清冷由木性恬淡隨人心
心積和平氣木應正始音
響餘纍動息曲罷秋夜深
正聲感元化天地清沈沈

This is the Chinese way of attaining unity. When we com-

Plate 3

Landscape   Shôkei

pare them, the Japanese seems trivial, insignificant, almost
an anticlimax:

水際もなくて古江の時雨かな　　　蕪　村

> In the drizzling rain at Furue,
> The edge of the water
> Is lost.　　　　　　　Buson

The Japanese way is put plainly in the following verse from
the *Zenrinkushu:*

> Yuima is disinclined to open his mouth,
> But on the bough, a single cicada is chirping.

維摩懶開口、
枝上一蟬吟。

The manner in which haiku poets made use of Chinese
poetry differs according to the individual poet. To take Bashô
and Buson as typical examples of this, Bashô constantly read
the Chinese poets for inspiration, and to enrich his own poetical
life. He was especially found of Tôhô, (who does not appeal
to me personally). In *Oku no Hosomichi*, the very first words
are an adaptation from some prose of Ritaihaku:

光陰者百代之過客

> Time is an endlessly passing traveller.

Bashô has

月日は百代の過客にして、行きかふ年も
又旅人なり。

> Months and days are eternal travellers; the passing
> years are travellers too.

Later on, we have phrases like

片雲の風にさそはれて、

> a solitary cloud invited by the wind,

行く春や鳥啼き魚の目は泪

> Spring departing,
> Birds weeping,
> Tears in the eyes of the fish.

These are echoes of Tôhô.

呉天に白髪のうらみを重ぬといへども

> Even if sorrow and anxiety weighed on me
> and turned my hair grey under a foreign sky,

comes from a poem by Hakurakuten:

今年九月來呉郷、
兩邊蓬鬢一時白。

In September this year I came to the province of Go;
Both sides of my disordered hair became suddenly
white.

The following passage,

雲端につちふる心地して

> Feeling as though earth were falling from
> the edges of the clouds,

comes from a verse of Tôhô:

已入風磴霾雲端。

Entering on the windy slope of stone, the edges
of the clouds rained dust.

Another example:

雨も又奇なりとせば、
雨後の晴色また頼もしと、

> In the rain, the scenery was wonderful, and
> after the rain I hoped that it would be more so.

This comes from one of Sotôba's two poems on Drinking on

the Lake, after the Rain Cleared Up.

飲湖上、初晴後雨、二首。

There is a description of Matsushima:

負へるあり抱けるあり、
　　兒孫を愛するがごとし

Some (islands) appear like a child on the
back, some like a child at the breast, some like
a man caressing his children or grandchildren.

This probably comes from Tôhô's 望岳, *Gazing at the Mountains:*

諸峰羅列似兒孫。

All the peaks in array look like children and
grandchildren.

There are some haiku of Bashô which are based more or
less directly upon verses of Tôhô, for example:

猿を聞く人捨子に秋の風いかに

Sad at the cry of the monkey,
Seeing the abandoned child in the autumn wind,
How would he feel?

This comes from 秋興八首; *Eight Poems of Autumn Diversion:*

聲猿實下三聲淚

Hearing the monkeys, indeed three tearful wails!

Bashô's verse occurs in the *Nozarashi Nikki,* and represents
a real experience while passing near the River Fuji. It is
different in feeling from the Chinese poem which provided part
of the thought.

These are concrete examples of the way in which the
thoughts and feelings of the Chinese poets were continually run-

ning through Bashô's mind. It shows what his ideals of literature were, though his idea of haiku included something quite new and original,—unique, indeed, in world literature. But with his haiku, all this Chinese poetical life is absorbed completely into his own, and there are few examples of direct borrowing. Some more are noted in individual haiku.

With Buson and several other of the older haiku poets, we find something quite different. In a great many of his verses we see Buson aiming at the same object as the Chinese. In extreme cases, of which there are quite a number, he takes whole phrases and embodies them in a new setting. Many examples may be found in the body of this work, but one may be set down here as typical. Buson's verse is:

春 夜 聞 琴

瀟湘の雁のなみだやおぼろ月

Listening to the lute one spring evening.

Tears
For the wild geese of Shôshô;
A hazy moon.

The River Shôshô is that which flows into the famous Lake Dôtei; it is well known for its Eight Views. The wild geese of Shôshô are mentioned in the poem of a famous Chinese poet Senki, found in the *Tôshisen:*

歸 雁

瀟湘何事等閒回
水碧沙明兩岸苔、
二十五絃彈夜月、
不勝清怨郤飛來。

RETURNING WILD GEESE

Why do they so blindly depart from Shôshô?
The water is blue, the sand is white, the moss
  on both banks green;
Should the lute of twenty-five strings be played,
  on a moon-lit night,
With the overwhelming emotion will they not
  return?

The lute of twenty five strings was played by Gaô and Joei, the two daughters of Gyô, who both died at this spot. The "tears" of Buson's verse is connected with the two sisters. The title is in the Chinese style, though it seems to be original with Buson. His verse is entirely Chinese in feeling and is, as far from the simplicity and directness of haiku as it is possible to go in seventeen syllables. Buson probably heard the *koto* being played one spring evening, and expressed his own feelings, using the scenery of Shôshô, the wild geese returning, the tears of Gaô and Joei, as the material, and adding the hazy moon, thus changing the season from autumn to spring to fit the romantic element. In other words, Buson's verse is literature, it is poetry,—but it is not haiku, except in the sense that we are willing to accept anything good or interesting in the haiku form as a contribution to culture and the pleasures of life. Contrast the above verse with a real haiku by Buson:

洗足の盥も漏りて行く春や
    It leaks too,
  The tub for foot-washing:
    Departing spring.

Here we have the harmony of an abstraction with a concrete

instance of it, which is nevertheless also a purely accidental accompaniment. This verse is not a very good one, but it is given as being at the opposite pole of poetic life and technique to the former.

Another of Ritaihaku, nearer to the spirit of haiku, but still somewhat diffuse:

宿清溪主人

夜到清溪宿。
主人碧巖裏。
簷楹掛星斗。
沈席響風水。
月落西山時。
啾々夜猿起。

LODGING AT AN INN AT SEIKEI

I reached Seikei at night,
Where my friend lives among the green rocks;
Between the pillars under the eaves,
Stars were hung,
Rustling of leaves and trickling of water close by;
When the moon fell behind the western hills,
The night-cry of the monkeys arose,—whee! whee!

As stated before, Japanese poets, particularly haiku poets, have a natural tendency towards the small, away from the magnificent, as though they felt there was something rather vulgar about the grand in nature. There are a few haiku certainly, which portray the vaster aspects of nature, for example:

あら海や佐渡に横たふ天の川　　　芭 蕉

A wild sea,
And stretching out towards the Island of Sado,
The Milky Way.　　　Bashô

Plate 4

Monkey   Tôhaku

Chinese poets, possibly from the geography and history of their native country, give us time and space *in extenso*. The past, in haiku, is nearly always the individual, not the historical past. Space is felt in the sky, both of the day and night, but there is little of the vast distances on earth, ranges of mountains and endless plains that we meet in the Chinese poets. In the following poem of Hakurakuten, the last two lines are quite un-Japanese both in their hint of moralizing and generality, and in the preference of the large and aged to the small and short-lived.

秋　　　・蝶

秋花紫蒙蒙。　秋蝶黃茸茸。
花低蝶新少。　飛戲叢西東。
日暮凉風來。　紛紛花落叢。
夜深白露冷。　蝶已死叢中。
朝生夕俱死。　氣類各相從。
不見千年鶴。　多捷百丈松。

THE AUTUMN BUTTERFLY

The purple flowers of autumn bloom in profusion,
The yellow butterflies of autumn flutter to and fro.
Flowers begin to droop, new butterflies are small;
East and west they flirt in twos and threes.
The sun goes down, a cold wind arises;
Flowers fall and scatter in the bushes.
Night deepens, the white dew is chill;
The butterflies have already perished in the thickets.
Born in the morning, they die that night,
In mutual accord with each other;
Have you not seen how the thousand year crane
Dwells so often in the lofty pine tree?

The following is called *Early Spring*, but this means rather *Thoughts in Early Spring*.

早　　春

雪消永又釋景和風復暄。
滿庭田地濕薺葉生檣根。
官舍悄無事日西斜掩門。
不開莊老巷欲與何人言。

EARLY SPRING

Snow is disappearing, ice is melting,
The landscape is softened, the wind is mild.
Gardens and fields are moist,
Young greens growing along by the fence.
In my house, all is quiet and leisure;
The westering sun floods slanting into the gateway.
If I do not open the books of R shi and Sôshi,
With whom should I wish to converse?

The last two lines have such remote connection with the title that we may say that they have none. The following again, is talking about a certain state; haiku is being in it.

睡　起　晏　坐

後亭晝眼足。　起坐春景暮。
新覺眼猶昏。　無思心正住。
淡寂歸一性、　虛閑遣萬慮
了然此時心　無物可譬喩
本是無有鄉、　亦名不用虔
行禪與坐忘、　同歸無異路

SLEEPING, AND ON WAKING, SITTING QUIETLY IN THE DUSK

In the rear arbour I slept all the afternoon.

Rising, I sat there, the spring scene darkening.
Having just awakened, eyes were still dim,
But my mind was at rest, without thought.
Quiet and unattached, it had returned to its unity;
Laying aside the myriad ideas, it was empty and
    still.
There is nothing by which we can hint
At the enlightenment of such a time.
It is simply the state of is—is not,
Called also, "the realm of the useless."
The state of Zen, and of "forgetful sitting,"
The same in essence, are not two roads.

This "forgetful sitting" Sôshi explains as "keeping down the body, causing the intelligence to retire, separating oneself from form, discarding all wisdom."

Rogers, Pope, Greene, and Cowper say:

Mine be a cot beside the hill.

Happy the man, whose wish and care,
A few paternal acres bound.

Sweet are the thoughts that savour of content.

O for a lodge in some vast wilderness.

This was little more than a literary convention in England, but in China and Japan actually practised. Nothing appealed more to the haiku poets than the Chinese poems of a life of solitude. Of the Chinese poets, the most famous in this respect is Tôenmei, whose prose and poetic descriptions of his retirement are classics also of Japan. As a shorter example, we may take the following poem of Hakurakuten:

晚 秋 閑 居

地僻門深少送迎
披夜閑坐養幽情
秋庭不掃携藤杖
閑蹋梧桐黄葉行。

A LIFE OF SECLUSION IN LATE AUTUMN

I live in a withdrawn, out-of-the-way place;
    Few come to visit me.
Putting on my clothes I sit quietly,
    And nourish my peace of mind.
The autumn garden, I do not sweep;
    With a staff of wistaria in my hand,
I slowly walk over the yellow paulownia leaves.

This is entirely in the spirit of haiku, especially the particularity, the concreteness and sensuousness of the last two lines.

Japanese poets have studied rain in all its aspects, the different kinds of rain, windy slashing rain, steady drumming rain, the shower, the noiseless, invisible rain that Hakurakuten describes in the following:

微 雨 夜 行

漠漠秋雲起、　悄悄夜寒生、
自覺衣裳濕、　無點亦無聲。

WALKING AT NIGHT IN FINE RAIN

Autumn clouds, vague and obscure;
The evening, lonely and chill.
I felt the dampness on my garments,
But saw no spot, and heard no sound of rain.

The relation between Hakurakuten, and Sôshi is a very strong and profound one. The second chapter of Sôshi, 齊物論, is made the subject of two poems by Hakurakuten who explictly aligns himself with Sôshi in his world view, and view of human nature:

齊 物 二 首

青松高百尺　綠蕙低數寸
同生人塊間　長短各有分
長者不可退　短者不可進
若用此理推　窮通兩無悶

其　　　二

椿壽八千春　槿花不經宿
中間復何有　冉冉孤生竹、
竹身三年老、竹色四時綠、
雖謝椿有餘、獨勝槿不足。

1

The lofty green pine tree is a hundred feet tall;
The lowly orchid, only a few inches of green.
Both live between the same heaven and earth;
Each has its share of length and shortness.
That which is long cannot retract;
Nor that which is short increase its stature.
A man who lives out this truth,
Will never know sorrow from riches or poverty.

2

Eight thousand years, and the Camellia has reached its spring;
The flower of a Rose of Sharon lasts only a day.
What is there between these two?

There is the bamboo, that grows on by itself.
The bamboo is old after three years,
Yet it is green in every season.
Though it cannot compare with the Camellia,
It far surpasses the Rose of Sharon.

The second verse, (it cannot be called a poem) is a version
of the end of the first chapter of Sôshi.

There is another of these philosophical-botanical poems
which is of interest:

問　　　友

種蘭不種艾、　蘭生艾亦生。
根荄相交長、　莖葉相附榮。
香莖與臭葉、　日夜俱長大、
鋤艾恐傷蘭、　溉蘭恐滋艾、
蘭亦未能溉、　艾亦未能除、
沈吟意不決、　問君合何如、

A QUESTION TO A FRIEND

I planted an orchid; I did not plant mugwort.
But the orchid came up and so did the mugwort.
Their roots and rootlets mingled and spread out;
Their stems and leaves intertwined and flourished.
The sweet-smelling stalks and the evil-smelling
    leaves
Both day and night grew longer and thicker.
If I weed out the mugwort, I may injure the
    orchid;
If I water the orchid, I shall nourish the mugwort.
As yet I am unwilling to water the orchid,
Neither can I get rid of the mugwort.
I ponder and ponder and cannot decide:
I ask you, what should I do?

This is the dilemma of the practical world as seen by the dichotomous intellect, solved by life, by living, which alone can be and not be, speak and be silent, exist and not-exist, at one and the same timeless moment.

Buddhism, the Chinese poets treated sometimes seriously and sometimes with ridicule; both attitudes were well-deserved. At the end of a short poem, *White Hairs*, Hakurakuten makes the following remarks concerning old age and death in particular, and human life in general:

由來生老死、　三病者相隨。
除却無生念、　人間無藥治、

In the nature of things, life, old age, death,
These three ailments follow one another for long.
Apart from belief in something beyond living,
Men have no remedy.

This 無生念 is the thought of and faith in something which is neither life nor death but something transcending both, yet livable in this world.

In the following poem, also by Hakurakuten, the Buddhist view of the body is expressed in a moderate, common-sense Chinese fashion:

逍　　遙　　詠

亦莫戀此身　　亦莫厭此身
此身何足戀　　萬却煩惱根
此身何足厭　　一聚虛空塵
無戀亦無厭　　始是逍遙人

PEACEFUL FREEDOM

I do not love this body of mine,

Nor do I hate it.
Why should I love it?
It is the source of all the desires and passions.
Why should I hate it?
It but an empty collection of dust.
Only by not hating and not loving it
Can we be free and at peace.

Here we see the thought of Sôshi mingled with the thought and terminology of Buddhism. Hakurakuten makes fun of Buddhism and Buddhist monks in the following:

戲 禮 經 老 僧

香火一爐燈一盞、白頭衣禮佛名經、
何年飲著聲聞酒、直到如今醉未醒

DERIDING AN AGED MONK FOR WORSHIPPING THE SUTRAS

Burning incense, lighting tapers,
A white-haired old monk is chanting the Thousand
    Buddhas' Names Sutra.
For how many years has be been drinking the
    wine of Sravaka?[1]
Up to now he has never wakened from his stupor.

Here, however, it is superstitious regard for the written word that he is attacking. Nevertheless, Hakurakuten was a free-lance and would have attacked even poetry itself, let alone Zen in any form. He assails Rôshi in his well-known verse:

讀　老　子

言者不知知者默、此語吾聞於老君。
若道老君是知者、緣何自著五千文。

[1] Hinayana doctrine of personal salvation.

READING RÔSHI

The speaker does not know; the knower does not
  speak:
Thus we have heard from Rôshi.
If Rôshi is to be called a knower,
Why did he write five thousand words?

He also criticises Sôshi's doctrine of the unity of all things,
the identity of contraries, in the following way:

讀　莊　子

莊生齊物同歸一、　我道同中者不同。
遂性逍遙雖一致、　鸞鳳終校勝蛇蟲。

READING SÔSHI

Sôshi reduces all things to one;
I believe that in unity there is diversity;
Though by their own nature they live in equal
  happiness,
A phoenix is slightly superior to a snake.

Nevertheless, in a poem written in his old age, an occasional
verse, 偶作, after describing a day of his life spent in quiet
meditation and walking alone in the fields, he concludes:

是非一以貫、　身世交相忘、
若問此何許、　此是無何鄉。

Perceiving that the relative is the absolute,
Forgetting both oneself and the world,
What condition is this, you ask?
It is the realm of [Sôshi's] Serene, Self-less Inacti-
  vity.

As an example of Chinese poetry that is pure haiku we may take the following:

夜　　雨

旱蛩啼復歇、殘燈滅又明、
隔牕知夜雨、芭蕉先有聲。

RAIN AT NIGHT

A cricket chirps and is silent:
The guttering lamp sinks and flares up again.
Outside the window, evening rain is heard;
It is the banana-plant that speaks of it first.

This is two haiku, rather than one; first:

> A cricket chirps.
> And is silent:
> The guttering lamp sinks.

It will be noted that this avoids the parallelism, more or less an inevitable accompaniment of rhyming verse. Haiku are both asymmetric in form and asymmetric in thought. It might be better to arrange the lines thus:

> The guttering lamp sinks;
> A cricket chirps,
> And is silent.

The second "haiku" is even more suitable to the haiku form, since it is the essence of the original poem:

> Evening rain:
> The *bashô*
> Speaks of it first.

Hakurakuten's verse is an example of George Moore's definition of "pure poetry,"

Plate 5

Bird and Apples   Chôshô

> Something that the poet creates outside of his own
> personality,

if we understand by this clear yet ambiguous statement, that
the world is reflected in the mind of the poet as in an undis-
storted mirror, the growth and life of the poet's mind being
identical with that movement of things outside him. By some
happy chance, the apparent peculiarities and idiosyncrasies
of the poet correspond exactly with the vagaries of the universe, and what he expresses as personal feeling within, is
law without; what he creates out of nothing, is what God
made out of the void. Pure poetry therefore appears to us
super-personal, extra-personal, and so it is, for such a poet
speaks not for himself, but for mankind. It should be remembered, however, in regard to poetry in general, and also for
some haiku, that a poet's own personal prejudices and whims,
weaknesses and over-emphasizings, may produce romantic,
subjective, lyrical verse that is nevertheless poetry because of
some subtle power the poet possesses and bestows on us, of
taking those personal elements and subjective attitude, and
standing outside even them. Such, for example, is the poetry
of Heine. The following verse by Shiki is of this kind:

工夫して花にランプを吊しけり

> Hanging a lantern
> On a blossoming bough,—
> What pains I took!

In view of the large number of quotations from Hakurakuten, it should be mentioned that his influence on Japanese
literature was very strong indeed from the ninth century
to the fifteenth. The Nô play, *Hakurakuten,* by Seami, is
a proof of this, and represents the persistent influence of

five hundred years. Sumiyoshi, 住吉 (or Suminoe, 住江) the god of waka, drives back Hakurakuten to China:

住吉の　神の力のあらん程はよも日本をば
從へさせ給はじ、速に浦の波立ち歸り給へ
樂天

The strength of the god Sumiyoshi is such that it will not allow you to conquer Japan; swiftly go back, Rakuten, over the waves of the bay.

As evidence of the wide-spread nature of the influence of Hakurakuten, especially among the ruling classes and the literati, we may quote the following anecdote from 皇朝史略, *A Brief History of the Emperors*, by Aoyama Enu, 1776–1842, concerning the Emperor Takakura, the eightieth Emperor of Japan, 1169–80:

高倉天皇幼時、有獻楓者。天皇愛之、命
藤原信成守之。一日、仕丁將飲酒、勵枝
爲薪以煖酒、信成見而大驚收仕丁、將之
罪、會天皇使信成上其樹、信成具奏其狀、
叩頭請罪、天皇從容曰、唐詩有云、林間
煖酒燒紅葉。誰敎仕丁作此風流。無復所
問。

When Takakura Tennô was young, someone presented him with a maple tree, which he treasured highly. He ordered Fujiwara Nobunari to take charge of it. One day, some palace workmen, intending to drink wine, cut off some branches to make a fire and warm it. Nobunari, seeing this, was greatly upset, seized them and prepared to punish them; the Emperor had told him many times to be careful about the tree. Nobunari

reported the matter in detail to the Emperor, pro-
strated himself, and asked to be punished. The
Emperor calmly replied, "A Tang poem[1] says,

> Burning the red autumn leaves, we warm wine
> in the forest.

Who taught the workmen such an elegant accom-
plishment?" and referred no more to the matter.

---

[1] This "Tang poem" is a verse by Hakurakuten.

V

Confucianism

Confucianism contributed a certain sobriety, reserve, lack of extravagance and hyperbole, brevity and pithiness, and a moral flavour that may sometimes be vaguely felt, but is never allowed to be separated, as it is in Wordsworth and Hakurakuten, from the poetry itself. The relation between haiku and Confucianism is all the more profound, the influence of the one on the other is all the more subtle, because of the apparent disparity between the two. But Confucianism is a much more poetical thing than most people suppose. In fact, as of Christianity and all other religions, one may say that what in it is poetical is true, using the word true in the sense of something that feeds the life of man, which can be absorbed into our own life and yet have a life of its own, which is organic and growing. For example, at the very beginning of the *Analects*, Confucius says,

有朋自遠方來、不亦樂乎

　　Is it not delightful to have a friend come from
afar?

Bashô repeats this in,

　　さびしさを問てくれぬか桐一葉

　　　　A paulownia leaf has fallen;
　　Will you not come to me
　　　　In my loneliness?

addressed to Ransetsu.

In Confucius, his love of music and poetry is never to be

forgotten. He devotion to the *Odes*, his not knowing the taste of meat for three months after hearing a certain piece of music,[1]—this is what gave him the power to influence the Chinese race for three thousand years. Men are poets and musicians in a sense that they are not philosophers and sages. Men do not live by bread alone, but by every poetic word that proceeds out of the mouth of God. Confucius said:

子曰興於詩、立於禮、成於樂（論語八、八）
Arise with poetry;
Stand with propriety;
Grow with music.

The mind is roused by poetry, made steadfast by propriety, and perfected by music. This poetic, musical, charming quality in the deeds and talk of Confucius naturally made him difficult to understand, and this is why he said,

得其門者或寡矣　　　（論語十九、二十八）
Few there be that find the door.

If Confucius had been a mere moralist, he could never have said this.

Confucius comes very close to Zen and haiku in the following passage:

子在川上曰、逝者如斯夫、不舍晝夜
（論語九、十六）
Standing by a stream, Confucius said, " It ceases not day or night, flowing on and on like this."

The Zen of this is not so much in the direct grasping of the meaning of something, as the expression of it without ex-

---

[1] 子在齋聞韶、三月不知肉味 （論語七、十三）

pressing it. This also is dangerous, but not so dangerous as words. Confucius himself said,

不知言無以知人也　　　（論語二十、三）

If you do not know (the meaning of) words, you do not know men.

An example of this is in such a sentence as " Without knowing propriety. we cannot establish ourselves."[1] If we take the words " know ", " propriety ", " establish ", in their ordinary, everyday, unpoetical, intellectual significance, this statement has little meaning, and that cold and pedantic, with no power to move us. But if we take " know " to mean " believe and have faith in ", " confide ourselves to "; " propriety " to mean " a harmonious mode of living ", " a poetical way of doing everything ", " a deep, inward rightness of relation between ourselves and all outward circumstances "; " establish ourselves " to mean " become a real human being, be cheerfully unaffected by the vicissitudes of fate "; then Confucius' " Stand with propriety " comes alive. We feel him putting into practice in his own person that which the words stiffen and disfigure as they try to manifest it forth. In the same spirit we are to read such passages as the following, all from the *Analects*:

人焉廋哉、人焉廋哉　　　（二、十）

How can a man conceal his nature? How can a man conceal his nature?

獲罪於天、無所禱也　（三、十二）

He who offends against Heaven has none to whom he can pray.

[1] Another translation of " Stand with propriety ".

祭神如神在。　　　（三、十二。）

He sacrificed to the spirits as if the spirits were present.

仁者安仁。　　　（四二）

A virtuous man finds rest in his virtue.

There are traces of Taoist elements in the *Analects*:

季康子患盜、問於孔子、孔子對曰苟子之
不欲、雖賞之不竊。　　　（十二、十八）

君子之德風、小人之德草、草上之風必偃。
　　　　　　　　　　　　　（十二、十九）

Kikô was worried about thieves, and asked Confucius concerning the matter. Confucius replied, "If you were desire-less, they would not steal, even for rewards."

The sage is the wind, ordinary people the grass; with the wind on it, the grass must bend.

The animism from which both religion and poetry sprang and which is still the fountain and motive force of all our religion and poetry today, may be illustrated, in early Chinese thought, from *The Doctrine of The Mean*, Chapter XVI:

子曰、鬼神之爲德、其盛矣乎、視之而弗
見、聽之而弗聞、體物而不可遺。

Confucius said, "The power of spirits, how abundant! We look, but do not see them; we listen, but do not hear them; yet they sustain all things, and nothing is neglected by them."

In Rôshi XIV, these are identified with the Way:

視之不見、名曰夷。聽之不聞、名曰希。
搏之不得、名曰微

> Looking at it, it is not seen, and thus is named colourless. Listening to it, we cannot hear it, and name it soundless. Feeling for it, we cannot get it, and name it formless.

In China, as in Japan, the gradual tendency, during three thousand years, was the mingling of what started as three distinct trains of thought, Confucianism, Taoism ,and Buddhism—to add a fourth, Zen. As a late example of this synthesis we may take the *Saikontan*, written by Kôjisei, 洪自誠. Details of the life of the author are not known, nor the date of the book, but it was already in existence in 1624. The *Saikontan* consists of three hundred and fifty nine short pieces of prose and verse, the shortest of fourteen characters, the longest of seventy four. This form of writing, epigrammatic, or something of a prose poem, became popular and indeed universal in the Ming Dynasty. The name *Saikontan* means literally " vegetable root discourses," and is used to imply that only a man leading a simple life is capable of being a poet or philosopher. It came into Japan probably through Zen priests[1] or Nagasaki merchants.

The following extracts will give an idea of his not always complete assimilation of Zen, Taoism and Confucianism. But the reader is all the more urged to apply each of the following extracts, whatever their ostensible purport, to poetry, religion and practical conduct, remembering that if these three are not one, they are not three.

---

[1] E.g. Ingen, 隱元, who became naturalized in Japan, where he arrived 1654, ten years after the birth of Bashô.

(七) 醲肥辛甘非眞味、眞味只是淡、神奇卓異
　　非至人、至人只是常。

Strong wine, fat meat, peppery things, very
sweet things, these have not real taste; real taste
is plain and simple. Supernatural, extraordinary
feats do not characterize a real man; a real man
is quite ordinary in behaviour.

(二一) 家庭有個眞佛、日用有種眞道、人能誠心
　　　和氣、愉色婉言、使父母兄弟間形骸兩釋、
　　　意氣交流、訥息觀心萬倍矣。

The true Buddha is in the home; the real Way
is everyday life. A man who has sincerity, who
is a peace-maker, cheerful in looks and gentle in
his words, harmonious in mind and body towards
parents and brethren, such a man is vastly
superior to one who practises breathing control
and introspection.

(六五)　　　　　心頭光明、暗室中有靑天、
　　　　　　　　念頭暗昧、白日下生厲鬼。

If the mind is clear, a dark room has its blue
sky; if the mind is sombre, broad daylight gives
birth to demons and evil spirits.

(九一) 貞士無心激福、天卽就無心處牖其衷、憸
　　　人著意避禍、天卽就著、意中奪其魄、可
　　　見天之機權最神、人之智巧何益。

The just man has no mind to seek happiness;
Heaven therefore, because of this mindlessness,
opens its inmost heart. The bad man busies
himself with avoiding misfortunes; Heaven therefore confounds him for this desire. How un-
searchable are the ways of Heaven! How useless
the wisdom of men!

(一五一) 水不波則自定、鑑不翳則自明、故心無可
　　　　　清、去其混之者而清自現、樂不必尋、去
　　　　　其苦之者而樂自存。

　　　Water not disturbed by waves settles down of
itself.　A mirror not covered with dust is clear
and bright.　The mind should be like this.　When
what beclouds it passes away, its brightness appears.　Happiness must not be sought for; when
what disturbs passes away, happiness comes of
itself.

(一六一) 道是一重公衆物事、當隨人而接引、學是
　　　　　一個尋常家飯、常隨事而警惕。

　　　The Way is common property.　It should be
pointed out to all we meet.　Learning is as ordinary as eating rice at home.　According to the
circumstances, it should be applied circumspectly.

(一七三) 爲鼠常留飯、憐蛾不點燈、古人此等念頭
　　　　　是吾人一點生生之機、無此便所謂土木形
　　　　　骸而已。

　　　The ancients left rice for mice, and did not
light lamps out of pity for moths.　These thoughts
of theirs are the operation point of humanity in
life.　Lacking this, a man is a mere earthen,
wooden body.

(二三一)　　　聽靜夜之鐘聲、晚醒夢中之夢、
　　　　　　　觀澄潭之月影、窺見身外之身。

　　　At the sound of the bell in the silent night,
I wake from my dream in this dream-world of
ours.　Gazing at the reflection of the moon in a
clear pool, I see, beyond my form, my real form.

(二三二)　　　鳥語蟲聲總是傳人之訣
　　　　　　　花英草色無非見道之交

Plate 6

Shiki soku ze ku

Takuan

學者要天機清徹胸次
玲瓏觸物皆有會心之處。

The song of birds, the voices of insects, are all
means of conveying truth to the mind; in flowers
and grasses we see messages of the Way. The
scholar, pure and clear of mind, serene and open
of heart, should find in everything what nourishes
him.

（二三三）人解讀有字書、不解讀無字書、知彈有絃
琴、不知彈無絃琴、以跡用不以神用、何
以得琴書之趣。

Men know how to read printed books; they do
not know how to read the unprinted ones. They
can play on a stringed harp, but not on a string-
less one. Applying themselves to the superficial
instead of the profound, how should they understand music or poetry?

（二三六）　會得個中趣、五湖之煙月盡入寸裡、
破得眼前機、千古之英雄盡歸掌握。

If you know the inner significance of things, the
misty moon of the Five Lakes is all within you.
If you understand the activity of human phenomena, the heroism and nobility of the great men
of all ages is in your grasp.

（二四八）　松澗邊、携杖獨行、立處雲生破衲、
竹窗下、枕書高臥、覺時月侵寒氈。

Walking alone, leaning on a staff, in a valley
of pine-trees, clouds rise round my monkish robes.
Sleeping with a book as my pillow by the window
beneath the bamboos, I wake when the moonlight
steeps the floor-cloths.

（二五八）　　狐雲出岫、去留一無所係、
　　　　　　朗鏡懸空、靜躁兩不相干。

A solitary cloud comes out of a mountain cave;
it stays or departs without reference to anything
else. The bright mirror of the moon hangs in
the sky; it is aloof from both quietness and
clamour.

（二六〇）　禪宗曰、饑來喫飯倦來眠、詩旨曰、眼前
　　　　　景致口頭語蓋極高寓於極平、至難出於至
　　　　　易、有意者反遠無心者自近也。

The Zen sect says, "When you are hungry,
eat; when you are weary, sleep". Poetry aims at
the description in common language of beautiful
scenery. The sublime is contained in the ordinary,
the hardest in the easiest. What is self-consious
and ulterior is far from the truth; what is mind-
less is near.

（二七四）身如不繫之舟、一任流行坎止、心似旣灰
　　　　　之木、何妨刀割香塗。

The body is like a boat adrift, floating along
or motionless in a deep pool. The mind is like a
piece of burnt wood; what matters if it is split
fuel, or varnished with scented laquer?

（二七九）讀易曉窓、丹砂研松間之露、談經午案寶
　　　　　磬宣、竹下之風。

Reading the Book of Changes at the morning
window, I rub a vermilion stick in the dew that
drips from the pine-trees. Discussing the sutras
with a visitor, the sound of the *kei*[1] is borne
away on the wind from the bamboos.

---

[1] A kind of clapper made of stone, used in a Zen temple.

(二八八）古德云、竹影掃階塵不動、月輪穿沼水無
痕、吾儒云、水流任急境常靜、花落雖頻
意自閒、人常持此意、以應事接物、身心
何等自在。

An ancient worthy says, " The shadow of the
bamboo sweeps over the stairs, but the dust does
not move. The disc of the moon passes through
water of the lake, leaving no trace." One of our
Confucians says, " The stream rushes down swiftly
but all is silent around. The flowers fall incessantly, but we feel quiet." If you have grasped
the meaning of this, in all your relations with
things, you are free in mind and body.

(二九一）　心地上無風濤、隨在皆青山綠樹、
　　　　　性天中有化育、觸處見魚躍鳶飛。

If your heart is without stormy waves, everywhere are blue mountains and green trees. If
our real nature is creative like nature itself,
wherever we may be, we see that all things are
free like sporting fishes and circling kites.

(三三二）興逐時來芳草中撒履閒行、野鳥忘機時作
伴、景與心會、落花下披襟兀坐、白雲無
語漫相留。

When in the mood, I take off my shoes and walk
barefooted through the sweet-smelling grasses of
the fields, wild birds without fear accompanying
me. My heart at one with nature, I loosen my
shirt as I sit absorbed beneath the falling petals,
while the clouds silently enfold me as if wishing
to keep me there.

(三四五）耳根以颭谷投響、過而不留、則是非俱謝。
心境如月池浸色、空而不著、則物我兩忘。

Just as a whirlwind roaring down a valley
leaves nothing behind it, so the ear is to have
nothing to do with right and wrong. Just as the
moon only reflects its light in a pool, so the mind,
empty and unattached, does not know itself and
the outside world as two things.

（三五五）波浪兼天、舟中不知懼、而舟外者寒心猖
　　狂罵座、席上不知警、而席外者咋舌、故
　　君子身雖在事中、心要超事外也。

When waves reach the sky, those in the boat
are unware of the danger, but onlookers are trembling with fear. A drunken diner is swearing and
cursing at the others, but they are quite unalarm-
ed, whereas those outside are "biting their
tongues" (in apprehension of a quarrel). Thus
with the superior man, his body may be im-
mersed in affairs, but his mind is above and
beyond them.

（三五八）茶不求精而壺亦不燥、酒不求冽而樽亦不
　　空、素琴無絃而常調短笛無腔而自適、縱
　　難超越羲皇可匹濤嵇阮。

Though my tea is not the very best, the pot
is never dry. My wine is not exquisite, but the
barrel is not empty. My plain lute, though string-
less, is always in tune. My short flute, though a
formless one, suits me well. I may not perhaps
be able to surpass the Emperor Gi, but I can
equal Kei and Gen.

（三五九）釋氏隨緣、吾儒素位、四字是渡海的浮囊、
　　蓋世路茫茫一念求全、則萬緒紛起、隨寓
　　而安、則無入不得矣。

Following Buddha's "adapting ourselves to
circumstances," and our Confucian "acting in

accord with one's position", these two phrases
are the life-buoy for us to pass over the sea of
life. The paths of life are illimitable. If we
desire perfection, all kinds of obstacles arise, but
if we obey our destiny, we are free everywhere.

As stated above, the general tendency in Japan has been
for the fusion of Buddhism, Confucianism and Shintô. Fujiwara Seika, born in 1651, a Zen priest who afterwards
abandoned Buddhism, was the founder of the Shushi[1] School
of Confucianism in Japan. He said that the three were
different in their principles, but the same as to the final state
to which their followers attain. Amenomori Hôshu, who died
in 1755, declared that Rôshi was the sage of emptiness,
Buddha the sage of mercy, Confucius the sage of sages.
What is known as the Yômei[2] School was really founded by
Rikushôzan,[3] who said,

> Self is everything; the mind constitutes the
> six classics.

Nakae Tôju,[4] one of the greatest men that Japan has produced, the virtual founder of the Yômei School in Japan, said
that Heaven and Earth and man appear to be different, but
they are essentially one. This essence has no size, and the
spirit of man and the infinite must be one.

Nakane Tori,[5] a priest of the Jidô sect, converted to
Confucianism, said what might be taken as the philosophic
basis of haiku:

[1] 1139—1200.
[2] 1472—1528.
[2] 1138—92.
[4] 1608—1648.
[5] Born 1694.

The aim of learning is but to abolish the
"fence" which separates man from man. In other
words, the distinction between he and I will be
abolished when we are truly educated.

The universe and humanity are one, and my
parents, brothers, and all men are my self. Sun,
moon, rain, dew, mountains, rivers, birds, animals
and fish are also my self. Therefore I should love
and sympathize with others, because they are my
self, and not separable from me.

Oshio Chusai[1] said,

Even the broken grass, or the fallen tree, or
the cut stone gives us sorrow, because we feel
they are in our minds.

It may be seen from the above extracts that during the
second half of the seventeenth century, that is, during the
lifetime of Bashô, Confucianism was making a remarkable
contribution to the culture of Japan, and to the nourishment
of the spirit of haiku. Especially to be mentioned during this
period are:

Fujiwara Seika, 藤原成家, Hayashi Razan, 林羅山,
Ishikawa Jôzan, 石川常山, Nakae Tôju, 中江藤樹,
Kaibara Ekken, 貝原益軒, Itô Jinsai, 伊藤仁齋,
Itô Togai, 伊藤東涯, Ogiu Sorai, 狙生徂徠.

To conclude this account, we may refer to a book called
Zenkai Ichiran, One Wave of the Sea of Zen, by Kôsen
Imakita. This consists of a long introduction and thirty
Cases, in which the author, a noted Zen priest of the Meiji
Era, shows how the best of the Confucian interpretation of
life, as represented in the writings of Confucius and Mencius,

[1] Born 1793.

is in accord with that of Zen. Kôsen started writing this work when he was forty three, in 1858, while living in Eikôji Temple at Iwakami in Yamaguchi Prefecture. It is a work of culture, humanity and insight, showing the Japanese mind at its best, its assimilative and appreciative character. Though apparently so far apart, Confucianism and haiku have this in common, that both aim at a life of perfection, in this world, in relation to outward things and practical affairs; both aim at the same poise of the mind.

It should be especially noted in this connection that Bashô was born and educated as a samurai. When Yoshitada Tôdô, his Lord, died in 1667, he left the castle town of Ueno in Iga province for Edo. From now on he studied Japanese classics under Kigin Kitamura, 北村季吟, died 1705, of the Teitoku school of haikai, Chinese classics under Itô Tanan, 伊藤淡庵, and later Zen under Bucchô, 佛頂, but for twenty three years, in the most impressionable part of his life, he had imbibed the theory and practice of Confucianism which ruled the samurai world.

We cannot, however, adduce very much direct evidence of the influence of the Confucian classics upon Bashô. He seems to have turned to the poets rather than to the philosophers. There is a passage near the beginning of *Oku no Hosomichi*, in which he describes a certain worthy but not very talented man called "Hotoke Gozaemon," ("Buddha Gozaemon") because of his honesty, in the words of the *Analects*:

剛毅木訥近仁。　　（子路第十三）

The steadfast, the persevering, the simple,
the modest, are near to virtue.

The following verses of Bashô have a specially Confucian flavour of *Jingichukô,* 仁義忠孝, Humanity, Justice, Loyalty and Filial Piety:

塚も動けわが泣く聲は秋の風
> Shake, O grave!
> My wailing voice
> Is the autumn wind.

手にとらば消えん涙ぞあつき秋の霜
> Should I take it[1] in my hand,
> It would disappear with my hot tears,
> Like the frost of autumn.

なでしこにかゝる涙や楠のつゆ
> The dew of the camphor tree
> Falls in tears
> On the pinks.[2]

This simple Confucianism developed into something deeper and wider, embracing all nature in its scope, without losing its human feeling:

やがて死ぬけしきも見えず蟬の聲
> Nothing intimates
> How soon they must die,—
> Crying cicadas.

大風のあしたも赤し唐辛子
> The morning
> After the gale too,
> Peppers are red.

---

[1] Composed on a lock of hair of his dead mother.
[2] This refers to Kusunoki and his son Masatsura, when they parted, in 1336, before the father's defeat and suicide.

初雪や水仙の葉のたわむ迄

> The first snow,
> Just enough to bend
> The leaves of the daffodils.

We may further illustrate the Confucian influence on haiku by the *Rules of (Poetical) Pilgrimage*, 行脚掟, of which there are at least three forms, ascribed to Bashô. The first to appear was in 1760, sixty six years after his death, in the *Goshichiki*:

一宿再宿すべからず、あたゝめざる蓙を
思ふべし

1. Do not sleep twice in the same inn; wish for a mat that you have not yet warmed.

腰に寸鐡たりとも帶すべからず、物而物
の命を取ることなかれ、君父の讐あるも
のは門外に遊ぶべし、いたゞきふまぬの
道忍びざる情あれば也

2. Do not gird even a dagger on your thigh; kill no living thing. Meet the enemy of your lord or father only without the gate, for " Not living under the same heaven or walking the same earth ",—this law comes from an inevitable human feeling.

衣類器財相應すべし、過たるはよからず
足らざるもしからず

3. Clothes and utensils are to be suitable to one's needs, not too many, not too few.

魚鳥獸の肉好むでくふべからず、美食珍
味にふける人は他事にふれやすき物也、
菜根を咬へ百事をなすべき語を思ふべし

4. The desire for the flesh of fish, fowl, and
   beast is not good. Indulging in tasty and
   rare dishes leads to baser pleasures. Remember the saying "Eat simple food, and
   you can do anything."

人の求めなきに己が句出すべからず、望
をそむくもしからず

5. Do not produce your verses unasked; if asked,
   never refuse.

たとへ嶮岨の境たりとも所勞の念起すべ
からず起らば中途より歸るべし

6. When in a difficult and dangerous region, do
   not weary of the journey; should you do so,
   turn back half-way.

馬駕に乘る事なかれ、一枝の枯枝を己が
痿脚と思ふべし

7. Do not ride on horses or in palanquins. Think
   of your staff as another thin leg.

好んで酒を飮むべからず、饗應により固
辭しがたくと微醺にして止むべし、亂に
及ばずの禁、幽亂起歲の戒祭にもろみを
用るも醉るを憎んで也、酒に遠ざかるの
訓あり、つゝしめや

8. Do not be fond of wine. If it is difficult
   to refuse at banquets, stop after you have
   had a little. "Restrain yourself from all
   rowdiness." Because drunkenness at the
   matsuri is disliked, the Chinese use unrefined
   saké. There is an admonition to keep away
   from saké; be careful!

船錢茶代忘るべからず

9. Do not forget the ferry-boat fee and tips.

他の短をあげ己が長を顕すことなかれ、
人を謗て己にほこるは甚賤き事也

10. Do not mention other people's weaknesses and
    your own strong points. Reviling others and
    praising yourself, is an exceedingly vulgar
    thing.

俳談の外雑話すべからず、雑話出なば居
眠して労を養ふべし

11. Apart from poetry, do not gossip about all
    things and sundry. When there is such talk,
    take a nap and recreate yourself.

女性の俳友にしたしむべからず、師にも
弟子にもいらぬ事也、此道に親炙せば人
をもて傳ふべし、惣じて男女の道は嗣を
立るのみ也、流蕩すれば心敦一ならず、
此道は主一無適にして成ず、能已を省べ
し

12. Do not become intimate with women haiku
    poets; this is good for neither teacher nor
    pupil. If she is in earnest about haiku, teach
    her through another. The duty of men and
    women is the production of heirs. Dissipation
    prevents the richness and unity of the mind.
    The Way of Haiku arises from concentration
    and lack of distraction. Look well within
    yourself.

主あるものは一針一葉たりとも取るべか
らず、山川江澤にも主あり、勤よや

13. You must not take a needle or blade of grass
    that belongs to another. Mountains, streams,
    rivers, marshes,—all have an Owner; be care-
    ful about this.

山川舊跡したしく尋入べし、あらたに私
の名を付する事なかれ

14. You should visit mountains, rivers and historical places. Do not give them new names.

一字の師恩たりとも忘るゝ事なかれ、一
句の理をだに解せず人の師となる事なか
れ、人に敎るは已を成じて後の事也

15. Be grateful to a man who teaches you even a single word. Do not try to teach unless you understand fully. Teaching is to be done after you have perfected yourself.

一宿一飯の主もおろそかに思ふべからず、
さりとて媚諂ふ事なかれ、如此の人は世
の奴也、此道に入る者は此道に交るべし

16. Do not treat as of no account anyone who puts you up even one night, or gives you a single meal. Even so, do not flatter people. Those who do such things are the rascals of this world. Those who walk the Way of Haiku should associate with others who walk it.

夕を思ひ且を思ふべし、且暮の行脚とい
ふ事は好まざる事也、人に勞をかくるこ
となかれ、しばしばすれば疎ぜらるゝの
言を思ふべし

17. Think, in the evening; think, in the morning. Travelling is not to be done in the beginning and ending of the day. Do not trouble other people.[1] Remember the saying, "If you trouble them often, they will be distant to you."

[1] There is such a sentiment expressed in the *Hôjôki*.

The above Rules are ascribed to Bashô, but the internal evidence seems to me against this. The central idea of most may well be Bashô's, but the language and verbosity do not seem to be his. It is, however, a very significant document as showing the influence the Confucian ideal of life had upon all the earlier haiku poets. When we read the above seventeen points we feel them to show a combination, imperfectly reconciled, of Buddhist, Confucian and poetical ideals, but they sound old-fashioned, and are interesting rather as fossils of something that was once alive,—in a word, they lack poetry, and thus have no immortality.

VI
Oriental Art and Haiku

The relation of oriental art to haiku is a very deep one. It is direct, in so far as a haiku poet may express his understanding pictorially as well as well as verbally, and the resultant haiku and haiga stand side by side on the same scrap of paper. It is indirect, in that the pictures he sees teach him how to look at and feel and listen to the world of nature. They show him where the value and meaning of things is, so that he may say in words what the pictures say in lines, concerning that mysterious interplay of the simple and the complicated, the general and the particular. For it must never be forgotten, that simplicity and brevity have meaning only because this is a world of multifariousness and complexity. The ukiyoe of Hiroshige would have no significance, were the scenery of Japan as plain and clear in outline as they.

Biological development is a gradual specialization of functions; it is the same with painting, and with poetry. Western landscape gradually detatched itself from portraits and became independent; in the course of time, all the different forms of literary expression, novels, dramas, essays, and so on, fell into separate categories. In just the same way, as is to be explained later, haiku separated itself from renga, and at about the same time, haiga, or haiku painting, became a certain type of artistic expression, doing in mass and line what haiku attempted to do in word and cadence.

We say " at about the same time," but it seems as if painting often precedes poetry in its grasp of the nature of things. When we compare the history of English landscape and that of nature poetry, we see how difficult it is to determine in the history of culture, which has been in advance, painting or poetry. It is best perhaps to assume a more or less alternating progress of both. In English nature poetry and landscape painting, we can follow a parallel course of development. Thomson's *Seasons* was published in 1730, but it was not until the middle of the century had been passed that the English landscape painters took over the work of the foreigners (chiefly Dutch) who were Thomson's contemporaries. Richard Wilson, 1714–82, a Welshman, has in his pictures, for example " The Summit of Cader-Idris ", or "A Welsh Valley with Snowdon Hill", a loneliness, serenity and majesty of mountain scenery which Wordsworth did not excel forty years later. Ruskin says of him,

> I believe that with the name of Richard Wilson
> the history of sincere landscape art, founded on
> a meditative love of nature, begins in England.

Gainsborough, during the Bath (portrait) period, 1760–74, painted the " Market Cart," and the " Harvest Wagon ". In his landscapes (one-fifth of all his paintings) he appeals somehow to the emotions. Constable says,

> On looking at them we find tears in our eyes,
> and we know not what brings them.

David Allan, 1744–66, John Robert Cozens, 1752–99, Thomas Girtin, 1775–1802, George Moreland, 1773–1804, all antedate Wordsworth and the other Romantic poets, whose contemporaries were J. S. Cotman, 1782–1842, J. S. Crome, 1768–1821, Turner, 1775–1851, Constable, 1776–1837. These have an intimacy with nature, an appreciation of detail, and grasp of the elementary and universal hardly attained by the poets.

In the case of Japanese painting and haiku, the matter is much more complicated. We find in the Chinese painters of the Tang and Sung Periods, in Sesshu and Hakuin Zenji something that does not appear in Japanese poetry at all until the advent of Bashô. Again, in theory, haiga should be something as original and remarkable as haiku, but in fact this is not altogether so. As stated above, paintings in the spirit of haiku may be found during the millenium preceding the death of Bashô, and haiga is rather an appendage than a companion art with haiku.

In Japanese literature, we have, roughly speaking, three types of poetry, *shi*, or Chinese poetry, waka, and haiku; and to them naturally correspond three types of painting[1], the poetical Chinese style, the lyrical or Japanese, and the intuitive. By "intuitive" is meant the kind of painting in which the nature of a thing, of a tree or flower or season or mood of a human being is implicitly expressed. From the most ancient times, in China, it was the custom to combine painting and poetry, these being the work of one man or of two, and it was quite natural that the same thing should take place when haiku became an independent poetic form.

Haiga are small sketches, either in indian-ink, black-and-white, or in simple colours, that endeavour to express in pictures what haiku do in words. Haiga as such seem to have begun their independent existence about the time of Sôkan, 1458–1546, that is to say when haiku began to be separated from renku.

---

[1] To speak more precisely, it is three attitudes towards the world, one of which will more or less predominate in any given picture.

By the age of Teitoku, 1570–1653, they already had their rather innocent, unprofessional air, as pictures by poets, not artists. We can find elements of haiga in many of the greatest Japanese artists, from Sesshu onwards, but one of the first to paint what can be called specifically haiga, was Shôkadô, 松花道, who died in 1640, four years before the birth of Bashô. He was a learned monk of the Shingon sect, and, it may be said, united the Bashô school of haiku which was about to rise, with the school of Zenga, or Zen paintings of the monks of the Ashikaga Period, 1338–1573, Ikkyu, Hakuin, Takuan, etc. Half a century after his death, Bashô wrote his famous haiku:

枯枝に烏の止りけり秋の暮

On a withered branch,
A crow is perched,
In the autumn evening.

This was to be a kind of standard for all haiku to come. (Bashô learned painting from one of his own pupils, Kyoroku). Among other painters of the time, Nonoguchi Ryuho, 野々口立圃, who died in 1669, learned haikai from Teitoku, and in his hands haiku was seen in pictures. From his time onwards, until the present day, haiga has had an existence as a special form of painting.

The qualities of haiga are rather vague and negative. The lines and masses are reduced to a minimum. The subjects are usually small things, or large things seen in a small way. The simplicity of the mind of the artist is perceived in the simplicity of the object. Technical skill is rather avoided, and the picture gives an impression of a certain awkwardness of treatment that reveals in hiding the inner meaning of the thing painted. The aim of haiku, according to Buson, is to express in ordinary language the inner poetical philosophy of all sublunary things. That is to say, the most delicate feelings and profound meanings of things are to be portrayed as though they were every-day occurences. Exactly the same is to be said of haiga. Moments of deep significance in our perceptions of the outer world are shown in crudeness, brevity, humour, with a certain inartistic art, an accidental purposefulness.

The combination of haiku and haiga is perhaps the most important practical question. One may spoil the other; but in the case of a complete success, how does one help the other? There seem to be two main ways of doing this. The haiga may be an illustration of the haiku, and say the same thing in line and form; or it may have a more independent existence, and yet an even deeper connection with the poem.

The illustrations of this book have been chosen to form, when chronologically surveyed, a pictorial parallel to the chart on page 3. In other words, we may trace in them the development from the philosophico-mystical Indian and Chinese origins of Japanese culture to the simplicity and nonchalance, the apparent crudeness and matter-of-factness of haiku.

The picture of Dainichi (Vairocana) in a Wheel of Sovereignty, facing page 5, is of the Kamakura Era, but it represents the Indian Buddhism which China, and finally Japan, brought down into daily life. Dainichi dwells in the Heaven beyond form, and is the essence of wisdom and of absolute purity. Compare this with the screen, facing page 137, by Kusumi Morikage, a contemporary of Bashô. We see a family of three cooling themselves in the evening under an arbour of evening-glories. There seems to be little connection between the picture of Dainichi aloof and glorious, and the poor family, but it has been the work of the Japanese to bring the calm of the Buddha into the evening, to transform the golden lotus into the humble convolvulus, so nearly a weed, the elaborate trappings of the Buddha into the human nakedness. This is not a degeneration or retrogression, but an incarnation, a re-making in blood and flesh of what was formed of thought and intuition. And strangely enough, the circle of Vairocana is still there in the full moon. To get the contrast in landscape, parallel with the above of persons, one should compare the two pictures facing pages 46 and 360.

The picture of Enô's enlightenment, facing page 207, is a very strange one, in that it lacks the violence and grimness of Zenga, Zen paintings. It is not fanciful, I think, to see in the quiet sweetness of this picture, so inward in its quality, something which was to develop into haiga, something that belongs rather to Jôdô and Shin than Zen. We may contrast his enlightenment with that of St. Paul. The subdued feeling of Shuai Weng's picture is far from the thunder and lightning on the way to Damascus. Yet Enô's listening to the words of the *Diamond Sutra* meant as much for the culture and religion of Japan as did St. Paul's conversion for those of Europe. Enô gave to Chinese and Japanese Zen its direction towards practicality which resulted in their application to haiku and the Way of Haiku in daily life. The verse is;

檐子全肩荷負、
目前歸路無差、
心知應無所住、
知柴落在誰家。

> The bundle is carried firmly on his shoulder;
> Before him, the way home has no obstructions.
> "Awaken the mind without fixing it anywhere",
> And he knows the house where the firewood burns.

The first line is the practical life, the second has a symbolic meaning. The third is the line of the *Diamond Sutra* that he hears as he stands outside the house to which he has brought the firewood. The last again has a symbolic meaning, but the literal and symbolic are not really different here.

The handwriting, facing page 73, says,

Form is emptiness.

This remarkable sentence, summing up in three words (four Chinese characters) the whole of Mahayana Buddhism, comes, like that of "Awaken the mind without fixing it anywhere", from the *Diamond Sutra.* The writing is by Takuan, a Japanese 17th century master of Zen. This "Form is emptiness" is the invisible seed which grew into what we call call Eastern Culture. This is is illustrated by Takuan's calligraphy itself. Writing, like everything else, when it is being done perfectly, is performed with the awakened Mind, without any desire of perfection, without any aim; it is done "meaninglessly". When we look at the handwriting, when we follow, dynamically and creatively the course of the brush, so definite and yet so yielding, we realize that the form of the characters is a no-form. Statically nothing exists at all; there is no writer, no brush, nothing written, only movement. And this movement is a no-movement, for to paraphrase Rôshi:

> A movement that can be moved (in speech or thought) is not an eternal movement.

Again, we have in this handwriting a perfect example of the "law" of "liberty". The form of the characters is absolutely fixed; yet the writer is absolutely free.

The interesting thing about Sengai's[1] picture of Tokusan and Ryutan, facing page 178, is the lack of beauty in the faces of the two people, and in the picture as a whole. Even if they had actually been a handsome couple, it would have been necessary to show them thus, because the picture is insisting on their deadly earnestness, on their souls, not on their appearance. We see a fundamental difference here between general Buddhism (and Christianity) and Zen, when we compare the face of Christ or Buddha and those of the Zen worthies. And just as Zen is more important than beauty, so the significance of the subject is more important than skill or technique in haiga.

The verse is:

點那箇心、
過現未來、
吹滅紙燭、
金剛爲灰。

Enlighten the Mind
Of the past, the present, the future.
Blow out the paper lantern,
And Mt. Kongo turns to ashes.

This means that the Mind is boundless, devoid of qualities; and when we are aware of It, when we are enlightened, the hardest and strongest thing in the world is as soft and weak as ashes. It is a practical application of the quotations from

[1] A celebrated painter-monk of the Rinzai branch of Zen. Died 1837.

the *Kongokyô, The Diamond Sutra,* on page 92.

The picture of A Papa on a Pine Branch, facing page 172, ascribed to the Chinese artist Mokkei[1], shows the direct application of Zen to art. Dr. Suzuki writes of this picture[2]:

> Is the pa-pa bird a kind of crow? It perches on an old pine tree symbolic of unbending strength. It seems to be looking down at something. The life of the universe pulsates through him, while quietness rules the enveloping nature. Here truly asserts the ancient spirit of solitude. This is when God has not yet given his fiat to the darkness of the unborn earth. To understand the working of the spirit in this, is not it the end of the Zen discipline?

It is rather another, a lighter yet still warm side of Mokkei which the Japanese artists have appreciated. For example, the picture of a monkey by Tôhaku, 1539–1610, facing page 52, is based on one of the three members of Mokkei's triptych in Daitokuji Temple. Haiku and haiga avoid the grim, the the violent, the dramatic and intense. They aspire to be deep without depth. Tôhaku portrays the old tree, pine-needles, bamboo leaves and monkey in the same spirit as Bashó's verse written about a hundred years later:

はつしぐれ猿も小みのをほしげなり

First winter rain;
The monkey also seems to wish
For a small straw rain-coat.

The Chinese were aware not only of the vaster aspects of nature, but saw the peculiar value of the small and appar-

[1] 13th Century.
[2] In *Essays in Zen Buddhism, III.*

ently insignificant. Such a picture as *Apples and a Small Bird*, by Chôshô, facing page 62, must have impressed the Japanese mind deeply. The painter is celebrated for his power of delineating fruit, but here he has adopted the Eastern method of hiding what it is wished to show. The apples are hidden in space by the leaves, and in composition by the bird, and yet they are the one essential of the picture. Chôshô, a painter of the 13th century, is recorded as getting up early every morning, and, going out into the flower garden, using the dew to paint the flowers, leaves, and insects.

The sketch by Sesshu, 1450–1506, facing page 120, was evidently a study for a larger, more ambitious work; this is shown by the absence of seals. It is too brilliant, too good for haiga, it lacks something, the warmth and human sentiment that infuse the more clumsy and less slick pictures by those who are concerned with the things represented rather than with the representation. The sketch shows, however, a simplification and grasp of essentials which are the aim of haiku.

Miyamoto Musashi, 1582–1645, who died one year after the birth of Bashô, continues the unconscious development towards haiga. His Shrike Screeching on a Dead Branch, facing page 271, has the quietness of eye, and the penetration into the nature of bird and bough, but it still aims at a perfection which for haiga and haiku is limited and finite. The great problem here is how to combine art with nature, nature that is always incomplete, never finished. It is the same paradox everywhere, to "reject people" yet value above all things "the human warmth"; to love and hate; to hold and to renounce; to be oneself alone and be all things; to paint the form and yet be conscious only of the spirit of the thing.

The Zenga, by Hakuin, 1683–1768, facing page 234, has strangely enough, a haiku added to it:

よしあしの葉をひつ布いて夕凉み

Spreading out
The reeds of good and evil,—
Cooling in the evening.

This picture has a concentration and intensity quite alien to haiga. It is a spiritual portrait, in the style of Blake, of Daitô Kokushi, 1282–1337, one of the greatest of early Zen priests in Japan.

A remarkably good haiga (though it may be called a Zenga) by Hakuin, who is perhaps the greatest of later Zen monks, is the painting of a *misosazai*, or wren, facing page 307; the tailless bird has the peculiar Zen flavour about it. The verse runs:

鴬になりが似たとてみそさゞひ

Its appearance
Is that of a nightingale,—
But it's a wren!

The verse is a kind of criticism of his own painting; it prevents the whole thing from being too lyrical, for the bough that is used for stirring the *miso* in the earthenware mortar seems to have a few leaves remaining on it, denoting a person of artistic sensibilities. The mortar is painted with great skill. Its irregular shape, the six dots that represent the grating inner surface, the white patches on the outside that represent the reflection of light on the glazed surface, the open beak of the tailless bird, all these things are well done. But it is a fact, the bird is too slender for a wren, and Hakuin rectifies this in his verse. The whole thing is an aiming at something of more value than perfection, through imperfection willingly chosen.

Bashô's sketch of the morning-glories, facing page 26, is real haiga. We feel the morning freshness; the dew is still on the leaves, and glistening down the slender reed that supports them. The verse is:

朝顔にわれはめし喰ふおとこ哉

> I am one
> Who eats his breakfast
> Gazing at the morning-glories.

The frontispiece, a picture of Bashô saying good-bye to his disciple[1] Sora, is by Buson. It is quite imaginary, in that Buson never met Bashô, but better so, since Buson is free to show us how he wished to see him. It is no romantic figure. Bashô is plain of countenance, simple in dress, an amiable, frail-looking creature, nothing about him to show him to be what he was, the greatest man Japan has produced. The picture illustrates Buson's transcription of *Oku no Hosomichi*, a short diary of travel, which breathes through it and in this illustration, Bashô's warm, unaffected simplicity.

The picture by Senna, 1650–1723, facing page 317, The Slope of Osaka, east of Kyôto, has grasped the spirit of the place, its mountains and cherry blossoms and pine trees. It has also something peculiarly Japanese, something that is

[1] The fact that the Japanese poets had disciples, the English poets not, is one of the most significant things in the comparative study of the two literatures.

almost unique to haiga, a certain childishness, a quality that we see, but can never reproduce, in children's pictures. The verse is:

會坂のかたまるころや初ざくら

At the time when
The Slope of Osaka hardens,
The first cherry blossoms.

In Kôrin, 1661–1716, contemporary of Bashô, we see the opposite tendency, a delight in painting for its own sake; he corresponds to Swinburne in English literature. So the picture of azaleas, facing page 114, has a superficial resemblance to haiga, but is utterly different in spirit and technique. The azaleas are only the excuse for a brilliant exhibition of significant form, but, form of what?

The following is an interesting use of pictures instead of words by Buson:

一つ埋み殘して若葉かな

Alone remains
Above the green leaves.

In the second example, the picture is found in the middle of the haiku:

日の光今朝や　の頭より

The light of day,—
From the head of the ² it came
This morning.

---

¹ A picture of Mt. Fuji.
² 鰯, a pilchard. This illustration is too good.

Plate 7

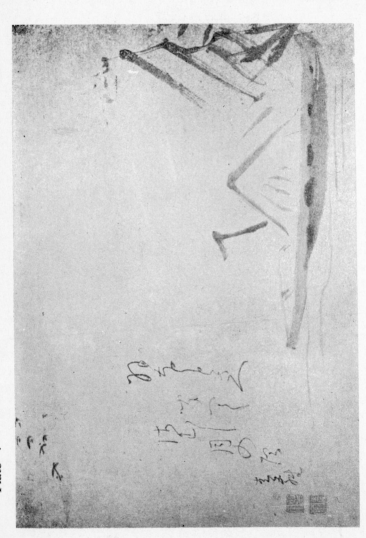

A Boat anchored at Night

Seira

The haiku and picture by Ryôta, 1707–87, facing page 192, is an example in which the connection between the two is rather distant. The verse is:

> ともしびを見れば風あり夜の雪
>> Looking at the light,
>> There is a wind,
>> This night of snow.

The wind is seen, not felt, and the mind trembles with the flame in the darkness surrounding it. The snow is falling, silent and invisible. This is the verse, but the picture is of the basket of charcoal, that is half out of the picture. It is black, but shines in the light of the lamp that is to be seen in the verse only.

Another haiga, facing this page, which has something rather Korean about it, portrays a boat by the shore at night. The verse is by Seira, died 1791:

> 羽をとさへ聞へてさむし月の夜　　青償
>> Even the sound
>> Of the wings is heard,—
>> A cold, moon-lit night.

The wild geese are seen, but not the moon, that shines down on the roof of the boat and on the reeds of the bank. The verse is one of sound, the picture of sight; it is the sound of birds, the sight of the reedy shore and moored sampan. It would have been better still, perhaps, to have omitted the wild geese from the picture.

Issa's picture of the morning-glory, facing page 344, has this verse:

> 朝顔の花でふいたる菴かな

> My hermitage
> Is thatched
> With morning-glories.

When he went out in the early morning he found that the
whole roof was covered with the flowers of the convolvulus;
his house was "roofed" with them. The verse is rather
simple, but the sketch, by being even more so, is in perfect
harmony with it. There is only one flower, which is used instead of the word *asagao*, and a short piece of vine, but everything is there. All the flowers sway in the morning breeze.
and Issa also is there, though his back is turned to us, gazing
at them.

In Issa's verse and illustration, facing page 365, we see
another side of his character, an invariable one perhaps, in
persons of strongly critical, cynical nature. The verse is:

又むだに口あく鳥のまゝ子かな

> Opening its mouth
> Uselessly still,
> The step-child of the bird.

Under the bird, it says: Both the Swallow and Issa.

We see here the self-pity into which tender-minded people
easily fall. (Herein lies the necessity for such haiku poets as
Kikaku, and for senryu). Issa was a step-son, and suffered
deeply because of his sensitive and love-desiring nature. He
compares himself to a baby swallow. The sketch of the
swallow is rather poor, but its angularity suggests, perhaps,
the unkindness of the foster-mother.

The verse by Tanehiko, 1782–1842, facing page 291, is
rather obscure, being based on an anecdote:

かつらぎの神やさくらの朝がへり

> The cherry blossoms,
> Returning at dawn from the Yoshiwara;
> Was it the goddess of Mt. Katsuragi?[1]

In the picture we feel the early spring morning; the willow tree gives the feeling of wantonness and enervation; the towel round the head of the man going home suggests the slight chill in the air; and the lantern the vagueness of the period between night and day. There is a balance between the four objects; the poem is one of them, and floats like an exhalation in the morning air.

For the treatment of pine-trees in haiga we may take the two illustrations facing page 243. In Ryôto's[2] picture, the tree is simplified to its farthest limits; it is to be noted how the ten, 十, of the poem joins the picture and the verse, which is:

十の指そろへて松のみどりかな

> The pine-tree,
> Ten fingers in a row:
> How green it is!

Gijôen's pine-tree is also original in vision and expression. The verse runs:

松脂をはなれかねてやせみの聲

> Can't it get away
> From the pine-tree resin?
> The voice of the cicada!

This means that there is something frantic in the sound of the crying of the cicada, as though it were stuck on the gum of the pine-tree, and could not extricate itself.

[1] There is a Nô play on this subject, *Katsuragi*.
[2] Died 1717.

The haiga on the inside of the covers of this volume is by Chora, 1729–1781. The verse, also by him, is:

呉竹のよよにあふひのまつりかな

Today, the Aoi Festival:
We greet again the many-jointed bamboos,
Generation after generation.

There is here a very complicated play on words, *yoyo* meaning " successive generations ", and the part of the bamboo between the joints. *Aoi* means " meeting day " and "Hollyhock ", the name of the festival held at the Kamo Shrine in Kyôto on the 15th of May. The picture, however, is very simple and child-like, characteristic of many of Chora's other verses.

To get clearly into our minds the difference between haiga and classical painting, we may compare the two illustrations on pages 46 and 360. The landscape by Shôkei, a Japanese of the later 15th century, is typical of Chinese romantic treatment. The mountains in the distance are the impossible creations of the dreaming artist, the pine-trees tragic in their intensity, the sage and attendant, the fisherman in his boat almost negligible among the overwhelming forms of nature. The haiga, by Isshô, died 1707, seems at first sight a mere smudge by comparison, a travesty of the other, but when we wait a little, the reeds in the water, the fisherman poling his boat, are seen to be something alive. There is no doubt who is the greater artist. or which is the better picture, but the haiga has something which the other has not,

The something that infects the world.

As an example of contemporary work, we may take the haiga of Shimada Tadao. The *kappa* or water-imp, portrayed facing page 218, sits gazing intently at the moon. There is a melon by his side. The verse is by Imozeni:

田や村や人聲もなき後の月
Not a voice
In field and hamlet:
The after-moon.

Another fine example is *Tilling the Field*, facing page 388. The man is somewhat kappa-like. He is not seen as contrasted with nature, but as an ephemeral movement among the changing seasons; now it is spring. He has something unreal about him, and his work is a dream within a dream world. Haiku has some weakness, an avoidance of power; it agrees with Pater that the end of life is not action but contemplation.

Coming at last to the point of the matter, the relation between Japanese art, particularly painting, and haiku, we may consider the question like this: what kind of pictures did Bashô see, in his first forty years, such as would have affected his creation of a new world of poetic life? The answer is that in Sesshu, Shôkadô, Kôetsu, Kôrin, Chokuan, Miyamoto Musashi, Itchô and so on, he must have seen done in art what he wanted to do in verse. He may have seen many great Chinese paintings of the Tang and Sung Dynasties, especially those of Mokkei and Gyokukaku, brought to Japan in the 15th century, who influenced greatly the painters of the Muromachi Period, 1334–1573, e.g. Kano Motonobu.

What Bashô wanted to do, however, was to condense without heaviness, to refine without dilettantism, to philosophize without intellection. This he could find done in pictures already. The trenchancy and unselfconsciouness of Zenga, their paradox and humour, must also have impressed him, but the priests were concerned with the expression of their own spiritual life, whereas Bashô wished rather to make manifest in a short compass the inner life of the things of the world. No doubt the life of the poet and the life of birds and trees and clouds are one, but there is a difference of emphasis, a certain gentleness, pathos, passivity in haiku which appears also in haiga as distinct from Zenga. To put it another way, Zen, that is, Zen as a body of religious experience, tends to underestimate the importance of love, of what Byron calls

the quiet of a loving eye.

Summing up, we may say that haiga justifies its existence in two ways, by its humour and by its roughness. The insistence on the fact that humour is to be seen everywhere, under all circumstances, which is the special virtue of haiku, is also the distinguishing quality of haiga, and one which keeps it most closely connected with this world and this life. Art comes down to earth; we are not transported into some fairy, unreal world of pure aesthetic pleasure. The roughness gives it that peculiar quality of *sabi* without age; unfinished pictures, half-built houses, broken statuary tell the same story. It corresponds in poetry to the fact that what we wish to say is just that which escapes the words. Haiku and haiga therefore do not try to express it, and succeed in doing what they have not attempted.

VII
WAKA

Before we deal with the relation of waka and haiku, let us consider the relation between waka and Chinese poetry. The *Manyôshu* consists of more than four thousand pieces, the great majority being waka, and the rest *naga-uta*, or long poems. Two or three hundred years before, Wani, 王仁, a Korean, had brought the *Analects* and the *Senjimon*, 千字文, (*A Thousand Characters*, written about 525 A.D.) to Japan, and the influence of Chinese thought and literature had begun. The *Kokinshu*, completed about 922, contains only five *naga-uta*, and this may well have been partly due to the influence of Chinese poetry, which, however long the poems may be, is meaty to the eye as well as the mind, whereas a long Japanese poem tends to be flimsy and vague.

As evidence of the way in which Chinese poetry was studied and compared to waka, we may take the *Rôeishu*, 和漢朗詠集, or *Collection of Clear Songs, Japanese and Chinese*. The date of publication is not known exactly, but the compiler, Fujiwara Kintô, 966–1041, son of Yoritada the famous poet, gave the two volumes to his daughter's bridegroom, Norimichi, as a wedding present in 1103. For a long time before this, Chinese poetry and waka had been sung or intoned by the people of the palace and the nobility in general. The *Rôeishu* consists of two parts, the first divided into seasons and subdivided into subjects, the second divided into subjects irrespective of seasons. For each subject, part of a Chinese poem, usually that of Hakurakuten, a part of a Chinese verse by a Japanese writer, and waka are given, the number of each varying. For example, in the first part, under Winter Evening, we have two lines from a poem by Hakurakuten:

一盞寒燈雲外夜、數盃溫酎雪中春

One cold lamp at night among the clouds;
Many cups of warm wine is spring in the snow.

Several old cronies are gathered together in a house high up in the mountains, and the cup passes round, gladdening their hearts as though spring had come.

The next is two lines of a Chinese poem, *Sitting up Alone at Night in Winter*, 冬夜獨起.

年光自向燈前盡、客思唯從枕上生。

The years passing with the guttering of the lamp,
The traveller's grief only grows at his pillow.

This verse describes the increasing loneliness of the traveller; as the night draws on the lamp goes out at his bed-side. It is by a Japanese poet, Aritsura, 在列, who afterwards became a monk, and took the name Sonkyô, 尊敬. Last, there is a waka by Ki no Tsurayuki, 紀貫之, 883–946, author of the *Tosanikki*, a classic of travel diaries, and one of the compilers of the *Kokinshu*. He is one of the greatest masters of waka.

おもひかねいもがりゆけば
冬のよの河かぜ寒みちどり鳴くなり

Filled with longing,
    I go to her I love;
The river wind is chill tonight,
    Plovers crying.

These three poems show how waka and Chinese verse were compared and contrasted by the Japanese poets. It is my own opinion that the *direct* effect of the one on the other was relatively small, owing partly to the great difference of form, and partly to that of national spirit.

One more point may be noted, the influence which Buddhism was exerting upon waka, even more indirectly than Chinese poetry. In the *Rôeishu* we find a comparatively long section entitled *Buddhist Affairs*, 佛事, and another called Monks, 僧. Besides many Chinese verses, there are waka by such famous priests as Kuya, 空也, 903–972, and Dengyô Daishi, 傳敎大師, 767–822, the founder of the Tendai Sect of Buddhism, and by the Emperor Murakami, died 967. Included is a piece of prose by Hakurakuten, in which he says that all his works are profane, but since everything, the mountains and valleys, the crying of birds and insects, is the Voice of the Law, he hopes that his verses may be included among the sutras and be a cause of his becoming a Buddha in the next world. Many of the literati of both China and Japan took this light view of Buddhism intellectually, but they could not avoid being deeply affected by it emotionally, in so far as they were poets.

In dealing with the relation between waka and haiku we may begin by describing Bashô's attitude and then give a more general account of the differences between the two.

Bashô,[1] the spiritual founder of modern haiku, lived during the second half of the seventeenth century. In the first half of the century, the Teitoku[2] school was flourishing. A typical example of his work is the following:

花よりも團子やありて歸る雁　　　貞　德

---

[1] *1644–94.*
[2] *1570–1653.*

> Dumplings
> Being better than flowers,
> The geese are returning there?

Teitoku has taken two elements and combined them, first the
popular saying *Hana yori dango*, meaning, something to eat
is better than something to look at, the material than the
spiritual. The other is a poem from the *Kokinshu:*

春霞立つを見すてゝ行く雁は
　　花なき里に住みやならへる

> They see the spring mist rising,
> But the wild geese depart,
> Wont to dwell
> In flowerless villages?

Teitoku has taken a quite beautiful old verse, abbreviated it,
and inserted in it a popular but not very elevated proverb.

Another example is the following, also by Teitoku:

まんまるにいづれどながき春日かな

> It arose a perfect sphere,—
> But how long it is,
> This spring day!

The word for sun and day are the same in Japanese, thus
making the pun and the verse possible. The sun is round,
but long in its passing through the sky. If we look at this
superficially, it is devoid of worth, but a historic feeling of
an organic kind, will allow us to see faint stirrings of religion
and poetry here, in the endeavour to attain a unity, or to see
variety in oneness, though with such inappropriate, intellectual
means.

Towards the middle of the century, the Danrin[1] school

---

[1] The name is taken from that of a disciple's house.

under S in[1] arose. This also made puns, combinations of scraps of learning, and wit, its chief objects. For example:

價あらば何かをしまの秋の景　　　宗因

Should it have such worth,
What would I not give
For the scenery of Autumn?

There is, in the original, an untranslatable play on words. Sôin composed the verse in praise of the island of Ojima at Matsushima. The name Ojima or Oshima is hinted at in *oshima no,* 惜まむ. The two expressions, "What is there not worth giving for the scenery of autumn?" and "The autumnal scenery of Oshima," are telescoped together. The rhythm of this verse is graceful, but the punning and artificiality, its unpoetical, unimaginative, one might say, irreligious character is evident.

A little later, that is, in the second half of the seventeenth century, there were great movements in haikai circles; Bashô and Onitsura appeared. The reasons for this phenomenon may be adduced in the social and spiritual conditions of the age, but the fact is that such matters are as inscrutable as the mystery of life itself. In any case, there was a general desire to raise haiku from its low state of punning and joking, to the high literary and spiritual level of waka. But just as Wordsworth, in contrast to the artificiality of the eighteenth century, inaugurated the "return to nature" of the nineteenth, so Bashô wished to make haiku something that waka was not, an expression of *popular* feeling, in the sense that it should express the intuitions of daily life. Another striking

[1] *1604–1682.*

similarity in the work of the two is in the matter of language.
As Confucius says,

不知言、無以知人也　　　（論語二十、二）

If you do not know words, you cannot know man,

and conversely, when language is changed, the hearts of men
are changed with it. Wordsworth wished to make use of

a selection of language really used by men,

and the aim of Bashô was to continue what began with the
Teitoku school and increased with the Danrin school, the
employment of popular phraseology, Chinese expressions and
other foreign words. Haiku poets wanted somehow or other,
by the use of 俳言, haiku words, to make haiku something
different from a short waka. This new vocabulary could be
used instead of 雅言, poetic diction, to express something they
felt in the poems of Ritaihaku, Tôhô, Hakurakuten, and in
the Zen poems of Kanzan, 寒山. Here was the spirit which,
in the case of Bashô, was more important than the form in
which it was to be expressed. In *The Empty Chestnut*, 虚栗,
edited by Kikaku in 1683, we read of

　　季杜が心酒を嘗めて寒山が法粥を啜る
　　tasting the wine of the hearts of Ritaihaku and
　　Tôhô, supping of the gruel of the law of Kanzan.

　　白氏が歌を假名にやつして初心を救ふた
　　よりならんとす
　　Writing in *kana* the poems of Hakurakuten is a
　　means of helping beginners.

Bashô was more interested in the spirit of Chinese poetry
than its form, but an example of his imitation of one of the
"tricks" of Chinese poetry, is seen in the following:

鬢風を吹いて暮秋嘆ずるは誰が子ぞ

Who is it that grieves,
The wind blowing through his beard,
For late autumn?

In one of his *Eight Poems on Autumn*, Tôhô says:

香稲咏餘　鸚鵡粒
碧梧捿老　鳳凰枝

This is his affected version, "The corn pecks the parakeet,"
with the same meaning, of

鸚鵡咏餘香稲粒
鳳凰捿老碧梧枝

The parakeet pecks at the remaining grains of
fragrant corn;
The phoenix dwells long on the branches of the
green paulownia.

Bashô has imited this kind of thing in transposing the words,
so that just as Tôhô says the grains are pecking the parakeet
and the green paulownia lives in the phoenix, Bashô's verse
actually says:

His beard blowing the wind.

This figure of speech of inversion, 例装法, paralleled in English
literature by the transferred epithet, was probably tried by
Bashô less as an ornament than as part of that effort of all
mystical poets to convey the idea of one in all, all in one.

It will be as well at once to indicate briefly the difference
between haiku and waka or renga. In *Three Volumes*,
三冊子, by Tohô, 土芳, a countryman and disciple of Bashô,
the following interesting passage occurs:

春雨の柳は全體連歌なり
田螺取る烏は全く俳諧なり

Spring rain falling on a willow tree is, generally
speaking, renga; a raven catching mud-snails is
simply haikai.

Renga, waka made by two or more people, deal with
"poetical" things; haikai, which replaced the mere pastime
of renga with aesthetical motives, and from which haiku broke
off, treat of "interesting" things.

In haiku, the gentlest, most melancholy and quiet aspects
of things are grasped with an energy, a concentration, an
élan, which seventeen syllables and no more are fitted to
express. Bashô occasionally tried to do in haiku what could
be better done in waka. The lyrical vague, the cloudy emotional, the dreamy forlorn,—this is the realm of waka, and
length is necessary for it.

人住まぬ不破の關屋の板庇
荒れにし後はたゞ秋の風

No one lives at the Barrier of Fuha;
　　　The wooden penthouse is fallen away;
All that remains
　　　Is the autumn wind.

Upon this, from the *Shin Kokinshu*, Bashô composed the
following:

秋風や藪もはたけも不破の關

The autumn wind:
Thickets and fields also,
Fuha Barrier.

This is much inferior to the waka. It omits the most poetical

part, the thought in the last two lines, and requires the waka
as a proscript, to enable the haiku to be understood at all.
We can expand the original and the translation:

> What was once the Barrier of Fuha,
> Now only fields and thickets:
> The autumn wind.

Here we get what Bashô had in mind, at the back of his
mind, it may be, which is not in the waka.

> All that remains
> Is the autumn wind,

has something a little false in the sentiment; the autumn wind
is not *all* that remains. The waka is aiming at this melancholy which is the truth but not the whole truth. The haiku
says that the autumn wind *is* the Barrier, is the fields and
thickets, is the very soul of the poet who gives the scene its
meaning and value. Bashô's verse is a failure, but it is a
failure of creative imagination struggling with the material
and the form.

Another verse which shows Bashô's preoccupation with
waka:

芋洗ふ女西行ならば歌よまん

> A woman washing potatoes;
> If Saigyô were here,
> He would write a waka.

Bashô realized the lyrical quality of his sensations and felt
that it required the form of waka.

Coming now to the general differences between waka and
haiku, we may say once more that waka aim at beauty, a
somewhat superficial beauty sometimes, that excludes all ugly
things. The aim of haiku is not beauty; it is something much

deeper and wider. It is *significance*, a poetical significance,
"a shock of mild surprise", that the poet receives when the
haiku is born, and the reader when it is reborn in his mind.
It would be impossible, for example, to rewrite the following
as waka:

> むさゝびの小鳥食み居る枯野かな　　　蕪 村
>
> > The flying squirrel
> > Is crunching the small bird,
> > > On the withered moor.　　　Buson

Haiku finds intensely interesting states of mind that have
no relation to beauty at all:

> 夜に入れば直したくなるつぎほかな
>
> > > > > 一 茶
>
> > After it was dark,
> > I began to want to change
> > > The way I grafted it.　　　Issa

Waka is what we may call in terms of pictorial art,
decorative. In terms of music, it reminds us of the Songs
without Words; for example:

> 淡海の海夕なみ千鳥汝が鳴けば
>
> > 心もしぬにいにしへおもほゆ　　　人 麿
>
> Ah, plovers, when you cry
> > On the evening waves of Omi,—
> How I grieve,
> > Remembering things of long ago !
> > > > > Hitomaro

The transition from the cry of the plovers to a melancholy mood, and a consequent recollection of old, unhappy,
far-off things is conventional but not insincere. This waka
succeeds, partly because it does not aim very high. In this
sense we can say that a poor haiku is better than a good

Plate 8

Azaleas   Kôrin

waka. Nevertheless, the mere length of waka enables the
poet to say things, to do things that cannot be done in haiku.
There is a natural sequence, a gradation of explicitness, for
example, that requires the thirty one syllables of waka. This
is illustrated in the previous verse, and in the following:

願くは花の下にて春死なむ
　　　その二月の望月のころ　　　西行

> My desire
> Is that I may die
> Beneath the cherry blossoms,
> In spring,
> On the fifteenth night
> Of the second month.　　　Saigyô

This is the day of Buddha's entrance into Nirvana, when
the cherry blossoms are at their best. The next verse is a
kind of after-echo of it:

佛には花の櫻を奉れ
　　　我がのちの世を人とぶらはゞ

> Lay cherry blossoms
> Before the Buddha,
> Should you wish to pray for my soul
> In the world to come.　　　Saigyô

Let us take a much later, but still famous waka:

うらうらとのどけき春の心より
　　　にほひ出たる山ざくら花　・　賀茂眞淵

> From the heart
> Of bright and balmy spring
> Are wafted forth
> These mountain cherry flowers.
> 　　　　　Kamo Mabuchi[1]

[1] *1697–1769.*

In this verse. the subject is the flowers of the mountain cherry
trees and their relation to spring; they represent the very
nature of spring in proceeding from it themselves. The
flowers are symbols of the new life of the world as the ice
and snow of winter dissolve and disappear. This verse is
characteristic of Mabuchi in his appreciation of the waka of
the *Manyôshu*. The word "wafted", which is literally
"comes smelling out", applies to the form and colour
as well as the actual scent. But for all its poetry and
beauty, Mabuchi's poem, in its symbolism and its making a
statement concerning the relation of the flowers and the spring,
remains waka and is not haiku.

限なく悲しきものは燈の
　　消えての後の寝覺めなりけり

香川景樹

> Waking at night
> After the light
> Has gone out,—
> An infinity
> Of grief.   Kagawa Kageki

How much more ordinary and plain and unpoetical is the
following haiku:

燭の火を燭に移すや春の夕　　　　蕪　村

> Lighting one candle
> With another candle;
> An evening of spring.   Buson

But the haiku seizes a moment of inexplicable depth. It does
not look before and after, but confines itself to the timeless,
when life suddenly deepens, and all the universe is present at
the lighting of a candle.

Waka says everything it wishes to say, expressing poig-

nant grief and yearning, conveying its meaning to the reader
without fail:

山里の春の夕暮きて見れば
　　いりあひの鐘に花ぞ散りけり
　　　　　　　　　　　　能因法師

Coming to the mountain village
　　One spring evening,
The evening bell was sounding,
　　Flowers falling.　　　　Nôin Hôshi

So many waka have titles, but haiku have none. because their
real subject is unmentionable.　Haiku are self-obliterating;
they are the real " Songs without words ".　In waka there is
still a kind of poetic haze between us and the thing.　The
music of the words and the cadence of the lines induce in us
a certain state of mind which we designate " poetic ", but in
haiku the melody and rhythm remove the barriers of custom
and prejudice between ourselves and the object.

When we say " object ", this does not mean that it is
necessarily a material thing.　It may be time, the length of a
spring day or shortness of a summer night.　But even this is
felt in a material way; spring is a manifold of sensations, and
the passage of time is as palpable as the flowing of a stream.

From the haiku point of view, waka say too much.　For
example, the following anonymous verse from the *Kokinshu*:

ほのぼのとあかしの浦のあさ霧に
　　島がくれ行く舟をしぞ思ふ

In the mist of morning
A boat has sailed away
　　Beyond the isle
In the Bay of Akashi;
My thoughts are with it.

When we say the last line, the pathos of parting with the unknown, to the unknown, is lost. What we gain in lyrical sweetness and historical associations, we lose in scope and freedom of imagination. It is like an illustrated novel, in which the pictures do not gibe with our visions of the characters. The same in true of the following verse:

ひさかたの天の香具山このゆふべ
　　　　霞たなびく春たつらしも　　人麿

> Evening mist is trailing
> Over Mount Kagu
> In the ageless sky;
> It must be
> That spring is here.　　　　Hitomaro

Compare this to the following, by Bashô:

春なれや名もなき山のうす霞

> Spring has come;
> A nameless hill
> Is shrouded in thin mist.

Here the historical association is not merely avoided, the point of the haiku lies in the very avoidance.

Other differences between waka and haiku besides the less lyrical approach, are the stronger grasp of essential poetry, a less general presentation and a more detailed and impressionistic method. Compare the following:

ひんがしの野にかげろひの立つ見えて
　　　かへり見すれば月かたぶきぬ　　人麿

> Seeing the heat waves
> Over the eastern moor,
> I looked back,
> And there was the moon,
> Sinking.　　　　Hitomaro

菜の花や月は東に日は西に   蕪 村

> Flowers of rape;
> The sun in the west,
> The moon in the east. ·   Buson

Hitomaro's verse is subjective, and has something trailing, lingering in its tone and cadence, partaking of the lyrical and vague. Buson's haiku is objective, descriptive, has no untidy edges, is abrupt in ending, with a conciseness that is almost harsh by contrast.

Bashô said,

俳諧は萬葉集の心なり
Haikai is the heart of the *Manyôshu*,

and this is undoubtedly true, but elimination of unessential elements means such a tremendous increase of power and significance that it is indeed " a new creation ".

俳諧は俗談平話を正さんが爲なり
Haikai has for its object the setting to rights
of common parlance and ordinary language.

This is one of those profound sayings which can and should be interpreted in a variety of ways. Bashô wanted our daily prose turned into poetry, the realization that the commonest events and actions of life may be done significantly, the deeper use of all language, written and spoken. Our lives are slovenly, imitative. We live, as Lawrence said, like the illustrated covers of magazines. Comfort is our aim, and dissatisfaction is all we achieve. The aim of haiku is to live twenty four hours a day, that is, to put meaning into every moment, a meaning that may be intense or diffuse, but never ceases.

Haiku often turns the weak subjectivity of waka into an

objectivity which is a more subtle subjectivity, or rather a region where "subjective" and "objective" lose their meaning and validity. Take for example the following waka by Ryôkan:

> むらぎもの心たのしも春の日に
> 　　　　鳥のむらがり遊ぶを見れば

> My heart rejoices,
> 　　　This day of spring,
> To see the birds
> 　　　That flock to play.

Compare this with Bashô's,

> 茱畠に花見顔なる雀哉

> Sparrows,
> 　　In the field of rape,
> 　　　With flower-viewing faces.

Both haiku and waka have a simplicity that belongs to the original character of the Japanese race, and is hardly to be paralleled in other literatures. It is sometimes rudely termed "playing on the soft pedal", and does in fact require a certain patience and repression of all desire for purple passages and poetic thrills. Even so, the simplicity of haiku is more gaunt and bare than that of waka.

> 六月や峯に雲おくあらし山　　　　芭蕉

> In the Sixth month,
> Mount Arashi
> 　　　Lays clouds on its summit.　Bashô

There is something at once simple and sublime about this verse. The simplicity is self-evident. Bashô's verse lacks both the feeling of movement and the artificiality of Milton's

Plate 9

A Sketch

Sesshu

Mountains, on whose barren breast
The labouring clouds do often rest.

It has not the strength and flow of the *Manyôshu*:

あしびきの山河の瀬の鳴るなべに
ゆづきが嶽に雲立ちわたる　　　人　麿

As the shallows
Of the mountain stream sound louder,
Clouds gather over
Yuzuki Peak.　　　　　　Hitomaro

But Bashô's verse has attained a vastness and aloofness that belongs to the subject. The simplicity is that of nature.

When we try to separate waka and haiku, we come across that law mentioned before, the law that the more the mind endeavours to distinguish two things, the closer they insensibly become; the more we assert their unity, the more they separate. Both waka and haiku are the activity of the spirit of man, and we must not exaggerate the differences between them. In general, we may say that waka is the feminine and haiku the masculine side of Japanese poetry, though haiku lacks the sterner, Miltonic elements. The " flavour ' of haiku, 俳句味, is rural, pastoral, bucolic, 田園趣味, but not idyllic, in the sense of ideal, unreal. We may also say that in contrast to waka, haiku is popular, democratic, plebeian.

Waka has a history of one thousand three hundred years, haiku has four hundred at most, two hundred and fifty from Bashô. Waka began as literature, haiku as a kind of sporting with words. Bashô made it literature, and yet something beyond and above literature, a process of discovery rather than of creation, using words as means, not ends, as a chisel that removes the rock hiding the statue beneath.

When the early haiku poets compared their verses with waka, they found in them the material they wanted, and yet somehow felt that it could have been given a more appropriate form, more condensed, and by saying less, meaning more. Such verses as the following especially must have inspired them to express the same insight more deeply in fewer words:

さびしさに宿を立ち出でゝ眺むれば
　　いづこもおなじ秋の夕暮　　　良暹法師

> Lonely,
> 　I left my hut;
> 　　Gazing around,
> Everywhere the same
> Autumn evening.　　　　　Ryôsen[1]

山ざとの稲葉の風にねざめして
　　夜深く鹿の聲を聞くかな　　　師　忠

> The wind in the rice leaves
> 　Wakes me at midnight;
> I listen to the distant cry of the deer
> 　In the mountain village.　Morotada[2]

思ほえず來ませる君を佐保川の
　　かはず聞せず歸しつるかも　　鞍作益人

> Unexpectedly you came,
> 　And I let you go back,
> The frogs of the River Saho
> 　Unheard.　　Kuratsukuri no Masahito[3]

尋ねきて花に暮せる木の間より
　　待つとしもなき山の端の月　　雅　經

[1] 11th Century.
[2] 11th Century.
[3] 8th Century.

Flower-viewing,
Shadows of evening fall,
But unawares,
Through the trees,
The moon over the mountain! Masatsune[1]

山邊より歸る我身を送りきて
あくれば門を月も入りけり　　　言　道

The moon,
Coming back with me
From the mountains,
Entered the gate
Together with me.　　　Kotomichi[2]

A last example with the haiku that it must have inspired:

ほとゝぎす鳴きつる方を眺むれば
たゞ有明の月ぞ殘れる

後德大寺左大臣

Looking
Where the *hototogisu*[3]
Had cried,
Only remaining
The moon of dawn.　Gotokudaiji Sadaijin

ほとゝぎす消え行く方や島一つ　　　蕉　芭

Where a *hototogisu*
Vanished —
A single island.　　　Bashô

Occasionally we come across haiku that should have been
waka, for example:

風薫る暮や鞠場の茶の給仕　　　乙　二

[1] *1170-1221.*
[2] *1798-1868.*
[3] A kind of nightingale.

> In the dusk, the breeze is fragrant;
> A maiden bringing the tea
>> To the football garden.   <small>Otsuji</small>

As an example of the way in which haiku sometimes drew from several sources at once, Chinese poetry, waka, and Japanese history, we may take the following verse by Buson:

青柳や我大君の草か木か

> The green willow,
> A tree or grass
>> Of our great Emperor.

This appears both simple and devoid of any poetical meaning, but some study of it will bring out unsuspected values. It has a proscript, 禁城春色曉蒼々, which is the second line of an eight-line poem by Koishi, 賈至, 718–772. The poem is entitled " Going early to the Taimei Palace, and Presenting it to Colleagues of Both Offices."

早朝大明宮呈兩省僚友

The first four lines are:

> 銀燭朝天紫陌長
> 禁城春色曉蒼々
> 千條弱柳垂青瑣
> 百囀流鶯遶建章

In the dawn, while the silver tapers are yet alight,
the road in the capital is long;
In the Palace, the spring scenery of early morning is bright and clear.
A thousand drooping branches of the willows hang over the green inscriptions on the wall;
A hundred voices of nightingales are heard around the Kenshô Palace.

Buson possibly read this in the *Tôshisen*, a selection of poetry of the Tô (Tang) Dynasty, which came to Japan early in the Edo Period, 1603–1867.

Then in the *Taiheiki*, 太平記, annals of Japanese history from 1318 to 1368, written by Kojima, 小島, a priest of Hiezan, who died in 1374, we have the following:

> Again, in the reign of the Emperor Tenchi, there was a man named Fujiwara Chikata, who employed four kinds of demons,......Because of these creatures, ordinary people being unable to withstand them, in the provinces of Iga and Ise, there was no one who obeyed the Imperial Rule. A man named Ki no Tomotake receiving an Imperial order, went to these provinces, and, composing a waka, sent it among the demons:
>
> > Even trees and grasses
> > > Are the kingdom of Our Lord;
> > Where can there be dwellings
> > > For demons?
>
> The four kinds of demons, reading this verse...... dispersed in every direction, and disappeared, losing their power everywhere, at last overcome by Tomotake.

Combining these two references, Buson has made poetry out of literature by getting us to perceive that the willow of its nature combines the beauty of the tree with that of the grasses. He has taken a Chinese poem of palace life, and the fantasies of the Japanese historian, and thus reinforced, added overtones to the willow that stands there with such slender grace.

VIII
RENKU

A haiku consists of seventeen syllables which may be broken into three parts, five, seven, five. It is the first part of a short poem, or tanka, which contains thirty one: 5, 7, 5; 7, 7. Haiku were first separated from the following fourteen (seven, seven) syllables during the 14th century. They are found in *The Tsukuba Collection*, 筑波集, compiled by Nijô Yoshimoto, 二條良基, 1320–88.

In the earliest times we have Long Poems, 長歌, and Short Poems, Tanka, 短歌. Then at a later date, at the beginning of the Christian Era, Short Poems began to be composed by two poets, one making the 5, 7, 5, the other the 7, 7, There is a legendary account of Yamato-takeru no Mikoto, 日本武尊, (81–112 AD), the third son of the Emperor Keikô, 景行, composing a Short Linked Poem, 短連歌, that is, a tanka or Short Poem made by two people. In the *Manyôshu*, a compilation made in the middle of the 8th century by Tachibana Moroe, 橘諸兄, 684–757, we find such short Linked Poems in the eighth Book. Long Linked Poems 長連歌, that is, a succession of 5, 7, 5; 7, 7; 5, 7, 5; 7, 7. etc. for fifty or a hundred or a thousand verses begin to appear in the later part of the Heian Era, 794–858. In the early part of the Kamakura Era, 1186–1339, such linked poems became exceedingly popular, and two schools arose, the serious, 有心派, Ushinha, and the comic, 無心派, Mushinha. The Mushinha gave the name Haikai Renga, "sportive linked poems", abbreviated to Haikai, 俳諧, to their compositions, and this became used of all such poetry and poetical exercises. The word haiku is a mixture of this expression, haikai, and hokku, 發句, the first poem of the Long Linked Verses, haikai plus hokku becoming haiku, about the middle of the 18th Century. "Haikai" sometimes means haiku, and some old people still use the word "hokku."

Haikai or renku has practically died out in Japan. The contempt of Shiki, 1866-1902, for this form of literary composition is often given as the reason for it. More probably, the inherent difficulty finding four or five real poets, in sufficient harmony of character and mood to accomplish the difficult task of writing one poem between them, may have caused the practice to stop.

The relation of haiku to renku is a little like that of ancient Greek statues to the temples in which they were enshrined. Only gradually did the statue begin to be carved for its own sake. Historically, and also for the purpose of understanding their mood and standpoint, the study of haiku needs to be preceded by some acquaintance with the nature of linked verses. It will be readily understood that linked poems themselves underwent development and changes both of form and spirit during over a thousand years. It is not possible to treat of this matter here, but we can give a short account of the way haiku developed out of waka through renku, (the name used for "renga" from about 1750).

In the age of the *Manyôshu*, waka were composed on the subjects of war and love, all the aspects of human life being included. To the simplicity of feeling was added the beauty of poetic expression. Some change took place by the time the *Kokinshu* was made in the 10th century. The poems are more "witty", have more polish, are more indirect than the earlier ones, but there is a common lyricism and subjectivity, a borrowing from nature to express the poet's feelings.

Coming to renku, or linked poems, we find in this common composition of several poets something more playful and artificial. People took to renku because it was easier than waka, and something free and easy came into them which is one of the marks of haiku. Renku reached the zenith of their popularity in the Muromachi Period, 1392–1490; Sôgi, d. 1502, was the greatest exponent of this form of verse. Waka itself gradually came to look for *yugen*, a mysterious subtlety, and *seijaku*, tranquillity of spirit, but it still relied on words to produce its effects and often fell into mere vagueness. The aims of waka and renku were not different, but the fact that renku had two or more authors, and that there was an opposition of the two parts of the verse, 上句, the upper, 5, 7, 5, and 下句, the lower, 7, 7, caused a clearness of atmosphere, an independence of the two parts, and a need for condensation and brevity in each. Again, this division made renku tend to become descriptive and objective rather than lyrical and subjective, since identity of mood is more difficult than similarity of subject. Further, in contradistinction to waka, which had a courtly origin, renku were practised by monks and recluses, and this ultimately gave haiku its Buddhistic, slightly pessimistic and escapist flavour, a certain passive " spectator " attitude to the world which it has never lost.

After Sôgi, renku began to lose its originality and power; rules increased and became more complicated. At the time of Sôkan, 1465–1553, new material was introduced, everyday words, unexpected thoughts, contradictions of form and matter, witty and humorous elements, which were ultimately to give haiku its different "meaning" from that of waka. By the time we reach Teitoku, 1570–1653, renku or haikai had become freer still, and this is his chief claim to fame, for his actual work consisted mainly of plays on words, and purely intellectual puns. Against this arose the Danrin Style, under Sôin, 1604–82, which tried to make this humour more spiritual and less verbal. When poetry was again in need of new life, Onitsura, 1660–1738, and Bashô appeared. All his life Bashô wrote renku, or haikai, and an example follows of Bashô's treatment of linked poems with his disciples in the mature period of his life.

A few of the most relevant rules may first be given. The hokku, 5, 7, 5, or starting verse has a season word in it, and sets the ball rolling; the ball indeed rolls just where the instinct of the participants wish it. The second verse 7, 7 fulfils the feeling of the hokku, fills out the picture, but the third verse, again 5, 7, 5, brings about a change, translating it to some new realm of poetic experience or imagination. It usually ends with て, -ing, thus leading the poem away from the hokku into pastures new. The season changes according to the will of the poets, but certain rules also govern it.

The example chosen is a chain of verses made in 1690, four years before Bashô's death, between Bashô, Kyorai, Bonchô and Shihô,[1] and found in a collection called 猿蓑, *The Monkey's Straw Coat*, edited by Bonchô and Kyorai. It contains haiku, renku, a travel diary by Bashô. The present selection is a series of renku called The First Winter Rain, *Hatsushigure*, 初時雨.

---

[1] Also read "Fumikuni".

鳶の羽も刷ひぬはつしぐれ　　　　　去　來
　一ふき風の木の葉しづまる　　　　芭　蕉

股引の朝からぬるゝ川こえて　　　　凡　兆
　たぬきをおどす篠張の弓　　　　　史　邦

まいら戸に蔦這ひかゝる宵の月　　　芭　蕉
　人にもくれず名物の梨　　　　　　去　來

かきなぐる墨繪をかしく秋暮れて　　史　邦
　はきこゝろよきめりやすの足袋　　凡　兆

何事も無言の内はしづかなり　　　　去　來
　里見え初めて午の貝ふく　　　　　芭　蕉

ほつれたる去年のねござのしたゝるく　凡　兆
　芙蓉の花のはらはらと散る　　　　史　邦

吸物は先づ出來されし水前寺　　　　芭　蕉
　三里あまりの道かゝへける　　　　去　來

この春も盧同が男居なりにて　　　　史　邦
　さし木つきたる月の朧夜　　　　　凡　兆

苦ながら花に並ぶる手水鉢　　　　　芭　蕉
　ひとり直りし今朝の腹だち　　　　去　來

いちどきに二日の物も喰ふて置く　　凡　兆
　雪げに寒き嶋の北風　　　　　　　史　邦

火ともしに暮るれば登る峯の寺　　　去　來
　ほとゝぎす皆鳴き仕舞ひたり　　　芭　蕉

痩骨のまだ起直る力なき　　　　　　史　邦
　隣をかりて車引きこむ　　　　　　凡　兆

うき人を枳殻垣よりくゞらせむ　　　芭　蕉
　いまや別れの刀さし出す　　　　　去　來

せはしげに櫛でかしらをかきちらし　凡　兆
　おもひ切つたる死ぐるひ見よ　　　史　邦

青天に有明月の朝ぼらけ　　　　　　去　来
　　湖水の秋の比良の初霜　　　　　　芭　蕉

柴の戸や蕎麥ぬすまれて歌をよむ　　史　邦
　　ぬのこ着習ふ風の夕暮　　　　　　凡　兆

押合うて寐ては又立つかりまくら　　芭　蕉
　　たゝらの雲のまだ赤き空　　　　　去　来

一構鞦つくる窓の花　　　　　　　　凡　兆
　　枇杷の古葉に木の芽もえたつ　　　史　邦

THE FIRST WINTER RAIN

Kyorai:　　　　　Its feathers
　　　　The kite has preened
　　　　　In the first winter rain.

Bashô:　　A gust of wind blows the leaves;
　　　They are quiet.

Bonchô:　　　　The breeches wet
　　　From morning,
　　　　　Crossing the river.

Shihô:　　A bamboo bow
　　　Threatening the badger.

Bashô:　　　　　Ivy creeps over
　　　The wooden door,
　　　　　Under the evening moon.

Kyorai:　　They keep from others
　　　The famous pears.

Shihô:　　　　　Dashing off
　　　Indian-ink sketches,
　　　　　Autumn passing pleasantly.

Bonchô: Comfortable
               Knitted socks.

Kyorai: Everything
               In the Silence,
                   Is full of peace.

Bashô: The hamlet first seen,
               The conch of noon is blown.

Bonchô: The frayed sleeping mat
               Of last year,
                   Is damp and grimy.

Shihô: The petals of the lotus flower
               Fall down by ones and twos.

Bashô: The soup
               Of Suizenji laver
                   Is the first success.

Kyorai: Seven miles and more
               Yet to journey.

Shihô: This spring also,
               Rodô's man-servant
                   Remains at his post.

Bonchô: The graft is taking
               Under the hazy moon of night.

Bashô: The mossy stone basin
               Stands beside
                   The cherry blossoms.

Kyorai: I am better of myself,
               Though this morning I was angry.

Bonchô: At one meal
               Eating
                   Two days' food.

Shihô: As if it is going to snow,
The north wind of the cold islands.

Kyorai: When it darkens
They climb up to the temple on
the peak
To light the lantern.

Bashô: The *hototogisu* have all
Sung their last song.

Shihô: Bony thinness;
Strength to rise,
Not yet.

Bonchô: Pulling the carriage
Into the neighbour's.

Bashô: She will let through
The fence of quince bushes,
Him who gives her the pains
of love.

Kyorai: "Well then, we must part;
Here is your sword."

Bonchô: Flurriedly
She combs
Her disordered tresses.

Shihô: See her, brooding
And frantic.

Kyorai: In the cloudless sky
Of dawn,
The wan moon.

Bashô: Autumn; in Lake Biwa,
The first frost of Mount Hira.

Shihô: A rustic door;
                   His buckwheat stolen,
                         He sings it in verse.

Bonchô: In the wind of evening,
                 Used to wearing wadded cotton
                     clothes.

Bashô: Packed in and sleeping with
                               others,
                   Again getting up
                         From this night's lodging.

Kyorai: The sky is still red
                 From clouds of the bellows.

Bonchô: A house making saddles;
                 Outside the window,
                         Cherry blossoms.

Shihô: In the old leaves of the loquat tree,
                 The buds are bursting.

I think few could make head or tail of this composite
poem; it is much worse than Blake's prophetic books. Nevertheless, it must be remembered that four living people once
sat down and composed this poem, one of them the greatest
poet Japan produced, and in his maturity. It is therefore
worth while to see what was going on in their minds as they
made this succession of verses. It is like a scroll picture that
is slowly unrolled before us. We are not supposed to look at
the whole thing as such, except in so far as it remains in our
minds as a record of changing scenes and moods. Each verse
is related to the verse before and after, but not to those at
a distance. Let us go through it again, verse by verse, ex-
plaining the obscurities and noting the association of ideas.

The season of each of the thirty six is given instead of the author. "Mixed" means that it is of no particular season.

> Hokku: Its feathers
> Winter   The kite preens[1]
>   In the first winter rain.

The emphasis is on the feathers rather than on the bird itself. It arranges its feathers already slightly wet with the rain.

> Side Verse:
> Winter   A gust of wind has blown the leaves;
>   They are quiet.

This verse fills in the scenery behind the kite, which stands out clearly. In a way, this verse precedes the hokku in time.

> No. 3   The breeches are wet
> Mixed   From morning,
>   Crossing the river.

Having shown us the forest with its almost bare branches on which a single kite is perched in the falling rain,[2] man is now drawn into the picture. A villager is seen fording the river, indifferent to wetting his breeches so early in the morning. Grammatically this verse is incomplete, leading to a change of subject, or a new aspect of the old one. The cold waters of the river flow across the page.

> No. 4   A bamboo bow,
> Mixed   Threatening the badger.

A bow was often hung near the thickets, on the edges of the fields to frighten away badgers, deer and wild boar. This

---

[1] Some take the subject of "preens" to be the winter rain.

[2] Actually, we are not to take, for example, the first *three* verses together as a poetic unit.

bow is a kind of scarecrow, but of course a superstitious one,
in the sense that it is a product of the mind of the farmer.
This bow is hanging near the river that the poor farmer is
crossing.

No. 5   Ivy creeps over
Autumn   The wooden door,
                 Under the evening moon.

A *mairado* is a kind of door in which there are a great
number of small cross-pieces of wood nailed on the planks.
At the end of the field where the badger-threatening bow is
hung, stands a mansion. Ivy creeps around the door, and
the moon slants over it. Some think that this is the gate of
a mountain temple.

No. 6   They keep from others
Autumn   The famous pears.

This verse seems to have a reference to passage from the
Tsurezuregusa, Section II, by Kenkô, 兼好, 1283–1350, in which
he tells of coming across a lonely, silent hermitage, that won
his admiration until he notice a fence all round an orange
tree in the garden, showing that the one who lived there still
had greed and selfishness in his heart.

No. 7   Dashing off
Autumn   Indian-ink sketches,
                 Autumn passing pleasantly.

This portrays the life of a hermit who paints what he likes, as
he likes. The not giving pears is evidently taken as due to being so far away from mankind, and the meaning is therefore
quite different from that of the anecdote in the *Tsurezuregusa,*

Plate 10

The Evening Cool   Morikage

No. 8   Comfortable
Winter   Knitted *tabi*:

This symbolizes a quiet self-sufficient life of poverty which is
nevertheless not grinding. This verse is somewhat Wordsworthian in its plainness and homeliness. It is hardly poetry,
but is part of it. *Tabi* are Japanese socks, with the big toe
divided.

No. 9   Everything,
Mixed   In the Silence,
                     Full of peace.

This verse does not lead us anywhere or develop the thought
of No. 8. It turns the apparent unpoeticality of the previous
verse into vagueness and abstraction, the arch-enemies of
poetry.

No. 10   The hamlet first seen,
Mixed   He blows the conch of noon.

It is said that there was a practice by Yamabushi, 山伏,
followers of the Shugendô, 修験道, an association formed by
the Shingon and Tendai Sects, of ascending mountains and
performing religious rites on the summit. When noon came,
a conch-shell was blown and the devotees descended the mountain. The connection between this and the previous verse is
that the ascent to the peak was done in silence. This verse,
by Bashô, is most dexterously appended to No. 9, which
seems to have come to a blind end. As we read on, we can
very easily see the difference of poetic calibre in the four
participants.

No. 11   The frayed sleeping mat
Mixed   Of last year,
                     Is damp and grimy.

This is related to the hamlet of the last verse, in connection
with midday, when the inhabitants are having a nap. It also
suggests travelling in poor inns, and leads on to verse 14.

> No. 12   The petals of the lotus
> Summer   Fall down by ones and twos.

There is a pool beside the inn, or temple, or poor farmer's
house, and into the water suddenly fall the petals of the lotus
flowers.

> No. 13   The soup
> Mixed   Of Suizenji laver
>   Is the first success.

"Suizenji" means the sea-weed which is grown at this place
in Kumamoto, Higo. In the small pavilion by the lotus pool,
the guests praise the taste of the soup with this seaweed in
it.   Bashô again pulls the poem back to the common things
of ordinary life.

> No. 14   Seven miles and more
> Mixed   Yet to journey.

That is to say, the sun is high in the heavens and we must
leave, for we have still far to go.

> No. 15   This spring also,
> Spring   Rodô's man-servant
>   Remains at his post.

Rodô, otherwise known as Gyokusen, 玉川, was a poet of the
Tô (Tang) Dynasty. He was also a Tea-man, and wrote a
book called The Tea Sutra, 茶経. His servant is mentioned
here as an example of faithfulness. He does not go home on

a holiday, but remains at work. The connection here with
the travelling of No. 14 is rather slight.

No. 16   The cutting is taking,
Spring   Under the hazy moon of night.

The connection between this and the previous verse lies in
the remaining of the man-servant and the continuing to live
of the slip that is planted. Also, the diligent servant of a
poet will go out at night in the moonlight to see how things
are living. A poet's servant may well become poetical like
his master.

No. 17   The mossy stone basin
Spring   Stands beside
              The cherry blossoms.[1]

The slip is putting forth its buds; the hazy moon above it
shines into the water of the old stone basin, used for rinsing
the hands, outside the verandah.

No. 18   Better of myself,
Mixed   This morning I was angry.

Looking at the cherry blossoms, the mind is unconsciously
quieted, not so much by their beauty, as by what their beauty
arises from, mindlessness, thusness, being what one is, without
affectation or self-seeking.

No. 19   At one meal,
Mixed   Eating
              Two day's food.

Sometimes we are to eat nothing, and like it, and at others
we make up for this meagre fare. This may be from caprice,

---

[1] Some take this "hana" to mean only flowers of some kind, a
flowering bush.

but it is better to take it as from necessity, from the nature of things, and then we see a connection between this fact and becoming calm of No. 18. When he was angry he missed a meal.

| No. 20 | As if it is going to snow, |
| Winter | The north wind of the cold islands. |

Fishermen are boldest and make as large catches ("two day's food") as possible, in the season just before the snow begins to fall. Shihô's task of continuing No. 19 has been most sucessfully performed.

No. 21	When it gets dark
Mixed	They climb up to the temple on the peak,
	To light the lantern.

We may think of this temple as being on the top of one of the mountains on the islands where the cold wind is blowing. No one lives in this remote place, and they must climb up there every evening to light the stone lantern.

| No. 22 | The *hototogisu*[1] have all |
| Summer | Sung their last song. |

On the road to the top of the peak and back again, through the forests that clothe the mountain, the cuckoos were heard from the beginning of summer, but now, after going so many times up the mountain to light the evening lamps, their voices are heard no more. Bashô had given us here, indirectly, a feeling of the passing of time, which in renku is most necessary to join the gaps between pictures and poetic ideas.

[1] Cuckoos.

No. 23   Bony thinness;
Mixed   Strength to rise,
                   Not yet.

The *hototogisu* have ceased their song with advancing summer, and the sick man is like them, unable to regain his former strength.

No. 24   Pulling the carriage
Mixed   Into the neighbour's.

This association of ideas is connected with the chapter Yugao of the *Genji Monogatari,* where Genji visits Daini's wet-nurse when she is ill. The gate being shut, he puts his carriage against the fence of Yugao's garden. In Bonchô's verse there is some alteration, but through it the connection is established between the "bony thinness" of No. 23, and the "neighbour" of No. 24.

No. 25   She will let through
Mixed   The fence of quince bushes[1]
                   Him who gives her the pains of love.

This continues the love-motif of the previous verse. and shows us a woman who has repulsed her lover, but now regrets it, and desires to meet him.

No. 26   "Well then, we must part;
Mxeid   Here is your sword."

The change of this verse is from meeting to parting. She gives him his sword as he goes.

No. 27   Hurriedly
Mixed   She combs at random
                   Her tresses.

---

[1] Thorny bushes.

While she is saying good-bye, she remembers, as only a woman can in the most trying circumstances, her personal appearance.

No. 28   See her, brooding
Mixed   And frantic.

She seems determined to take her own life. (Some commentators take this verse as referring to the man after he has left the house.)

No. 29   In the cloudless sky
Autumn   Of dawn,
                    The wan moon.

There is a sudden change here from man to nature, from the relative to the absolute, from motion to rest.

No. 30   In Lake Biwa, in autumn,
Autumn   The first frost of Mt. Hira.

Hira is the name of a mountain north of Hieizan, north-east of Kyôto. It is famous for its view of snow in the evening, being one of the Eight Views of Omi. This verse continues the description of scenery of the previous verse, making the location more definite. The mountain is reflected in the lake.

No. 31   A rustic gate;
Autumn   Having his buckwheat stolen,
                    He sings it in verse.

This poet can alchemize all his troubles into poetry, living on the slopes of Mount Hira on the shores of Lake Biwa. There is a waka by Chôkei Sôzu, 澄惠僧都, composed on hearing that the buckwheat of his neighbour had been stolen:

盗人は長袴をば着たるらん
　　そばをとりてぞ走り去りける

> The thief
> 　　Must have worn long *hakama*,
> ⎰Tucking them up at the sides,⎱
> ⎱Taking the buckwheat,　　 ⎰
> 　　As he ran away.

The bracketed part shows the pun on *soba wo torite*. *Hakama*
are a kind of skirt-like trousers.

> No. 32　　　　In the wind of the evening,
> Winter　　　 Learning to wear wadded cotton
> 　　　　　　　　clothes.

The poet who is sensitive to the poetry of losing his buckwheat, is sensitive to cold also, and puts on his warm winter
clothes sooner than other people.

> No. 33　　　　　　　Packed in and sleeping with others,
> Mixed　　　　Again getting up
> 　　　　　　　　From this night's lodging.

Bashô describes, from his many years of experience, the
miserable life of an itinerant poetry-teacher in Old Japan.

> No. 34　　　　The sky is still red
> Mixed　　　　From clouds of the bellows.

This red light from the forge is what the traveller sees when
he rises early in the morning after an uncomfortable night's
lodging. Some think that "tatara" refers not to a bellows
but to some place, for example, 多々良濱, north of Fukuoka.
It may be best to take it as merely an ornamental adjective
of sky, another way of saying "the burning sky".

No. 35   A house making saddles;
Spring   Outside the window,
                       Cherry blossoms.

This continues what the traveller sees on the outskirts of the
town, an artizan making saddles.

No. 36   In the old leaves of the loquat tree
Spring   The buds are bursting.

This also is in the garden of the harness-maker. The poem
ends with spring, and the particular.

If the reader will read once more the whole thing on pages
131–4, he may well find that it is still almost as obscure as before.
This is partly because of the inherent difficulty of this kind
of literature, partly due to lack of training, and to reading it
too quickly. At all events, we have here a kind of com-
munistic poetry, and in it we may see the poetic life being
lived by four old Japanese poets, both individually and in
communion. Part of its worth lies precisely where we cannot
grasp it, in the overlapping, in the interpenetration of one
scene with another, of man with nature. It was on this kind
of thing that Bashô, Buson and Issa were brought up, and it
is not only the historical origin of haiku, but must have
influenced greatly the separate haiku which these and lesser
poets composed. Every haiku, that is, has a kind of fluidity
which is different from vagueness. This fluidity makes it
less static, less circumscribed; we see things in their manifold
relations, at the same time as we see them as solitary objects.

IX
Nô, Ikebana, Cha no Yu

There are three arts, Nô, *Ikebana* (Flower Arrangement) and *Cha no Yu* (The Art of Tea) which have played some part in the origin and development of haiku. Their direct influence was slight, but their indirect influence perhaps correspondingly great, for each in its own sphere had already done what haiku was to do in its seventeen syllables. They could be, and were, drawn upon as material for haiku, but their most significant relation to haiku was the analogy that Bashô and the early writers of haiku must have seen in them. It should be noted once for all, that art and poetry and drama, learning and religion, architecture and music, are far closer to one another in the East than in the West. In this sense, the East is easy to understand; if you know one properly, you know all,—but an understanding of western architecture is no guarantee of an appreciation of Bach, nor that of Kantian metaphysics. The multifarious incoherence of the various forms of Western culture gives them a kind of vitality and indeterminate direction of development which makes Eastern culture seem a little monotonous, a little lifeless in comparison. The truth is that the East knows how to live, but does not do it; the West does not know. As D. H. Lawrence said,

> Life and love are life and love, a bunch of violets is a bunch of violets, and to drag in the idea of a point is to ruin everything. Live and let live, love and let love, flower and fade, and follow the natural curve, which flows on, pointless.

It is this natural curve which we see in the various forms of Eastern culture; this pointlessness is what we feel so deeply in each of them.

Nô

In a Nô play, the action takes place in a world where movement represents stillness, and the stillness is not immobility but a perfect balance of opposed forces. Passionate grief and weeping, for example, are represented by very slowly raising one stiff hand to within some inches of the eyes, and as slowly lowering it. As we watch this, we think of Emily Dickinson's lines:

> What fortitude the soul contains,
> That it can so endure
> The accent of a coming foot,
> The opening of a door.

There is that peculiar contradiction in the reality of the feelings, and the unreality, the conventionality of the acting; it is a real world and yet a dream world. This is perhaps what Bashô refers to in the following:

> 花 の 陰 謡 に 似 た る 旅 寝 か な
> On a journey,
> Resting beneath the cherry blossoms,
> I feel myself to be in a Nô play.

This verse is noteworthy; not only is the language of the verse that of Nô, but we see Bashô's strong impression from the Nô plays he had seen, how he had identified himself with the priest who, for example, in *Hachi no Ki*, begins the play saying,

行方さだめぬ道なれば、行方さだめぬ道なれば
來し方も何くならまし

Uncertain the journey's end, our destination,—
uncertain too, the place from whence we come.

When Bashô was looking at the Nô play, he was on a journey;
when travelling, he finds himself an actor in a Nô play. The
dream and the reality, life and art, poetry and the work-
a-day world, the historical past and the momentary present
are one thing.

The earlier haiku poets drew on many sources for their
poetic material. Besides the seasons, and their own daily
life, there were waka, the *monogatari* or historical tales,
Chinese poetry, Buddhist legends. Another store-house of
material was Nô. Kikaku especially was given to using suitable passages and "translating" them into haiku. An example is the following:

青柳に蝙蝠つたふ夕はえや

The bat
Flying from willow to willow
In the evening glow.

This is taken from the Nô play called 遊行柳, *The Willow of
the Yugyô*. Yugyô Shônin was the name given to each of
the head monks of Yugyôji Temple in Kanagawa Prefecture,
the main temple of the Jishu Sect. In the play, the Yugyô
goes on a pilgrimage and meets an old man who directs
him to the narrow road where the willow tree stands that was
made famous by Saigyô's waka:

道のべにしみづ流るゝ柳かげ
しばしとてこそたちとまりつれ

> The clear water of a stream
> Flows beneath the shade
> 　　Of a willow by the roadside;
> It was long indeed
> That I stood there.

The old man thinks that if such a saint were to lift up his voice and intone the sutra, even trees and plants would become Buddhas. He disappears and the Yugyô reads the sutras all night. Later the old man reappears in a more august form: he was really the spirit of the willow tree. He dances to express his pleasure at being able to go to Paradise, and his first words are:

> 青柳に鶯つたふ風の舞
> 　　柳花苑とぞ思ほえにける

> The windy-feather dance of the *uguisu* from the willow,—it calls to mind the court music called *Ryukaen*.

Kikaku has taken this, and changed the *uguisu* into a bat, something less beautiful and poetic, but more odd and humorous, and therefore more significant. Humour is found in Nô, but separated from the main body of the play in comic farce, interludes called Kyôgen. The humour of haiku is found everywhere, even where least expected or noticed; perhaps chiefly there.

Ikebana

Flower Arrangement is building a world of grace in a world of nature. *Ten-chi-jin*, heaven, earth, and man, are brought together in asymmetrical harmony in the simple-elaborate forms of branch, leaf and flower. There is a selection from the multifariousness of nature, and an infusion of mind in matter. For but a few hours (in theory, the whole thing should be dismantled in the evening, and not allowed to gather the dust of succeeding days) it is the free spirit and not merely the blind forces of nature which decides the length of the branch and the force of upthrust, the relation of variety to uniformity. The branch grows according to its own nature *and* according to the will of man.

As in haiku, the aim is to reduce the complexity, the wild lawlessness of the material, to that point, and not beyond it, where the true nature of the thing is revealed to the poetic eye. A simplicity is reached in which there is a perfection of balance between law and example. Truth strikes us dumb with astonishment in the particular thing, and the particular thing is seen as itself, and yet as all things. We see heaven in a wild flower, wherever it may be, for after all, heaven is within our hearts, but we see it best when alone, before the alcove, deprived, it is true, of its natural life, but endued with a supernatural, a Natural one which surpasses the other:

鵜の眞似を鵜より功者な子供哉　　　一　茶

> The children imitating the cormorants,
> Are more wonderful
> Than the real cormorants.　Issa

Flower Arrangement began about the same time as Cha no Yu, 1478, with the Eighth Ashikaga Shôgun Yoshimasa, 義政, 1435–1490, at the end of the Civil War of Onin, when he built on a hill east of Kyôto a palace called Kinkakuji. Here he enjoyed for the next ten years a quiet and secluded life of art. Flower Arrangement and Cha no Yu are thus entirely aristocratic in origin, though later they spread throughout all classes of society. It is worth nothing that Yoshimasa lived a kind of semi-Buddhist life during this time. Sôami, 宗阿彌, one of the Shôgun's favourites, painter, poet, and Tea-man, was especially interested in Flower Arrangement and Gardening.

Ikenobô Ono, 池の坊小野, a monk of Rokkakudô, 六角堂, and a friend of the Shôgun, was the founder of the best-known school of Flower Arrangement. One of his most famous successors was Ikenobô Senkô, 専好, of the seventeenth century, and during this time, the Emperors took great interest in Flower Arrangement; in the Shishinden, 紫宸殿, all the best Flower Masters showed their skill. The Emperor Gomizu-no-o, who died in 1680, fourteen years before the death of Bashô, lived in retirement for fifty years after his abdication, devoting much of his time to the art. He also left his mark on the Detached Palace and gardens of the Shugakuin of Kyôto.

Flower Arrangement has changed much during the four hundred and fifty years of its history. Cha no Yu and Nô have changed very little, if at all, and this difference is due to the significant fact that Flower Arrangement is very close to the life of people, varying according to the age, the living conditions, the size of the room, and every alteration in daily life, whereas the other two are held in separate rooms of fixed size and special purpose, and no change is felt necessary or desirable.

The early Tokugawa Period, when Bashô was living, was marked by the aristocratic patronage above mentioned, *rikka*, 立花, the formal style, being in the ascendant duing this time.

Towards the end of the century, however, the Nageire,[1] or informal, natural style, 投入, was beginning to spread throughout the country, and in the succeeding century, the eighteenth, this tendency increased.

The difference between the formal style and the natural is worth noting. The formal style, usually called Seika, with its (later 19th century) *ten-chi-jin*, heaven-earth-man branches, fixed positions and lengths, its centrally balanced asymmetry and faintly artifical air, is rather far from nature. It is the world seen under the aspect of law. In Nageire, the branch is put in the vase and allowed to go more or less where it will, and changes are made in accordance with the original nature of the branch; nothing is forced or twisted. Nageire is especially associated with Cha no Yu, where the straight lines and formal patterns of the room make the Seika style unsuitable. Another difference of the greatest importance in itself, and also in its relation to haiku, is that Seika has a kind of perfection attained in it, whereas Nageire is incomplete, leaves something for the imagination.

Rikyu, the great Tea-man, whom Bashô admired so much, was also great at Flower Arrangement. What is interesting, however, and relevant to the connection between haiku and Flower Arrangement, is the fact that he wrote nothing about either, believing that such matters could not be conveyed through words. It is here that we see the greatness of Bashô, who found a way (also incommunicable in words) of expressing in words, in seventeen syllables, what Rikyu portrayed

[1] Nageire means " something flung into ", and describes the way in which the branch lies as if fallen in the vase or vessel. It was originally used of a branch arranged in a boat-shaped container suspended from the ceiling.

in Tea and in Flowers. However, Rikyu is reported by
a pupil of his, Minami Bô, as teaching that the worst thing
in Nageire is the attempt to show something artistic. This is
exactly paralleled in haiku, where it is the thing itself, and
not poetry about it, which is portrayed, and again in Zen,
for the desire of enlightenment is the greatest of all obstacles
to it.

A verse that shows Bashô's deep understanding of the
real meaning of Flower Arrangement, its *raison d'etre*, is the
following, written about 1685:

米のなき時は瓢に女郎花

> When there is no rice,
> The *ominaeshi* flower
> In the gourd.

The gourd is a kind of flower-vase used in Flower Arrangement. Bashô's verse may be taken as the poet's version of
the saying:

武士は食はねど高揚枝

> The samurai, though he has not eaten, picks
> his teeth.

The illustration shows an Ikenobô arrangement of plum
and *senryô* by Ichimura Sôshin, in a bamboo receptacle.
The plum and the *senryô* are quite separate in their shape
and form, but by the genius of the arranger, the natural
material has an inner unity. It is a splendid example, in
flower arrangement, of

> Difference is identity,
> Identity is difference.

Plate 11

Plum and Senryô   Ichimura Sôshin

Cha no Yu

Bashô's pratice of the Art of Tea is important in the history of culture, for the qualities of mind which it exemplifies are also precisely those which he wished to express in the seventeen-syllabled verse then at his disposal as an instrument of joy and power. *Wa, kei, sei, jaku*, the four qualities of the Art of Tea, harmony, 和, respect, 敬, purity, 清, and tranquility, 寂, are those of the state of mind of the writer and reader of haiku. The harmony of the guests, and of them with the sound of trickling water, the pine trees, the simmering of the kettle; the sight of simplicity and orderliness, the touch of the bowl and the bitter flavour of the tea. The respect of the guests for each other, (all men are equal in the tea room,) the respect for the master of tea, Rikyu, (this is a kind of hero-worship,) and the writer of the picture hanging in the alcove; respect for the flowers standing there in all their simplicity and perfection, for the tatami and the posts and the roof, and for the motes that play in the sunbeams. Purity is in the body, in the things round us; but above all in the mind. When there is any feeling of competition, of enmity with nature, of desire to *use* things instead of having them *be*, when anything is *wanted*,—purity is no longer there. Tranquility comes from nature to us, and we return it to nature. We may say that tranquillity is something that man gives to things, but this presupposes a non-existent division between the two, to remove the illusion of which is the function of the Art of Tea. The relation of all this to haiku may be illustrated by a verse of Bashô:

白菊の目にたて〻見る塵もなし

The white chrysanthemum;
Not a speck of dust
To meet the eye.

According to the 笈日記, *Oi no Nikki, The Diary of the Travelling Altar,* this verse was written in praise of Sonojo and the beauty of her poetic life, 園女が風雅の美をいへる一章なるべし. However, it applies equally to both poetess and flower in its expression of harmony, respect, purity and tranquillity.

The way the Tea-master walks even, his unconsciousness, his walking-as-if-he-were-not-walking, this practical "living" of the Mahayana philosphy, is what Bashô wanted to do and at last succeeded in doing in haiku. The thing is seen neither objectively nor subjectively; it is both itself and all things, everything and nothing; here in the mind and there under the sky. This was the extraordinary discovery-invention of this very ordinary man. He had only to put the spirit of of Rikyu, of Sôshi and Rôshi, of Buddha and Enô, of Saigyô and Hakurakuten into the form given to him, the 17 syllables,— but what a feat it was. The apparent inanity and meaninglessness of things was once more conquered by the spirit of man.

Tea in Japan was from the beginning associated with Zen, for the cultivation of tea was introduced into Japan by Eisai, 榮西, 1141–1215, the founder of the Rinzai Branch of Zen, who composed a book called *Kissayôjôki,* 喫茶養生記, in praise of the its health-giving qualities.

The founder of the Tea Ceremony was Jukô, 珠光, died 1502. There is a story of Jukô's *mondô* with Ikkyu Zenji, in which we may see the deep connection between Zen and *Cha no Yu,* so deep that it cannot be brought out into the light of our intellectual day.

Ikkyu asked him what was the essential element of his Tea-drinking. Jukô replied that it was according to the Quiet Mind of Tea-drinking, 喫茶靜心法 of Senkô (Senkô is Eisai). Ikkyu then asked about Jôshu's Tea-drinking ("Have a cup of Tea") and Jukô was silent. Ikkyu then had a cup of tea brought and presented to him, and just as he was about to drink it, shouted "Kwatz" and smashed it with his iron rod; Jukô remained quite still and unperturbed, thus showing his power to drink tea-less Tea.

The actual relation of Bashô to *Cha no Yu* is as follows. The young lord whom Bashô served, Tôdô Shinshirô, was devoted to the Art of Tea. When he died, Bashô went to Kyôto, where Tea was being practised everywhere. It was here that Jukô and Jôô[1] taught the principles of Tea. In 1671 Bashô went to his native place, Iga, and stayed with his brother. There he produced the *Kai-ôi*, 貝おほひ. Here is his comment on a verse by Fukutsu, 不屈:

掃除して瓢箪たゝきや炭ほこり

Cleaning the room,
When the gourd is flicked,
Charcoal dust arises.

炭とりへうたんをたゝきて掃除したるは、
手もまめなる處あらはれて、奇麗なる發句也。

"Doing the cleaning, and flicking with a duster the charcoal-container made of a gourd,"—this shows energy; the hokku is a beautiful one.

A large gourd used to contain charcoal is one the articles of the Tea Ceremony. The above passage is the first in which we see Bashô's interest in and understanding of *Cha no Yu*.

[1] 紹鷗, 1503–55. Pupil of Jukô, and teacher of Rikyu, 1521–91.

After this, Bashô returned to Edo, and spent five painful but not useless years there, 1673–1677, part of the time as water-works superintendant, the rest struggling to make a living as a haikai teacher. He published collections of verses by himself and his pupils, and among these renga and kasen,[1] 歌仙, occur a remarkably large number of verses by Bashô with references to Tea. It was about this time that Bashô's poetical growth, so tardy up to now, suddenly underwent a remarkably quick development. From now on to the end of his life, there are various references to Tea in verses and letters which show that Bashô did not lose interest in it. There have been few who understood the Way of Tea as well as Bashô did, and there can be little doubt that it played an important part in the origin of real haiku at his hands.

In a letter, written within a year or two of his death, to Yôwa, 用和, inviting him to his own house, Bashô says:

此四五日以前に木節氏へ參候て風興存寄りて
此の一句口すさみ候

秋ちかき心よするや四疊半

Four or five days ago, I went to Mokusetsu's[2] house, and receiving much aesthetic pleasure, I hummed the following verse:

> Autumn is near;
> I feel drawn towards
> The four-and-a-half-mat room.

The "four-and-half-mat room" is the room for the Tea Ceremony, and upon the approach of autumn, the most poetical

---

[1] One of the many kinds of renku, a group of thirty six verses.
[2] A physician, and a pupil of Bashô's; he attended Bashô at his death in Osaka.

season, the thoughts of Bashô turn especially towards the Tea Room where the mind is quiet, and yet entirely in this world of sound and sight and feeling. Bashô says later:

愚庵へも松風など御同道

> Please come together with the wind in the pine-trees to my hut.

This language also is redolent of the Tea Ceremony, for the sound of the wind in the pine-tree is one of its many pleasures.

There is a verse by Ransetsu, one of Bashô's best disciples, that shows his interest in *Cha no Yu*:

松蟲のりんともいはず黒茶碗

> The *matsumushi*[1]
> Does not make a sound:
> The black bowl.

This particular bowl was by Nonko, 嫩古, (sometimes written 能無賀有, meaning "talentless and rejoicing") one of the most famous Japanese potters. He died in 1657. He excelled in black bowls which have no immediate or popular appeal, but grow more and more meaningful as we gaze at and lovingly handle them. Ransetsu's verse means: the *matsumushi* has a sweet voice, but when it is silent, still it sings to the spirit ditties of no tone. In the same way, this black bowl, of no great worth to the casual eye, has a deep beauty that is enhanced when the moon is full, or the cherry blossoms are in bloom. The highest art of the artist is to hide rather than to reveal beauty.

[3] A kind of cricket.

X
SHINTÔ

The relation of Shintô to haiku is a vital one, but owing to the obscurity of the nature of Shintô it is difficult to write clearly on this subject. With Shintô and its boring and repulsive mythology, haiku has little to do, directly or indirectly, but primitive, or crude Shintô, which still persists throughout Japan, both expresses the national character and affects it. As far as it concerns haiku, there are two aspects of this Shintô which we must describe, animism and simplicity.

Animism, the belief in indwelling spirits, together with animatism, or simple nature worship, was and is the essence of non-political Shintô. Waterfalls, great trees, deer, monkeys, pigeons, tortoises, crows and many other creatures are sacred at various shrines. Motoori[1] says,

> The term *Kami* is applied in the Nihongi[2] and Manyôshû[3] to the tiger and wolf...... There are many cases of seas[4] and mountains being called *Kami*. It is not their spirits which are meant. The word was applied directly to the seas or mountains themselves as being very awful things.

To the Japanese mind, there does not exist that tremendous gulf between us and God on the one hand, and animals,

[1] 本居, 1730–1801.
[2] Written in 720.
[3] Compiled c. 750.
[4] Aston quotes Wordsworth here, most aptly:
Listen, the mighty Being is awake,
And doth with his eternal motion make
A noise like thunder, everlastingly.

trees and stones on the other. It is said with some truth that they have a feeble grasp of personality, and haiku shows a democracy among its subjects which derives from this. Take the following as an example. The brush and the poet, all have their own "personalities"; the spirit of life is working in all of them:

灯火に氷れる筆を焦しけり　　　太魯

> The frozen brush
> Was burnt
> In the flame of the lamp.　Tairo

The poet sits in poverty and solitude, holding the frozen tip of his writing brush in the flame. Not a sound is heard. He sits there "tasting" the cold, listening to the silence. But see the faithfulness of matter. The frozen brush in the flame may be momentarily forgotten by the poet, but God does not forget it; *he burns it.*

> If we are faithless, he abideth faithful, for
> he cannot deny himself.

Simplicity is an even more important factor in haiku. In Shintô there is no reference to a future life, nor is there a sense of sin, a sense of the guilty past, once purification is performed. And this purification is a physical, not a moral or spiritual one. We have such sayings as:

> To do good is to be pure; to commit evil is
> to be impure. The gods dislike evil deeds, be-
> cause they are impure.[1]

These, however, date from far later times. The simplicity of Shintô, like that of Zen and of haiku, is entirely non-moral.

[1] *Shintô Gobusho*, 13th Century.

It resembles that of the children whom we are to be like if we wish to enter the kingdom of heaven. The simplicity of Shintô, in its teachings, its ceremonies, and its buildings, its directness and lack of moral and intellectual complications, undoubtly had a great effect upon the composition of haiku. When a Japanese, in sincerity of heart, in cheerful godliness, goes to a shrine, claps his hands and bows to the spirit of place, to his ancestors, to the powers and the power of nature, he is not far from the state of mind which sees the thing as it is, and records it in the simplest and fewest words:

雨に折れて穂麥に狹き徑かな　　　　丈草

> Bent over by the rain,
> The ears of barley
> 　　Make it a narrow path.　　　Jôsô

Aston's *Shintô, the Way of the Gods*, a work full, it is true, of the most disparaging and doubtful statements, concludes with the following words:

> Shintô will long continue to survive......in that lively sensibility to the divine in its simpler and more material aspects which characterizes the people of Japan.

ZEN,
THE STATE OF MIND FOR HAIKU

Zen as it is related to the mind of the haiku poet is dealt with under thirteen headings:

1. Selflessness.
2. Loneliness.
3. Grateful acceptance.
4. Wordlessness.
5. Non-intellectuality.
6. Contradictoriness.
7. Humour.
8. Freedom.
9. Non-morality.
10. Simplicity.
11. Materiality.
12. Love.
13. Courage.

These are some of the characteristics of the state of mind which the creation and appreciation of haiku demand.

I
Selflessness

It is a condition of *selflessness* in which things are seen without reference to profit or loss, even of some remote, spiritual kind.

He who loves God will not desire that God should love him in return with any partial or particular affection.

霧時雨富士を見ぬ日ぞおもしろき　芭　蕉

Misty rain;
Today is a happy day,
Although Mt. Fuji is unseen. Bashô

Carlyle too expresses this idea of not demanding anything from life, from nature, in his own boisterous way:

My brother, the brave man has to give his life away. Give it, I advise thee—thou dost not expect to *sell* thy life in an adequate manner?... Give it, like a royal heart: let the price be Nothing. Thou *hast* then, in a certain sense, got all for it! The heroic,—and is not every man, God be thanked, a potential hero?—has to do so, in all times and circumstances.

The courageous spirit that inspired Carlyle to write this enabled Hayashi Gahô, a Japanese Confucian scholar of the mid-seventeenth century, to see the fundamental likeness of the scholar, or poet, and the warrior. In the *Sentetsu Sôdan*, 先哲叢談, eight volumes relating anecdotes of Japanese Confucian scholars, edited by Hara Zen, 原善, we read:

[1] Died 1820.

Hayashi Gahô was strong of will and a remarkable character. He loved learning, was widely read, and of great knowledge. He once said, "The warrior takes up his weapons and fights; dying, he attains a glorious renown. The scholar, studying books, establishes his own views, for which, of course, he is willing to lose his life."

林鵝峯爲人剛毅好學、博覽多識。
嘗曰、武人執兵而戰、効死建功。
學者讀書立言、爲隄生命、固其所希也。

This losing of one's life, when attained in the will, is a state of rest and ease:

> To enjoy true happiness, we must travel into a very far country, and even out of ourselves; for the Pearl we seek for is not to be found in the Indian, but in the Empyrean Ocean.

When we are in this condition, we can look at anything and everything and see with its eyes, hear with its ears, fly with its wings:

蝶消えて魂我に返りけり　　　　　和　風

> The butterfly having disappeared,
> My spirit
> Came back to me.　　　　Wafû

It was in this same condition that Shelley was able to write, in *Prometheus Unbound*:

> As the sharp stars pierce winter's crystal air,
> And gaze upon themselves within the sea.

In this state Blake said, of the skylark, when it begins to sing,

All nature listens to him, and the awful sun
Stands still upon the mountain looking on this little
  bird
With eyes of soft humility, and wonder, love and
  awe.[1]

In this selflessness there is only nature and the bird, but in
the following verse, the song of the bird alone remains, nature
and skylark all swallowed up in its thrilling notes:

聲ばかり落て跡なき雲雀かな　　　　鞍　風

The skylark:
  Its voice alone fell,
    Leaving nothing behind.　　Ampû

One more example from Emerson, where it is the insentient things whose own Buddha nature stirs within them.

And the poor grass shall plot and plan
What it will do when it is man.[2]

The grass, the stars, the skylark are thus

The human soul of universal earth,
Dreaming of things to come,[3]

and at the same time, the poet himself. The artist has the
same object, and the same means to attain it. In *Modern
Painters*, Ruskin tells us of the youth of Turner, how he
strove to enter into the very being of things, their boundaries
and curves and angles, their weight and stress and movement.
Below London Bridge among the ships and boats he " studied "
their essential nature.

[1] *Milton.*
[2] *Bacchus.*
[3] *The Excursion.*

That mysterious forest below London Bridge
—better for the boy than wood of pine, or grove
of myrtle. How he must have tormented the
watermen, beseeching them to let him crouch anywhere in the bows, quiet as a log, so only that
he might get floated down there among the ships,
and round and round the ships, and with the
ships, and by the ships, and under the ships,
staring and clambering;—these the only quite
beautiful things he can see in all the world, except the sky; but these when the sun is on their
sails, filling or falling, endlessly disordered by
sway of tide and stress of anchorage, beautiful
unspeakably.

How near this is in fact, yet how far distant in time and
place, in feeling and expression, from Ippen's[1] simple waka:

唱ふれば我も佛もなかりけり
南無阿彌陀佛、南無阿彌陀佛

> When uttered,
> There is no I,
> No Buddha:
> " Namuamidabutsu,
> Namuamidabutsu."

Heard in the calm night of late spring, in their own
language, the frogs say the same thing:

たゝずめば遠くも聞ゆ蛙かな。   蕪 村

> Standing still,—
> The voices of frogs,
> Heard in the distance too.   Buson

[1] 1239-89, 一扁上人。

In truth, the frogs are silent; it is the frog nature of the
poet which is suddenly heard speaking in his breast.

This selflessness is the immediate and sufficient cause of
Selffulness, interpenetration with all things. S shi says,

> Only " he who has arrived " knows and under-
> stands that all things are one. He does not take
> himself as separate from things, but identifies
> himself with them in their essential activity.

> 唯達者知通爲一。 爲是不用。 而寓諸庸。
> 　　　　　　　　　　（內篇、 齋物論第二）

For some, self-identification with their fellow man is the
easier path. William Morris points to the obscure workings
of this instinct, in the following passage:

> Do you know, when I see a poor devil drunk
> and brutal, I always feel, quite apart from my
> aesthetical perceptions, a sort of shame, as if I
> myself had some hand in it.

St, Paul says the same thing:

> Who is weak and I am not weak?
> Who is offended and I burn not?

Bashô, with the same spirit that uttered the words,

> Thou shalt love thy neighbour as thyself,

asks,

> 秋深き隣は何をする人ぞ
> > It is deep autumn:
> > My neighbour—
> > How does he live, I wonder?

For some, the realization of the self-lessness of things
comes through a realization of non-ego, 無我.

本らいもなきいにしへの我なれば
死にゆくかたも何もかもなし   一 休

> Myself of long ago,
> In nature
> Non-existent:
> No final destination,
> Nothing of any value.   Ikkyû

For others, however, self-identification with nature, with
animals or " with rocks and stones and trees," comes easier.
Sôshi speaks of a man Tai Shi:

泰氏其臥除々。其覺于々。一以已爲馬。
一以已爲牛。(應帝王第七。)

> He was quietness itself when asleep, in perfect
> repose when awake. Now he became a horse,
> now an ox.

This same state is hinted at in various parts of the Old
(not the New) Testament, for example in *Job:*

> Thou shalt be in league with the stones of
> the field, and the beasts of the field shall be at
> peace with thee.

It is expressed more familiarly by Keats in *Meg Merrilies:*

> Her brothers were the craggy hills,
> Her sisters larchen trees;
> Alone with her great family,
> She lived as she did please.

This state is expressed yet more intimately, because only
the poet's willow tree nature is felt, in the following:

五六本よりてしだる丶柳かな   去 來

> Five or six,
> Drooping down together,—
> Willow trees.   Kyorai

For yet others, this self-identification is felt in a vaster, more general way with all life, with life as a whole, with Buddha, with God. The fifth of the seven short sentences found in the rubbish heaps of the Nile in 1887, and ascribed to Christ, is,

> Jesus says: Smite the rock and thou shalt find me; cleave the wood and there am I.

All sounds are the Voice of God,

> For it is not ye that speak but the spirit of your Father which is in you.[1]

The *Zenrinkushu* says,

> The voice of the mountain torrent is from the one great tongue;
> The lines of the hills—are they not the Pure Body of Buddha?

溪聲便是廣長舌。山色豈非清淨身。

All things, loving and dying, are God living and dying:

> Warum ist Gott Mensch geworden? Darum, dass ich derselbe Gott geboren würde! Warum ist Gott gestorben? Darum, dass ich der ganzen Welt und allen geschaffenen ersterbe!

Eckhart speaks of the identity of Man and God in the strongest possible terms:

> „Ihm gleich" bezeichnet noch immer eine Fremd-heit und Ferne. Zwischen Gott und der Seele ist aber weder Fremdheit noch Ferne. Darum ist die Seele Gott nicht gleich, sondern vielmehr ist

[1] John, 10,4.

> sie mit ihm "allzumal gleich," und *dasselbe das*
> *er ist.*

Spinoza speaks also of the illusion of our individual separateness, and says, with that purity and warmth that
characterize him,

> The greatest good is the knowledge of the
> union which the mind has with the whole of
> nature.

This "knowledge," however, is not one of the head, because
the *whole* of nature, its wholeness, could not possibly be
known except by the whole of our own nature, by its
complete emptiness and selflessness.

II
Loneliness

Another aspect of the state of Zen is *loneliness*. The underlying rhythm of thought rather than the thought itself, of the following lines from *In Utrumque Paratus*, expresses Matthew Arnold's feeling of this state:

> The solemn peaks, but to the stars are known,
> But to the stars, and the cold lunar beams;
> Alone the sun arises, and alone
> Spring the great streams.

At some time in our life we must come to know with Sue,

> I am one of the eternal Virgins, serving the eternal fire,[1]

and to feel with the arisen Christ,

> How good it is to have fulfilled my mission and to be beyond it.
> Now I can be alone, and leave all things to themselves, and the fig-tree may be barren if it will, and the rich may be rich. My way is my own alone.[2]

This is the real loneliness, but needs to go one step further beyond this

> Noli me tangere,

into the realm of

> And yet I am not alone, because the Father is with me.

[1] *St. Mawr.*
[2] *The Man who Died.*

It may be well here to note the use of words in Zen, the way in which silence and speech are one thing. In all true Zen language and conversation, that is to say, whenever two minds are really in communion, any given word connotes its logical opposite *as well*. So if we say " selflessness," it means, in conjunction, " selffulness." " Loneliness " is *also* a state of interpenetration with all other things. Thus Bashô says, aspiring to be in this state:

うき我を淋しがらせよかんこ鳥
Ah, *kankodori*,
Deepen thou
My loneliness.

The *kankodori* is a bird which lives among the mountains far from the haunts of men, so that its very shape and form are almost unknown. Its voice is somewhat like that of the wood-pigeon and is always heard in the distance. It is said to announce by its cry the approach of rain and of its coming cessation. In haiku the season is summer.

Sabishisa, loneliness, is the haiku equivalent of *Mu* in Zen, a state of absolute spiritual poverty in which, having nothing, we possess all. It is a state in which we

rejoice with them that do rejoice, and weep with
them that weep,

rejoice with the joy of the murderer and weep with the re-latives of the murdered man. It is not a state in which we pick and choose what we are to rejoice and weep with. It is not a state of Olympian indifference in which positive and negative feelings cancel out. Take the following well-known lines:

Plate 12

A Hakke on an Old Pine   Mokkei

> So the two brothers and their murdered man
> Rode past fair Florence to where Arno's stream
> Gurgles through straiten'd banks......
> > ......They passed the water,
> Into a forest quiet for the slaughter.[1]

All men are dead men, and I who write this. And in so far as we are one with God we not only acquiesce in this murdering, but are ourselves the murdering brothers of Isabella, and her murdered lover.

But there is a danger here, when we take examples from poetry or drama, that we may persuade ourselves that it is not the actual murder with which we sympathise but with the artistic elements of the whole. The following remarks of Stevenson, in *A Gossip on Romance*, give us a hint of how we are to look at things:

> One and all, at least, and each with his particular fancy, we read story-books in childhood, not for eloquence or character or thought, but for some quality of brute incident. That quality was not mere bloodshed or wonder. Although each of these was welcome in its place, the charm for the sake of which we read depended on something different from either...... ......Crusoe recoiling from the footprint, Achilles shouting over against the Trojan, Ulysses bending the great bow, Christian running with his fingers in his ears, these are each culminating moments in the legend.

These "culminating moments" are broken points in the line of *Mu*; they are moments of "Loneliness," of self-lessness, of universal life in which nevertheless the individual is not

[1] *Isabella, XXVI.*

swamped, but still stands clear and distinct.

How is this state of loneliness to be attained? How is the ordinary state of solitary sadness, in which Bashô still found himself, うき我, to be changed into that in which we can also say, of all things and all persons, as Virgil says to Minos,

> Non impedir lo suo fatale andare:
>> vuolsi così colà dove si puote
>> ciò che si vuole, e più non dimandare.

> Impede not his fated going:
>> Thus is it willed, where can be done
>> What is willed; and ask no more.

Bashô tells us that for him it is the *kankodori*, its cooing voice in the distance, that can work this miracle of grace in his heart. Wordsworth says the same thing:

> Though babbling only to the Vale
> Of sunshine and of showers,
> Thou bringest unto me a tale
> Of visionary hours.

> Thrice welcome, darling of the Spring!
> Even yet thou art to me
> No bird, but an invisible thing,
> A voice, a mystery!

Nature says of Lucy,

> The floating clouds their state shall lend
> To her, for her the willow bend;
> Nor shall she fail to see
> Even in the motions of the Storm
> Grace that shall mould the Maiden's form
> By silent sympathy.

In his *Journal*, in 1840, Thoreau writes of himself and a raindrop:

> While these clouds and this drizzling weather shut
> all in, we two draw nearer and know one another.

The Chinese poetic expression of loneliness may be exemplified by the following poem of Hakurakuten:

閒　夕

一聲早蟬歇、　數點新螢度。
蘭釭秋無煙、　竹簟清有露。
未歸後房寢、　且下前軒步。
斜月入低廊、　涼風滿高樹。
放懷常自適、　遇境多成趣、
何法便之然、　心中無細故。

EVENING QUIET

Early cicadas stop their trilling;
Points of light, new fireflies, pass to and fro.
The taper burns clear and smokeless;
Beads of bright dew hang on the bamboo mat.
Not yet will I enter the house to sleep,
But walk awhile beneath the eaves.
The rays of the moon slant into the low verandah;
The cool breeze fills the tall trees.
Letting loose the feelings, life flows on easily;
The scene entered deep into my heart.
What is the secret of this state?
To have nothing small in one's mind.

Hakurakuten makes here the Wordsworthian mistake of saying too much. This is where the genius of haiku comes in, with its apparent poverty of form and material. Haiku are

lonely in their very appearance and lack of richness of tone
and rhythm.

牛つんで渡る小舟や夕しぐれ　　　　子 規

> With a bull on board,
> A small boat passes across the river
> Through the evening rain.
>
> Shiki

Loneliness and poverty, the poverty of " Blessed are the poor
in spirit," are almost synonyms.　It is for this reason that
Socrates is reported to have said, and exemplified in his life
and death,

> Those who want fewest things are nearest to the
> gods.

St. John of the Cross, d. 1591, in *The Ascent of Mount Car-
mel*, gives instructions as to how to mortify and calm the four
natural passions of joy, hope, fear, and grief:

> Strive always, not after that which is most easy,
> but after that which is most difficult.
> Not after that which is most pleasant, but after
> that which is most unpleasant.
> Not after that which giveth pleasure, but after
> that which giveth none.
> Not after that which is consoling, but after that
> which is afflictive.
> Not after that which ministers to repose, but after
> that which ministers to labour.
> Not after great things, but after little things.
> Not after that which is high and precious, but
> after that which is lower and despised.
> Strive not to desire anything, but rather nothing.

The loneliness of haiku is not that of the poet as a recluse,
not that of desolate places and forgotten men, though it may
be induced by them or be in resonance with them:

梨さくやいくさのあとの崩れ家　　子規

> By a house collapsed,
> A pear tree is blooming;
> Here a battle was fought.　　Shiki

It is in the absence of things that never were:

菜の花や鯨もよらず海暮れぬ　　蕪村

> Flowers of rape:
> No whale approaches;
> It darkens over the sea.　　Buson

It is in the painful things that happen when we are happy,
in the pleasant things that happen when we are sorrowful:

苦の娑婆や櫻が咲けばさいたとて　　一茶

> A world of grief and pain:
> Flowers bloom;
> Even then......　　Issa

It is above all in a nameless realm where the human and
the non-human, love and law, meet and are one:

秋の暮灯ともさんと問ひに來る　　越人

> An autumn eve;
> She comes and asks,
> "Shall I light the lamp?"　　Etsujin

Compare this to the case of Tokusan:

一夕於室。外暗坐。龍潭問。何不歸來。
山對曰黑。潭乃點燭與山。山擬接。
龍便吹滅。山乃禮拜。　　（傳燈錄十五）

> Tokusan was sitting outside doing Zazen. Ryu-
> tan asked him why he didn't come back inside.
> Tokusan answered, "Because it's dark." Ryutan
> then lit a candle, and handed it to him. When
> Tokusan was about to take it, Ryutan blew it
> out. Tokusan[1] prostrated himself.

Etsujin's enlightenment is weak, diffused, temporary, in
one part of the personality only, but it is still a perception of
truth in its living form, non-abstract, wordless, inexpressible
but unmistakable. It is an entering into Loneliness through
the loneliness of evening, the loneliness of autumn. Let us
provide an explanation of the haiku,—not that this will give
the poetic experience to one who has not had it.

The poet sits looking out at the fast-dying day, the last
of all days, that so quickly, so slowly is passing. The autumn
evening darkens, and the poet's wife comes to ask him if she
shall bring a light ; she does not carry it with her, but only
comes to ask. She bows, and as she raises her head and
looks at him with her mild eyes, he thinks of the lamp with
its feeble light in prospect. The faint, everyday kindness and
tenderness of his wife, the irrevocability of the fall of day
are seen in the flame that is not yet present, but must come.
It also is warm and yet aloof, and in the light that enlightens
his mind, the poet perceives. *as one thing*, the inevitability of
nature, and the loving-kindness of man.

The common or garden loneliness that we all feel is not
something entirely different from the "loneliness" that we
have been here illustrating. It may be a prelude to the
other; it may be the cause; it may *be* the other, when the

[1] Teh-shan, 779–865.

Plate 13

金剛為灰
吹滅紙燈
呈現末末
盡那箇心

Tokusan and Ryutan   Sengai

energy of the religious and poetic life suffuses it.

And Jesus said unto him:

The foxes have holes, and the birds of the air have nests, but the Son of Man hath not where to lay his head.

此の道や行く人なしに秋の暮　　　　芭蕉

Along this road
Goes no one,
This autumn eve.　　　　Bashô

III
Grateful Acceptance

It is a statue of *grateful acceptance* of all that is inside us and outside us, our own shortcomings as well as those of others. This is the thought George Herbert is getting near, when he says that often he is

> Not thankful, when it pleaseth me,
> As if Thy blessings had spare days.

In everything we are to take cheerfully the inevitability of

> First the blade, then the ear,
> After that the full corn.

西吹ばひがしにたまる落葉哉　　　　蕪 村

> Blowing from the west,
> Fallen leaves gather
> In the east.　　　　　Buson

What Christ points to in the growth of the grasses of the field, and Buson in the fallen leaves of winter, Dante represents in the tones and cadences of the following passage:

> ' Questo misero modo
> Tengon l'anime triste di coloro
> Che visser senza infamia e senza lodo.
> Mischiate sono a quel cattivo coro
> Degli angeli, che non furon ribelli
> Nè fur fedeli a Dio, ma per sè foro.
> Caccianli i Ciel per non esser men belli,
> Nè lo profoundo inferno gli riceve,
> Chè alcuna gloria i rei avrebber d'elli.'

Ed io: 'Maestro, che è tanto greve
    a lor, che lamentar gli fa sì forte?'
  Rispose: 'Dicerolti molti breve.
Questi non hanno speranza di morte,
    E la lor cieca vita è tanto bassa,
    che invidiosi son d'ogni altra sorte.
Fama di loro il mondo esser non lassa,
    misericordia e giustizia gli sdegna;
    non ragioniam di lor, ma guarda e passa.'
                  Inferno, III, 34–51.

In this passage we feel, quite apart from the morality, pro-
bability or truth of the facts reported, the inevitability of
whatever happens. Religion, poetry have to do with the
actual goings-on of the universe. False religion, which is
nothing more than magic disguised, twists the past, present
and future, builds them nearer to the heart's desire. False
poetry does the same thing, though with less disastrous
results. It also is a world of escape, a world of literature,
but not of life. If this is so, it might seem that science can
be our only salvation from unreality. This is true up to a
point. It can indeed save us from what is unreal, but it
cannot give us more than a mechanically correct universe in
place of phantasy. It cannot tell us what life is, nor can it give
it to us more abundantly. This is the function of poetry, but
as in the passage from the *Inferno* above-quoted, we have to
look for poetry, that is, for reality, in the most unlikely places
also, in the mere sounds of the lines, in the perverse denial
of truth, and the impossible desires of human beings, in the
tremendous castles of intellectual air that they have erected,
in the lies and sophistries which are only inverted truths.

But at all extremes of thought and feeling there arises

the perception that the active acceptance of the inevitable is life, the life of perfection. In the following passages, from every race and time, in every mood and verbal incarnation, we feel the same cheerful attitude which alone marks the saint and the sage:

> Das Notwendige verletzt mich nicht: amor
> fati ist meine innerste Natur.[1]

年くれぬ笠着て草鞋はきながら　　　芭蕉

> The year draws to its close;
> But I am still wearing
> My *kasa* and straw sandals. Bashô

He whose mind is fixed upon true being, has no time to look down upon the little affairs of men, or to be filled with jealousy and enmity in the struggle against them; his eye is ever directed towards fixed and immutable principles, which he sees neither injuring nor injured by one another, but all in order moving according to reason: these imitates, and to these he would, so far as he can, conform himself.[2]

たふるればたふるゝまゝの庭の草　　　良寛

> The grasses of the garden,—
> They fall,
> And lie as they fall. Ryôkan

> To bear all naked truths,
> And to envisage circumstance, all calm:
> That is the top of sovereignty.[3]

---

[1] Nietzsche, *Ecce Homo*.
[2] Plato, *Republic*, 500.
[3] Keats, *Hyperion II*, 203.

A free man thinks of 'nothing less than of death; and his wisdom is a meditation not on death but on life.[1]

He sees things under a certain species of eternity.[2]

Whether he comes into his own now, or in a thousand years, he sits content.[3]

とも かく も あなた まかせ の 年 の 暮　　一 茶

Even so, even so,
Submission before Yonder—
The end of the year.　　　　　Issa

Speaking of the necessity of death:

"Well, gov'ner, we must all come to it, one day or another."
"So we must Sammy," said Mr. Weller the elder.
"There's a providence in it all," said Sam.
"O'course there is," replied his father, with a nod of grave approval. "Wot'ud become of the undertakers without it, Sammy?"

Lost in the immense field of conjecture opened by this reflection, the elder Mr. Weller laid his pipe on the table and stirred the fire with a meditative visage.[4]

When Rôtan[5] died, Shinshitsu came to offer his condolences. He (simply) raised his voice in lamentation three times and went away. A disciple asked, "Were you not a friend of his?" "I was!" "Then was it right for you to offer condolences in that way?" "Formerly I took him to

---

1 Spinoza, *Ethics, iv, 67.*
2 *Ib. II, 44.*
3 Whitman.
4 *Pickwick Papers.*
5 Literally, "Old Lobeless Ears", that is, Rôshi.

be a Man; now (I realise) he was not. I went
in and offered my condolences. Old men were
weeping as though for their own children, young
people were lamenting as if for their own mother.
The reason for this must have been that he uttered uncalled-for words, wept uncalled-for tears.
This was fleeing from Heaven, multiplying emotions, forgetting whence he had recieved (his
nature). The ancients called this, "the punish-
ment of not being in accordance with Heaven."
It was the right time for the Master to come; it
was the right time when he went."[1]

老聃死、秦失弔之、三號而出。弟子曰、
非夫子之友耶。曰然。然則弔焉若此可乎。
曰然。始也吾以爲其人也。而今非也。向
吾入而弔焉。有老者哭之。如哭其子。少
者哭之、如哭其母。彼其所以會之。必有
不蘄言而言。不蘄哭而哭者、是遁天倍情、
忘其所受。古者謂之遁天之刑。適來夫子
時也。適去來夫子順也。

（內篇養生主第三）

Underneath are the everlasting arms.[2]

His detachedness and his acceptance of something in destiny which people cannot accept. Right
in the middle of him he accepted something from
destiny which gave him the quality of eternity.[3]

......such as, that a red hot poker will burn you
if you hold it too long, and that if you cut your
finger very deeply with a knife, it usually bleeds.[4]

[1] Sôshi.
[2] *Deut.* 33, 27.
[3] *St. Mawr.*
[4] *Alice in Wonderland.*

地車のとゞろと響く牡丹かな   蕪村

> The heavy wagon
> Rumbles by:
>   The peonies quiver.   Buson

Wilt thou have me govern, or live privately, or stay at home, or go into exile, or be a poor man or a rich? For all these conditions will I be Thy advocate with men—I will show the nature of each of them, what it is.[1]

When Chi-tzu of Godasan became enlightened, he expressed his understanding of Zen by saying, "Nuns are naturally women."

尼さんは元來女がなるものです。 （傳、一）

It may be that what Father says is true;
If things are so, it does not matter why.[2]

有漏ぢより無漏ぢへかへる一やすみ
　あめふらばふれ風ふかばふけ   一休

> A rest on the wayside
> From the Leaky Road
>   To the Never-Leaking Road;
>   If it rains, let it rain;
>   If it blows, let it blow.   Ikkyu

One of the many lessons that one learns in prison is, that things are what they are, and will be what they will be.[3]

稲妻や昨日は東今日は西   其角

---

[1] Epictetus.
[2] Charlotte Mew, *The Quiet House*.
[3] *De Profundis*.

Summer lightning!
Yesterday in the East,
　　Today in the West.　　　Kikaku

A man is on duty here; he knows not how
or why, *and does not need* to know; he knows
not for what he is here, *and must not ask.*[1]

It loved to happen. ($\phi\iota\lambda\epsilon\iota$ $\tau o\upsilon\tau o$ $\Upsilon\iota\nu\epsilon\varsigma\theta\alpha\iota.$[2])

Zen, like haiku, is an attitude of mind. Though expressed
negatively, we may say, "Never refuse to give anything.
Never refuse to receive anything." Whatever it is, take it,
"for it is all God offers." It is this manner of doing things,
or not doing things, in which the poetical, the religious life
comes to be lived. Eckhart therefore says:

Gott sieht nicht an, was du für Werke tust,
sondern nur, welche Liebe, welche Andacht, und
welche Gemut du bei deinen Werken hast.

Once, when Ikkyû went to Sumiyoshi (which means
"Good-to-live-in") and saw a funeral there, he said,

來てみればこゝも火宅の宿なるを
なに住吉と人のいふらん

When we come and see,
Here also
　　Is the burning house,—
Why do people say
"Good-to-live-in"?

But to this an old man replied,

[1] Stevenson.
[2] Marcus Aurelius, x, 21.

よしあしと思ふ心をふりすてゝ
たゞ何もなく住めば住みよし

> Get rid of the mind that thinks
> This is good, that is bad;
> Simply live
> Without such thoughts,
> And it is Good-to-live-in.

This feeling of thankfulness is a rare thing in the world. There is no greater difference between men than between grateful and ungrateful people. Johnson says in his *Tour to the Hebrides*.

> Gratitude is a fruit of great cultivation; you do not find it among gross people.

When this feeling of gratitude is applied to things, this is poetry; when it is applied to all things as a whole, it is called religion, but haiku and Zen are different from both in this respect, that they deal with every thing as all things. When one thing is taken up in the mind, all things are to be present there. The feeling that is attendant upon such a state of mind is gratitude. In the expression of it, we speak as though we and the universe were two distinct things:

> The world which was ere I was born,
> The world which lasts when I am dead,
> Which never was the friend of *one*,
> Nor promised love it could not give,
> But lit for all its generous sun,
> And lived itself and made us live.[1]

But this word " generous " expresses a warm feeling of unity in which the giving and receiving are one. The sun which

[1] Arnold, *A Wish*.

shines without us lives within us; our warmth of feeling is
not something different from the heat of the sun. And so
quite rightly we can command the sun to shine and the
flowers to bloom. We not only gratefully accept but gently
order those things to happen which must happen. When
Michizane stood in his garden for the last time before his
exile to Kyushu, in 901, he said:

東風吹かばにほひおこせよ梅の花
　　あるじなしとて春を忘るな

When the wind blows from the east,
Send out your perfume
O plum flowers;
Though the master be not there,
Forget not the spring.

This lyrical feeling towards nature, Issa converts into a closer
and more everyday experience:

山水に米をつかせて畫寢かな

I take a nap,
Making the mountain water
Pound the rice.

We get the reverse action in the following, also by Issa:

扇にて尺をとらせる牡丹かな

The peony
Made me measure it
With my fan.

We see then that this grateful acceptance may and must
rise from a merely passive to an active cooperation with
something that is in reality not different from our own essential nature. There are indeed four attitudes to the world,

(depending on our attitude to our own being): opposition, resignation, cooperation, and domination. We are continually moving among them. Zen is the last. It is the spirit in which Wordsworth says to the already singing birds and frisking lambs of spring-time,

> Then sing, ye Birds, sing, sing a joyous song!
> And let the young lambs bound
> As to the tabor's sound!

IV
Wordlessness

It is essentially a *wordless* state, in which words are used, not to express anything, but rather to clear away something that seems to stand between us and the real things which (in being not in fact separate from ourselves) are then percived by self-knewledge.

> There was an old man who supposed,
> The street door was partially closed,
>> But some very large rats
>> Ate his coat and his hats,
> While the futile old gentleman dozed.[1]

This is a time

>> When the light of sense
> Goes out, but with a flash that has revealed
> The invisible world.[2]

Another example from Lear:

> Ploffskin, Pluffskin, Pelican jee!
> We think no birds so happy as we!
> Plumpskin, Ploshkin, Pelican jill!
> We think so then, and we thought so still!

This illustrates what Thoreau says at the end of *Walden:*

> The volatile truth of our words should continually betray the inadequacy of the residual statement. Their truth is instantly translated; its literal monument alone remains.

[1] Lear.
[2] *Prelude VI, 610.*

Eckhart says,

> Gott hat keinen Namen...In ihrer Namen-
> losigkeit sind Gott und Seele eins.

Christ, in trying to find a name for what is essentially nameless, calls himself a gate, a king, a vine, a shepherd, a thief
in the night. This danger of mistaking words for things is
coupled with that of being killed by the words of life themselves:

> Woe is me,
> The winged words on which my soul would pierce
> Into the heights of Love's rare universe,
> Are chains of lead around its flight of fire.[1]

Lawrence expresses the same thought with a different metaphor:

> A world dark and still, where language never
> ruffled the growing leaves, and seared their edges
> like a bad wind.[2]

Christ regrets his preaching and teaching:

> What a pity I preached to them. A sermon
> is so much more likely to cake into mud, and
> close the fountains, than a psalm or song.[2]

It is asserted by two of the most eloquent men of genius that
the world has ever produced, that the truth is inexpressible:

> If the abysm
> Could vomit forth its secrets...but a voice
> Is wanting, the deep truth is imageless.

(Said by Demogorgon in answer to Asia asking about the
origin of evil.)

[1] *Epipsychidion.*
[2] *The Man Who Died.*

The Great Way does not express itself;
Perfect Eloquence does not speak.[1]

夫大道不稱、
大辯不言。

If this be so, how is it possible for us to convey to one another the fact of our perception of the same truth? In his
essay on Wordsworth, Matthew Arnold says,

> Poetry is nothing less than the most perfect
> speech of man.

What kind of speech is this?

ものいはず客と亭主と白菊と   蓼 太

They spoke no word.
The visitor, the host,
And the white chrysanthemum.

                                                            Ryôta

Yet it may be words just as much as silence:

夕べの嬉しさ足洗ふ時の二言三言   灰 斗

This evening,....the happiness,
While I washed my feet,...
Those two or three words.   Kaito

Haiku take away as many words as possible between
the thing itself and the reader. English poetry too often uses
words as the vice-gerents of God. This is dangerous, and
the words may become the fetters of the spirit. When a haiku
fails, we are left with the bare object devoid of significance,
because of insufficiently powerful selection and rejection. When
an English poem fails, we are left with mere words, nonsense
syllables. Some haiku, for all their brevity, are too long:

[1] Sôshi.

Plate 14

The Charcoal Basket
Ryôta

浅ましや蟲鳴く中に尼一人   言 水

> How pitiful!
> Among the insects,
> A solitary nun.   Gonsui

The first line is not only redundant, the pathos of the
scene disappears when we mention it, when we think of it.
The chirping of the insects in the autumn field, and the nun
standing there alone, this is enough, and anything more is too
much. But mere brevity is not poetry. This is especially
true when intellectual elements are omitted. For example,

鯛は花は見ぬ里もありけふの月   西 鶴

> There are hamlets
> That know not sea-bream or flowers,
> But all have today's moon.

This, by Saikaku, is literally "Sea-bream, flowers, not-see-
ing villages there are also, today's moon." This is not poetry
because the intellectual elements are not subdued into the
poetic attitude. There is a hiatus, the words come between
us and the object. We can say of the good haiku what Alcott
says of the good teacher, and what people should bear in
mind in their imitation of Christ,

> The true teacher defends his pupils against his
> own personal influence. He inspires self-distrust.
> He guides their eyes from himself to the spirit
> that quickens him. He will have no disciples.

Certain poets, certain kinds of poetry have a browbeating
effect upon us, and this is an illustration of the power words
exert. We must never allow them to be anything but tools
and servants. Humpty Dumpty says,

" There's glory for you ! "

" I don't know what you mean by glory," Alice
said. Humpty Dumpty smiled contemptuously.
" Of course you don't, ... till I tell you. I meant
there's a nice knock-down argument for you."

" But glory doesn't mean a nice knock-down
argument," Alice objected. " When I use a word,"
Humpty Dumty said in rather a scornful tone, " it
means just what I choose it to mean ... neither
more nor less."

" The question is," said Alice, " whether you
can make words mean so many different things."

" The question is," said Humpty Dumpty,
" which is to be Master ... that's all ".[1]

An illustration of this may be taken from *Dombey and
Son*. Dickens shows how the word " considering " is used to
reveal a whole world of the mind, a soul-state:

" I am pretty well, considering ". Mrs Pipchin
always used that form of words. It meant considering her virtues, sacrifices and so forth.

We must use the strongest language, and say that nothing
is more dangerous, more octopus-like and insidious than words.
A man says, " The proper place for a dog is outside the
house ! " and I hate him for it, not realizing that he and
I are talking about two entirely different things with the same
name. Or to put it more exactly, what he is looking at and
what I am looking at are not the same thing at all. What
he dislikes, I would also, if I were looking at it. What I love,
he would too, could he see it. But it is the crude and vague
word " dog " that misleads us, makes us misunderstand and

[1] *Alice in the Looking-Glass*, Chap. **VI**.

feel antipathetic to each other. If the word 'dog", apparently
so clear and concrete, is thus ambiguous and unmanageable,
how much more so are such words as God, liberty, mankind,
music. It may be said that increase of wisdom means a free-
ing of oneself from the chains with which we are increasingly
bound as our vocabulary enlarges.

> Shades of the prison-house begin to close
> Upon the growing boy.

There are times when words lose their own power and
serve us in humility and truth, when our thoughts peacefully
arrange themselves in conformity with the order of things.
Yet it still remains true that the squeaking of the nib I write
with it has more meaning and less error in it than anything
I can write down. What after all do all those years of
Buddha's teaching amount to? As Dôgen says,

> 山の色、谷のひゞきもみなながら
> 　　我が釋迦牟尼の聲のあとかな
>
> The colours of the mountains,
> The echoes of the valleys,...
> All, all are
> The form and voice
> Of Shakamuni.

V
Non-intellectuality

Zen is *non-intellectual*.

Philosophy will clip an angel's wings,

says Keats, and Eckhart gives the reason for this:

> Der Mensch soll sich nicht mit einem gedachten
> Gott begnügen; wenn der Gedanke vergeht, so
> vergeht auch der Gott.

What a man knows, and the only thing he knows, is God.
In so far as he knows God, he is God, since all knowledge is
self-knowledge. This is what we mean when we say that all
men have the Buddha-nature. What we think about things
is quite different from what we grasp as the thing itself.
Again Eckhart says:

> Alles was man von Gott erdenken kann ist
> all zusammen nicht Gott.

Thought, like passion, deepens intuition, but can in no way
substitute for it. Through this comes the inexplicability of
life, of poetry.

From this fact of the non-intellectuality of Zen and haiku,
we can see a deep meaning in the proverb

> Comparisons are odious,

and this explains the failure, as poetry, of such haiku as the
following:

名月や草木に劣る人の影   梅室

> The bright autumn moon:
> The shadows of tree and grass,—
> And those of men!   Baishitsu

Notice further that, naturally enough, the moonlight has no (poetical) connection whatever with the shadows that are being contrasted with one another. There is the same mistake in another verse by the same author:

さてはあの月が鳴いたか時鳥

> Why, was it the moon
> That cried?
> A cuckoo!

There was the intuition of identity, the first thought, 第一念, that allowed itself to be overridden by the second. When we use the intellect alone, we arrive nowhere. As Alice says,

> "I'm sure I'm not Ada, for her hair goes in long ringlets, and mine doesn't go in ringlets at all, and I'm sure I can't be Mabel, for I know all sorts of things, and she, oh! she knows such a very little! Besides, *she's* she and *I'm* I and— oh dear, how puzzling it all is!"

Poetry has as its (unconscious) philosophic basis, the fact that all things are changing, unfixed, unfixable, contradictory, that a mountain is not a mountain, and yet at the same time it is a mountain.

手把鋤頭, 步行騎水牛。　（禪林句集）

He holds the handle of the hoe, but his hands are empty;
He rides astride the water-buffalo, but he is walking.

Hence poetry and science, religion and science are truly antipathetic. Science objectifies, abstracts and generalises.

Poetry identifies, lives in and through the thing, ultimately particularises. As part of this paradox, the poet unites himself with the object, which like Baalam's ass, speaks with the voice of a man.

Further, there is the question of whole and part. The intellect can understand any part of a thing as a part, but not as a whole. *It can understand anything which God is not.* The divinity of a thing is manifested in its wholeness. So since love is the personality as a whole, we love God and he loves us; we know a thing, and the thing knows us; we know each other as wholes. Any partial understanding, the understanding of part of a thing, is evil, though not always what we call specifically moral evil. So the scientific knowledge of a thing is, in its divorce from the suchness, the wholeness of that thing, potentially bad, and bad in actuality when the thing is used without regard to its suchness, but scientifically, partially, intellectually. Eckhart says,

> Gott will wohl dass die Seele auch das wahr-
> nähme, was Gott selbst nicht ist. Er will aber
> nicht dass sie etwas liebhabe ausser ihn, denn er
> hat sie zur Einung mit sich geschaffen.

And here, in connection with the question of the misuse of the intellect, we may sound a note of warning. The intellect not only complicates but generalises. *Beware of over-simplification.* If we cannot keep our balance, as life does, between variety and unity, let us choose, if we must, variety, as being the less dangerous, the less intellectually tempting. If we try to force all poetry into some one theory (which we may call Zen, but is not) we shall find ourselves servants, not masters of the intellect; we shall be twisting meanings, trying to twist life, and be twisted by it. Poetry can make use not only of Zen, but of the absence of it:

田を賣りていとど寝られぬ蛙哉　　　北　枝

>　　I sold the field,
>　And all the more could not sleep,
>　　　For the frogs.　　　Hokushi

We do the will of God even in disobeying Him. Enlightenment and delusion are not two different things. The ordinary man is Buddha. Let us take poetry in the same way that we must take life, as it comes, regardless of theories and prepared explanations. The unity will be there, never doubt it, but should we try to force it, our dead interpretations will be condemned by the life of the poetry itself. This is the point of the opening paragraphs of Pater's essay on *Style*, and of

>　　Judge not, that ye be not judged.

And just as poetry cannot be explained, but only repeated, religion, that is, life in perfect accord with reality, cannot be verbally interpreted:

逆順縦横時、佛亦不能辨。　　　（禪林句集）

>　When moving in all directions,
>　Even the Buddha cannot discourse upon it.

The Psalmist said,

>　　The Lord is my Shepherd: I shall not want.

Whenever we read this we know, deep down in our hearts, that it is true. But when we think about it, above all, when parsons preach upon it, we know, intellectually speaking, that it is false. Religiously speaking, it is self-evident. But what

we know by intuition is far more subtle than any explanation
we can give of it. St. Augustine says,

> Si nemo me quaerat, si quaerenti explicari
> velim nescio.[1]

The words of David do not refer to material things, since
we may and do lack food and warmth and are deprived of
even the bare necessities of life. Does it then refer only to
spiritual matters, to the love of God *in vacuo*, or to some
other such abstraction? This can hardly be so, for what
sort of shepherd is it that loves his sheep but will not give
them grass, or protection from the elements? What kind of
protector is it that showers down on us indiscriminately,
plague, earthquake, whirlwinds and all the forms of sudden
death by land and sea, not to speak of madness and lingering
death in life?

The truth, the deep and painful, the almost unbearable
truth that we intuitively realize when we read the words of
the Psalm, is that we want nothing. All the joys and sorrows,
the triumphs and agonies of mankind are ours. They are
our heritage as man, as sons of God, as Buddha !

> Joy and woe are woven fine,
> A clothing for the soul divine.

To desire happiness only is the cardinal error of man. To
accept all

> With plain, heroic magnitude of mind,[2]

is the Way. And as for explanations of it all,

[1] *Confessions, XI, 14.*
[2] *Samson Agonistes.*

若識琴中趣、
何勞絃上聲。 （草堂錄）

If you know the meaning within the lute,
Why trouble about the sound of the string?

The following is an example of an "explanation." Gaunt
says:

> All places that the eye of heaven visits
> Are to a wise man ports and happy havens.
> Teach thy necessity to reason thus;
> There is no virtue like necessity.
> Think not the king did banish thee,
> But thou the king: Woe doth the heavier sit
> When it perceives it is but faintly borne.
> Go, say I sent thee forth to purchase honour,
> And not the king exiled thee. Or suppose
> Devouring pestilence hangs in our air,
> And thou art flying to a fresher clime.
> Look! what thy soul holds dear, imagine it
> To lie that way thou go'st, not whence thou
>   com'st.
> Suppose the singing birds musicians,
> The grass whereon thou tread'st the presence
>   strew'd;
> The flowers fair ladies, and thy steps no more
> Than a delightful measure or a dance;
> For gnarling sorrow has less power to bite
> The man that mocks at it, and sets it light.[1]

With the exception of the first two lines, which have some Zen
in them, this is all true enough,—yet false. The most momentary *experience* of the goodness of evil, the indifference of
circumstances, the willing of destiny, is worth all the philoso-

---

[1] *King Richard II, 1, 3.*

phizing in the world. The mistake is visible in the words:
reason thus—, think not—, suppose that—, say—, imagine—.
Again, Gaunt goes on too long. In the teaching of Zen, as
with the sermons of Christ, the brevity is part of their power;

> The water a cow drinks turns to milk;
> The water a serpent drinks turns to poision.

牛飲水成乳、蛇飲水成毒。　　　（禪林句集）

> Blessed are the pure in heart,
> For they shall see God.

These, like Gaunt's

> There is no virtue like necessity,

convince, without attempting to persuade. Bolingbroke answers Gaunt in the following lines:

> O, who can hold a fire in his hand
> By thinking on the frosty Caucasus?
> Or cloy the hungry edge of appetite
> By bare imagination of a feast?
> Or wallow naked in December snow
> By thinking on fantastic summer's heat?
> O! no, the aprehension of the good
> Gives but the greater feeling to the worse.
> Fell sorrow doth never rankle more
> Than when it bites, but lanceth not the sore.

There is perhaps a limit then, to the scope of

> Nothing is, but thinking makes it so.

No amount of thinking, that is, faith and belief of the profoundest kind, will make a sharp knife blunt or a dead man
alive. Faith cannot remove mountains. But it can keep the
mountains in their place, (so long as they stay there,) and

as they move, it moves them. This following of events, not leading them, is instantaneous; is in the will. It does not make painful things pleasant or vice versa:

長者長法身、短者短法身。　　（禪林句集）

A long thing is the long body of Buddha;
A short thing is the short body of Buddha.

When the mind is quiet, it can accept such statements and be satisfied with them, but once we elaborate them, the mind, the intellectual part of the mind, is aroused to work by itself. In the *Essay on Man*, Pope says,

All nature is but art, unknown to thee;
All chance, direction which thou canst not see;
All discord, harmony not understood;
All partial evil, universal good;
And spite of pride, in erring reason's spite,
One truth is clear, whatever is, is right.

This is all true enough, but dead, cold truth that has not life enough to enter into the heart. When Shelley[1] repeats this we feel a great difference:

The One Spirit's plastic stress
Sweeps through the dull dense world; compelling there
All new successions to the forms they wear;
Torturing th'unwilling dross that checks its flight
To its own likeness, as each mass may bear;
And bursting in its beauty and its might
From trees and beasts and men into the Heaven's light.

In these words the truth slides unresistingly into our minds, because that truth is sublimed into the form which

[1] *Adonais*, 43.

can be instantly received by our deepest instinct. The problem for haiku, both in composition and in appreciation, is the same as for life itself: how to retain and assimilate the intellectual elements that distinguish the upper from the lower animals, into the instinctive life common to all. Sometimes, indeed, we are able to express what we mean better by our silence than in any other way:

元日のこゝろ言葉にあまりけり　　　　大　櫻

New Year's Day:
What I feel, has been too much
For the words.　　　　Daiô

The incohate, chaotic mass of thought-emotion, which is the fount of our existence, sometimes emerges, crystallized into words. In being expressed, it loses something of its primitive vitality. If only we can express by not expressing, we can have our cake and eat it too, and this is what the poet has tried to do in the above verse. Nevertheless, merely to say a thing is inexpressible is not to express it. But our feelings on New Year's Day are peculiarly difficult to put into words, though so insistent. Look at the following advice of an old Cambridge professor to a young student, who told him of some difficulties and doubts that tortured him:

> "Difficulties! Doubts!" echoed the old gentle-
> man. "Take a couple of glasses of port. If that
> don't dispel them, take two more, and continue
> the dose till you have found ease of mind."
> 　　　　　　　　Baring-Gould, *The Rev. M.M.*—

This "ease of mind" is what Spinoza calls man's "eternity" as distinct from his immortality in time, which Spinoza denies:

> If we pay attention to the common opinion of
> men, we shall see that they are conscious of the
> eternity of their mind; but they confuse eternity
> with duration, and attribute it to imagination or
> memory, which they believe will remain after
> death.   *Ethics*, V, 34, note.

In other words, when men think, when they use their intellects,
they suppose that the eternity they feel at certain moments
is a promise, a foretaste of their immortality in time. This
is why St. John of the Cross says, in *The Dark Night of the
Soul*,

> If a man wishes to be sure of the road he treads
> on, he must close his eyes and walk in the dark.

Bashô says the same thing in a less poetic way:

> 稲妻にさとらぬ人の貴さよ
>
> How admirable,
> He who thinks not, " Life is fleeting,"
> When he sees the lightning!

VI
Contradiction

Zen is often conveyed by some intellectual *contradiction*, explicit or implicit, expressed in the form of paradox or dilemma, that is somehow resolved by a living experience. In the Bible and elsewhere, these contradictions are applied to the great problems of human life.

Is there a God?
> He that cometh to God must believe that he is.[1]

What is man?
> God said, Let us make man in our own image, after our likeness.[2]
> As for man, his days are as grass.[3]

Who am I?
> Lear, speaking of himself, says,
> > His body is perfectly spherical.
> > He weareth a runicible hat.

Have we free will, or is everything predetermined?
> Thou shalt love.
> The perfect law, the law of liberty.[4]

How can we attain eternal life?
> To preserve life, it must be destroyed;
> When it is completely destroyed, for the first time there is rest.

護生須是殺、殺盡始居安。　　　（禪林句集）

---

[1] *Heb.* 26.
[2] *Gen. 1, 6.*
[3] *Ps. 104, 15.*
[4] *Jas. 1, 26.*

Plate 15

任公泉開贊
知累落主流家
心知應る可能
目前歸無差
媛子全員猗負

The Enlightenment of Enô

Shuai Weng

What is the nature of God?
>   It is like a tiger, but with many horns;
>   Just like a cow, but it has no tail.

似虎多雙角、如牛欠尾巴   （禪林句集）

How can we have faith?
>   Lord, I believe; help thou mine unbelief.[1]

How can we become enlightened?
>   'Tis heaven alone that is given away,
>   'Tis only God may be had for the asking.[2]

What is the most important thing we possess?
>   Nothing is so precious that we cannot afford to
>   throw it away.[3]

How can we be saved?
>   And he asked himself a last question; from what
>   and to what, could this infinite whirl be saved?[4]

What shall a man do now, and what shall be his
recompense hereafter?
>   His reward is with him, and his work before him.[5]

How shall we avoid suffering?
>   Bear ye one another's burdens, and so fulfil the
>   law of Christ.[6]
>   For each man shall bear his own burden.[7]

What is the relation of God to the Universe?
>   Wer die ganze Welt mit Gott nähme, der hätte
>   nicht mehr, als wenn er Gott allein hätte.[8]

[1] *Mk. 9, 24.*
[2] Lowell.
[3] Jacks, *Religious Perplexities.*
[4] *The Man Who Died.*
[5] *Is. 40, 10.*
[6] *Gal. 6, 2.*
[7] *Gal. 6, 5.*
[8] Eckhart.

What should our relation be with our fellow man?

> Let the dead bury their dead.[1]
> Love thy neighbour as thyself.[2]

Blake's *The Clod and the Pebble* tells the same story; it is the theme of Keats' *Song of Opposites*, but comes out most clearly in the following famous dilemma:

> The executioner's argument was that you couldn't cut off a head unless there was a body to cut it off from....... The King's argument was, that anything that had a head could be beheaded, and that you weren't to talk nonsense.
>
> The Queen's argument was, that if something wasn't done about it in less than no time, she'd have everybody executed all round. (It was this last remark that made the whole party look so grave and anxious.)[3]

What must a man believe?

> The man asked him, " Why do you carry a cock?" "I am a healer," he said, "and the bird hath virtue." "You are not a believer?" "Yea! I believe the bird is full of life and virtue."[4]

Paradox and contradiction are only so to the intellect, to the mature, civilized man. The child, the savage, the poet, the visionary, take these in their stride. And therefore it is not strange but characteristic of poetry that we feel no call to "understand" it, to explain it. There is nothing special about it, nothing mysterious, nothing separate from ourself,

---

[1] *Matt. 8, 22.*
[2] *Matt. 5, 43.*
[3] *Alice in Wonderland.*
[4] *The Man Who Died.*

nothing separable in our experience. Rinzai was asked what the esoteric teaching of Daruma was. He replied,

若有意、自救不了。

"If there is any meaning in it, I myself am not saved."

And when the interlocutor grumbled,

既無意云何二祖得法。

"If it was meaningless, how was it the 2nd Patriarch (Eka) received the law?"

Rinzai could only bawl,

得者是不得。

"This receiving is a non-receiving."

If we aim at consistency, which Emerson calls "the hobgoblin of little minds", all the life and virtue in us will dry up. At one New Year, Issa said:

めでたさも中位なりおらが春

> A Time of Congratulation;
> About average for me,—
> This is my spring.

This has the spirit of Matthew Arnold's lines. Issa felt himself, like the solemn hills, the mute turf, the stream, the lonely sky,

> to bear rather than rejoice.

But on another occasion Issa says quite the contrary:

我が春も上上吉ぞ梅の花

> Plum blossoms:
> My spring
> Is an ecstasy.

This is Browning's

> God's in his Heaven;
> All's right with the world!

The truth is not between the two, or an alternation of them; the truth is the very contradiction itself. Thus Coleridge, in speaking of the poet, tells us that he brings all the contradictory faculties of mankind into subjection by the imagination, and this power is shown

> in the balance or reconciliation of opposite or discordant qualities; of sameness, with difference; of the general, with the concrete; the idea, with the image; the individual, with the representative; the sense of novelty and freshness, with old and familiar objects; a more that usual state of emotion with more than usual order.[1]

This is indeed eminently true of haiku, and has its counterpart in the Incarnation, where, however, the immanence of the "all-men-god" and "all-things-god" of Mahayana philosophy is restricted to the transcendence of the "god-man" conception of Christian theology.

> It is true greatness to have in one, the frailty of a man and the security of a god.[2]

For the poet, his frailty belongs to the breaking and jolting of things, the destruction of art and culture, the paradoxes of morality, the necessity of suffering and death; his security is in the free-flowing of life itself within all those phenomena. There is a beautiful paradox hidden in a well-known

[1] *Biographia Litteraria, XIV.*
[2] Quoted from Seneca by Bacon in *Of Adversity.*

passage from Traherne's *Centuries of Meditation*, a passage
that is a poetical elaboration of Buddha's

天上天下唯我獨尊

Above the heavens, and below them, I only am
the Honoured One,

uttered by him when he was born.

You never enjoy the world aright, till the Sea
itself floweth in your veins, till you are clothed
with the heavens, and crowned with the stars,
and perceive *yourself to be the sole heir of the
whole world,* and more than so, because *men are
in it who are every one sole heirs as well as you.*

Paradox is the life of haiku, for in each verse some particular thing is seen, and at the same time, without loss of
its individuality and separateness, its distinctive difference
from all other things, it is seen as a no-thing, as all things,
as an all-thing. Coleridge, in his definition of poetry adum-
brates this paradoxical state when he says that a poem
proposes to itself

such delight from the whole as is compatible with
a distinct gratification from each component part.

Just as one part of a long poem is to be enjoyed while
the whole is held in the mind, so a haiku is to be read with
the object clearly before the eye, while the season, the world
in one of its four aspects, is occupying the whole of the mind.
This is because every object, every flower, every creature is
in itself all that is, while at the same time it is itself and
nothing else.

The power of the imagination is the power of our Buddha nature, our profoundest instinct, a state of what the Indian mystics call *samadhi*. It is this condition of activity which Enô describes in the *Rokusôdangyô*:

動靜無心、凡聖情忘。能所俱泯、性相如
如無不定時也。　　　　　　　　（第 七）

> In activity as in quiescence, to let your mind
> abide nowhere, to forget the difference between
> sage and fool, not to discriminate between subject
> and object, to see the essence and the form as
> one,—this to be ever in *samadhi*.

How different they sound, Thoreau's words:

> Sometimes, as I drift idly on Walden Pond
> I cease to live and begin to be.

Yet this is also *samadhi*.

Here are some couplets by Angelus Silesius, (Johann Scheffler), 1624–1677. He became a Catholic in 1663, and composed both religious lyrics of sentiment and nature, and verses in which he expresses with the utmost boldness the philosophic intuitions of Eckhart. In them the paradoxical element is so strong, or rather, so obvious, that the poetical feeling suffers. In other words, the discord is over-emphasized at the expense of the harmony, yet it is a deep spiritual pleasure sometimes to hear these clashes of powerful intellectual counterpoint.

> Bist du demütiglich wie eine Jungfrau rein,
> So wird Gott bald dein Kind, du seine Mutter
> sein.

Mensch, werde Gott verwandt aus Wasser, Blut
  und Geist,
Auf dass du Gott in Gott aus Gott durch Gott
  selbst!

O Wesen, dem nichts gleich! Gott ist ganz ausser
  mir,
Und inner mir auch ganz, ganz dort und ganz auch
  hier!

VII
Humour

Humour is an indispensable element of poetry and religion that has been so often laid aside and forgotten, with disastrous results. (The Roman Catholic religion is an honourable exception to the rule that Christianity is humourless in all its creeds, and general attitude). It was not a mere accident that haiku grew out of the sportiveness of poetasters, and became serious, became literature in the hand of Bashô. The lightness, directness, lack of sentimentality (the deadly enemy of all true laughter), the central paradox that lies somewhere concealed in every haiku comes, not from, but through, such early verses as the following:

まん丸に出づれど長き春日かな　　　宗 鑑

Emerging a perfect sphere,
And yet how long it is,—
The spring day.[1]

Sôkan (1458–1546)

月に柄をさしたらばよき團扇かな　　宗 鑑

A handle
On the moon,—
And what a splendid fan!　Sôkan

歌軍文武二道の蛙かな　　　　　　　貞 室

The frog
Has both arts,—
Of song and of battle.

Teishitsu (1609–1673)

---

[1] There is is a pun here on 日 = " sun," and " day."

鼻息の嵐も白し今朝の冬　　　松　意

> Even the storm of breath
Is white,
> > This winter morn.　Shô-i (17th Cy.)

早乙女やよごれぬものは歌ばかり　來　山

> The women planting the rice,—
Everything about them dirty,
> > Except their song.

> > > Raizan (1653–1716)

Haiku betrays its origin in one of its subjects, a strange and undignified one for literature, the Loves of the Cats.

寝て起て大欠して猫の戀　　　一　茶

> > Having slept, the cat gets up,
And with great yawns,
> > > Goes out love-making.　Issa

鬚につく飯さへ見えず猫の戀　　太　祇

> > Loves of the cat;
Forgetful even of the rice
> > > Sticking on his whiskers.　Taigi

おそろしや石垣崩す猫の戀　　　子　規

> > How awful!
They have broken the stone wall,—
> > > Cats in love!　Shiki

Lear says:

> There was an old man who said "Hush!
> I perceive a young bird in this bush!"
> When they said, "Is it small?" he replied, "Not at all;
> It is four times as big as the bush!"

This states the general ununderstandability of things, due to their being apparently spacial in essence, but not really so; but when we state it in words, no one, not even the writer, knows what he is talking about. When we read Lear's verse, we know something immediately, something that cannot be put into words of sense and logical validity, but that requires some quite other expression.

In the following verse of Lear, the cow is the universe, whose heart we try to soften in so many different ways.

> There was an old man who said, " How
> Shall I flee from this horrible cow ?
> I will sit on this stile,
> And continue to smile,
> Which may soften the heart of the cow."

Senryu originated in the eighteenth century with Karai Hachiemon, 1718–1790, whose pen-name was Senryû. They are more cynical and less refined than haiku, but what is more important, they lack the element of interpenetration which is the religious aspect of all haiku. There are lines of Lamb's *The Housekeeper* which may be written out as a senryû. The subject is the snail:

> Wheresoe'er he roam,
>   Knock when you will,
> He's sure to be at home.

The following are rather above the average in poetic value, especially the first. It is after all, to some extent a personal matter. If you emphasize the humour, it is a senryû; if you look more at the poetry it is a haiku:

道問へば一度にうごく田植笠

Asking the way,
>   All the bamboo hats
Move together.

團扇賣少しあふいで出して見せ

The fan-seller
>   Pulled one out,
Showing how to fan oneself.

かみなりをまねて腹掛やつとさせ

Imitating thunder,
>   At last managing
To get his vest on.

It was once thought that if anybody was naked, the
thunder would carry off his navel. A mother uses this saying
to get her wilful child to put on his undershirt, making a
noise imitating thunder.

無きものゝやうにとらへるところてん

>   Taking out the gelidium jelly,
Is like picking up
>   Nothing.

This jelly is transparent, and usually kept in water, and
when we try to take it out, it looks as if we were picking
up something invisible, non-existent.

The humour of haiku and Zen is far more fundamental
than this rather obvious kind. It goes down to something
deeper than the unconscious where repressions wait with ill-
concealed impatience. It goes beyond this into the realm
where a thing is and is not at the same time, and yet at the
very same time *is*. Let us take an example, a difficult one:

塚も動け我泣聲は秋の風　　芭蕉

Shake, oh grave!
The autumn wind
Is the voice of my wailing

Bashô

This verse was composed upon the death of Isshô, a contemporary poet. We may think about it like this. Our faith moves mountains. Our love moves the sun and the other stars. With our violent grief nature itself is compassionate, and the tomb trembles in the autumn blast that is one with our sighing.

The wind may blow, and we may weep in extreme anguish, but the grave will not move. Our faith does not move a mole-hill, let alone a mountain. The sun shines upon the just and upon the unjust. This contradiction, like that given before,

> The Lord is my shepherd:
> I shall not want;

with the actual facts of human life, owes its power to the truth, and the very untruth, that it exposes. To put it another way, every truth has in it a kind of untruth that draws us by its very absurdity, the incongruousness of the fact in its self-contradictory nature. We know in our bones that there is something odd, something queer about everything, and when this contradictoriness has a deep, religious, poetical quality, when the whole thing stands revealed and we see right through it to this side, we weep with uncontrollable joy, or laugh with irrepressible grief.

All real laughter, all laughter from the belly, is to some extent a realization of truth, truth that the normal mind with

Plate 16

A Kappa   Shimada Tadao

its diffused consciousness and prominent intellectuality can not only never attain, but can and does continually avoid or obscure. The strange thing is that this world which we wish to be free from, is yet the one that we really desire to live in, somehow or other. And when you come to think of it, is not the strength of the paroxism of delight (we even speak of a man "dying of laughter") that we have in jokes and wit, an evidence that we are momentarily enlightened, Buddhas, raised above morality and religion, beyond life and death, into a timeless, spaceless realm that overflows with perpetual happiness, which is nevertheless this world of hopes and fears, remorse and apprehension?

All the varieties of humour may be paralleled by Zen experiences and by haiku. Here follow some examples that the reader is to make out for himself:

1. The laughter of disillusionment.

When Rinzai became enlightened at the hands of Obaku, he said,

> "There isn't much in this Buddhism of Obaku's."

黃蘗佛法無多子。

晝見れば首筋赤きほたるかな　　　芭 蕉

By daylight,
The nape of the neck of the firefly
Is red.　　　　　　Bashô

2. The laughter of studied idiocy.

Bashô said to the assembled monks, "If you have a stick, I will give you it. If you have not a stick, I will take it away from you."

芭蕉[1]和尚示衆云儞有柱杖子我與儞柱杖子。
儞無柱杖子我奪儞柱杖子。（無門關第四十四）

(Compare the problem of beheading the bodiless cat in
Alice in Wonderland, page 208).

蛇逃げて我を見し眼の草に殘る　　　　盧　子

> The snake slid away,
> But the eyes that glared at me,
> Remained in the grass.　　　Kyoshi

3.　Spontaneous idiocy.

As the roof was leaking, a Zen master told two monks
to bring something to catch the water. One brought a
tub, the other a basket. The first was severely repri-
manded, the second highly praised.

柴の戸や錠の代りにかたつむり　　　　一　茶

> A brushwood gate;
> For a lock,
> This snail.　　　Issa

4.　Hyperbole.

盡大地撮來如粟米粒大。　　（碧巖錄、五）

　　(Seppô) picked up the terrestrial globe between
finger and thumb, and found it no larger than a grain
of millet.

乞食かな天地を着たる夏衣　　　　其　角

> The beggar,—
> He has heaven and earth
> For his summer clothes!　　　Kikaku

[1] This is a Korean monk, not the haiku poet.

5. Dilemma.

A monk asked Fuketsu, "Both speaking and silence belong to the relative world; how can we escape both these errors?" Fuketsu said,
　"I always think of Kônan in March;
　Partridges chirp among the scented blossoms."

風穴和尚因僧問。語默涉離微如何通不犯。
穴云、長憶江南三月裏、鷓鴣啼處百花香。
　　　　　　　　　　　　（無門關、二十四）

6. Scatalogical humour.

A monk asked Unmon, "What is the Buddha?"
"A dry shit-stick," replied Unmon.

雲門因僧問、如何是佛。門云、乾屎橛。
　　　　　　　　　　（無門關、二十一）

　　鶯が梅の小枝に糞をして　　　　　鬼　貫
　　　　　　The uguisu
　　　　Poops
　　　　　　On the slender plum branch.
　　　　　　　　　　　　　　　　　Onitsura

7. Dry humour.

A certain monk said to Hôgen,
"I, Echô, ask you, 'What is the Buddha?'"
Hôgen answered, "You are Echô!"

　擧。僧問法眼。慧超咨和尚。如何是佛。
　法眼云。汝是慧超。　　　（碧巖錄、七）

　蝸牛そろそろ登れ富士の山　　　　　一　茶
　　　　O snail,
　　　Climb Mt. Fuji,
　　　　　But slowly, slowly!　　　　　Issa

I cannot forbear quoting from *Reminiscences of Scottish Life
and Character*, by Dean Ramsay:

> A gentleman sitting in the stage-coach at
> Berwick, complained bitterly that the cushion on
> which he sat was quite wet. On looking up to
> the roof, he saw a hole through which the rain
> descended copiously, and at once accounted for
> the mischief. He called for the coachman, and
> in great wrath reproached him with the evil under
> which he suffered, and pointed to the hole which
> was the cause of it. All the satisfaction, how-
> ever, that he got was the quiet, unmoved reply,
> "Ay, mony a ane has complained o' *that* hole."

8.　Breaking with conventionality.

When Hyakujo called the monks before him, he set
a water-bottle on the floor, and telling them not to call it
a water-bottle, asked them what they would call it.

Isan came forward and kicked it over.

(See *Mumonkan, 40*)

御幸にも編笠ぬがぬ案山子かな　　　圓 水

Even before His Majesty,
The scarecrow does not remove
His plaited hat.　　　　Dansui

9.　Dropping from the sublime to the ridiculous.

> A monk once said to Jôshu, "I have just entered this
> monastery. I beg of you to give me some instruction
> and guidance."
> Jôshu said, "Have you eaten you your breakfast?" The
> monk replied, "I have." Jôshu said, "Then wash your
> bowls." The monk came to a realization.

趙州因僧問、某甲仁入叢林乞師指示、州云、
喫粥了也末。僧云、喫粥了也。州云、洗鉢盂法。
其僧有省。　　　　　　　　　　（無門關、七）

夕貌の花で涕かむ娘かな　　　　　　一　茶

The young girl
Blew her nose
In the evening-glory.　　　　　　Issa

VIII
Freedom

The *feedom* of Zen comes out in a great variety of ways.
What is real freedom?

> But what am I to do?" said Alice. "Anything
> you like," said the Footman, and began whist-
> ling.

Freedom is not doing what you like, but liking what you do.
When we are in pain, grief and loneliness, we are safe. We
can think as Satan did in Hell,

>   Here at least
> We shall be free; th'Almighty hath not built
> Here for his envy, will not drive us hence.

This is the freedom that Buson felt one day, sitting alone
in the darkness, remembering his father's face, his mother's
voice:

> 父母の事のみ思ふ秋の暮
> > It is evening, autumn;
> > I think only
> > > Of my parents.

It is freedom from likes and dislikes, not in the sense that
we become indifferent or insensitive, but that likable things
are not sentimentalized or falsified:

> 遺羽子にまけし美人の怒かな　　　　　子　規
> > Beaten at battledore and shuttlecock,
> > The beautiful maiden's
> > > Anger!
> > > > > > > > Shiki

In the same way dislikable or ugly or disgusting things are found interesting and meaningful. Haiku endeavours to take away what Coleridge called

The film of familiarity and selfish solicitude.

Harder to overcome and be free of are the customs of language and the associations of words. The word "snore," with its humorous connotation, overwhelms the poetry of the following two haiku, the first with its strange mixture of the immaterial, the human, and the insect world; the second with its pathos:

秋の夜や夢と鼾ときりぎりす　　　　水 蚓

> An autumn night;
> Dreams, snores,
> The chirping of crickets.　　Suiô

其人の鼾さへなし秋の蟬　　　　其 角

> Even his snores
> Are heard no longer:
> Autumn cicadas.　　Kikaku

Written on the death of Kôsai, 工齋, pupil of Bashô, the second verse means that though the cicadas are still singing on into autumn, the least intelligent and intelligible of human sounds, his snores, are now inaudible in death.

It is freedom from what men ordinarily consider possible and impossible.

則至人固不知利害乎。王倪曰。至人神矣。大
澤焚。而不能熱。河漢冱而不能寒。疾雷破山。
風振海。而不能驚。若然者乘雲氣。騎日月。而
游乎四海之外。死生無變於己。而況利害之端
乎。　　　　　　　　　　　　（莊子內篇二。）

"Does a Real Man know what profit and loss is?" Ogei said, "The Real Man is a spiritual being—an absolute entity, above relativity. If the Great Ocean were dried up with heat, he would not feel hot; were the Milky Way frozen solid, he would not feel cold. Did thunderbolts rive the mountains, and tempests shake the seas, he would remain unmoved. Such a man can mount the clouds, ride upon the sun and moon, sport beyond the four oceans. Life and death cannot change him. How then should profit and loss get at him?"

Such a man is like God, with whom all things are possible. In such an enlightened mood Christ shouted,

> I say unto you, that God is able of these stones to raise up children unto Abraham.

Confucius, with all his sobriety, has a passage in harmony with the spirit of Christ's words:

唯天下至誠、爲能盡其性、能盡其性、則能盡
人之性能盡人之性、則能盡物之性、能盡物之
性則可以贊天地之化育、可以贊天地之化育、
則可以與天地參矣。　　　　　　(中庸廿二)

Only he who has attained to (perfect) sincerity under Heaven can exhaust (the infinite possibilities of) his nature. He who does this, can exhaust the nature of man, and thereby the nature of (all other) things, thus attaining (the power of) taking part in the transforming and life-giving (activity) of Heaven and Earth, and as Man, making a Third with them.

There is freedom from fear as to the results of one's actions:

生不受天堂、死不怕地獄。 （禪林句集）

Alive, I will not receive the Heavenly Halls;
Dead, I fear no Hell.

There is freedom from the bounds of time and place.

Alles was noch künftig ist in tausend und aber
tausend Jahren—wenn denn die Welt so lange
steht—, das hat Gott jetzt gemacht, und alles
was manch tausend Jahr vergangen ist, das soll
er heute noch machen.[1]

How are we to attain to this?

God is not tyed to Time or Place, who is everywhere at the same time; and this we shall know,
as far as we are capable, if wherever we are,
our Desires are *to be with Him*.[2]

"To be with Him" does not mean to be in any kind of
Heaven in space or time. It means to feel pain and pleasure
just as God does, but having no fear that pain will come or
pleasure flee away, since they are the web and woof of our
temporal and spacial existence. It means to be free of life
and death, in the sense that we know

we begin to die when we live, and long life
is but a prolongation of death.... Whatever hath
no beginning may be confident of no end.[3]

This is the freedom earnestly desired by the Stoics, expressed by Virgil in the words,

Felix qui potuit rerum cognoscere causas,
Atque metus omnes, et inexorabile fatum
Subjectis pedibus, strepitumque acherontis avari.[4]

[1] St. Augustine, quoted by Eckhart.
[2] William Penn.
[3] *Hydriotaphia.*
[4] *Georgics*, 2, 490.

But rather than in such solemn tones, this is better said by Stevenson in *Aes Triplex*, expressed with the very sprightliness and vitality, the buoyancy and fun that this freedom implies:

> If we clung as devotedly as some philosophers pretend we do to the abstract idea of life, or were half as frightened as they make out we are, for the subversive accident that ends it all, the trumpets might sound by the hour and no one would follow them into battle—the blue-peter might fly at the truck, but who would climb into a sea-going ship? Think (if these philosophers were right) with what a preparation of spirit we should affront the daily peril of the dinner table; a deadlier spot than any battle-field in history, where the far greater proportion of our ancestors have miserably left their bones!

笠もなき我を時雨るゝ何となんと   芭蕉

> To be rained upon, in winter,
> And not even an umbrella-hat,—
>   Well, well!   Bashô

Freedom from creeds general statements, -isms and -ologies, may seem to make the intellectual life so much the poorer. It may seem to strike at the root of Christianity. But this is not so:

> The temple thereof, founded some eighteen centuries ago, now lies in ruins, overgrown with jungle, the habitation of doleful creatures: nevertheless, venture forward; in a low crypt, arched out of falling fragments, thou findest the altar

still there, and its sacred Lamp perennially
burning.[1]

只たのめ花もはらはらあの通り　　　　　一・茶

> Simply trust:
> Do not the petals flutter down,
> Just like that?　　　　　Issa

Freedom from morality, from notions of progress, from
all abstract ideals, from preconceived values that the mind
is supposed to bestow on things,—and what is left? Spengler
says,

> For the man who in these things has won
> his unconditional freedom of outlook beyond all
> personal interests whatsoever, there is no depen-
> dence, no priority, no relation of cause and effect,
> no differentiation of value or importance. That
> which assigns relative ranks amongst the indivi-
> dual detail-facts is simply the greater or less
> purity and force of their form-language, their
> symbolism, beyond all questions of good and evil,
> high and low, useful and ideal.[2]

We must have freedom from the idea, and freedom from
the fact of seeking for happiness, seeking for beauty or significance. So Buson says,

さびしさのうれしくもあり秋の暮

> An autumn eve;
> There is joy too,
> In loneliness.

To escape from the feeling that happiness is an end in
itself is a lifelong task. But we can at least be free of the

---

[1] *Sartor Resartus.*
[2] Introduction, 11.

notion, implanted in us indirectly from our earliest years, that we have a right to certain things, among them and perhaps chief, happiness. In *Sartor Resartus*, Carlyle says:

> But the whim we have of Happiness is some-
> what thus. By certain valuations, and averages,
> of our own striking, we come upon some sort
> of average terrestrial lot; this we fancy belongs
> to us by nature and of indefeasible right. It is
> simple payment of our wages, of our deserts;
> requires neither thanks nor complaint; on such
> overplus as there may be do we account Happi-
> ness; any deficit again is Misery.[1]

Thomas Jefferson put this into words that never fail to move us, yet which are almost universally misunderstood:

> We hold these truths to be self-evident,—that
> all men are created equal; that they are endowed
> by their Creator with certain unalienable rights;
> that among these are life, liberty, and the pursuit
> of happiness.

But Carlyle has a word which breaks through all the sophistries and hair-splitting:

> Love not Pleasure: love God.

Love all that was, is, and must be. Love things.

> This is the Everlasing Yea, wherein all cont-
> radiction is solved: wherein whoso walks, it is
> well within him.

Matthew Arnold puts it more grimly and no less emphatically than Carlyle:

[1] Chapter IX.

Couldst thou, Pausanius, learn, how deep a fault
 is this;
Couldst thou but once discern thou hast no right
 to bliss.

When we know this without bitterness or regret, when
we acquiesce, agree, or even perhaps desire that it be so, we
understand for the first time the meaning of freedom.

¹ Empedcles.

IX
Non-morality

Zen is *non-moral*. About morality as such, pure morality, there is something hard and mechanical and dead that often makes us wish to do without it. So-called "good" actions are, as far as the morality of them is concerned, cold, and move us to a merely cold admiration. It is in the *manner*, rather than the action or its results, the manner of the person who does it, that the value lies. This has very little to do with the "manners" of the person, the amiability in which the action is clothed. In *The Revolutionist's Handbook*, Shaw says,

> If you hit your child, be sure that you hit
> him in anger.

At bottom, this "manner" is the poetry of the action. It has nothing to do with the morality of it. For example,

むつとして戻れば庭に柳かな   蓼 太

> Angry and offended,
> I came back:
> The willow tree in the garden.

Ryôta

This is not poetry at all. Yet here, as always, we come upon the same difficulty in the treatment of any problem. Poetry is one thing, morality is another, and yet they are one thing, ... and yet they are two things. However we may treat the problem, whether we take poetry and morality as one thing or as two, we are bound to fall into some error or other, simply because, like you and I, this and that, is and is not, they are both one thing *and* two things.

On the one hand, morality is of such importance that Eckhart in one of his sayings rates it above religion, above God himself:

> Dem gerechten Menschen ist es so ernst um die Gerechtigkeit: wäre Gott nicht gerecht, sie achteten nicht eine Bohne auf Gott.

Thoreau in *Walden* says,

> Our whole life is startlingly moral. There is never an instant's truce between virtue and vice.

Matthew Arnold says in his essay on Wordsworth,

> A poetry of revolt against moral ideas, is a poetry of revolt against *life;* a poetry of indifference toward moral ideas is a poetry of indifference toward *life.*

Buddha taught that by fulfilment of the moral laws a man may enter into Nirvana. He never suggested that any other means was possible. Christ's teaching is exactly the same. The Rich Young Ruler fails as a candidate for the Kingdom of Heaven because his morality did not go far enough. The righteousness of the Scribes and Pharisees must be exceeded, ... but by righteousness, not by anything supposedly transcending it.

On the other hand, there is the fact that morality has in it something against life. This was felt by Christ just as strongly as by Nietzsche. We see it in the cleansing of the temple, the cursing of the fig-tree, the abuse of his enemies, the wasting of precious ointment on his own feet.

Then said Jesus, let her alone, against the day of my
burying hath she kept this.   For the poor ye have
always with you: but me ye have not always.[1]

Engo puts the matter in a yet more striking way:

若是本分人、 須是有驅耕夫之牛、
奪飢人之食底手脚。   (碧巖錄、第三則)

If you are a real man, you can freely drive
away the farmer's ox, or snatch the food from
a starving man.

Machiavelli has said what all the teachers of morality and
professional good men were afraid to say:

Among the wonderful deeds of Hannibal this
one is enumerated: that having led an enormous
army, composed of various races of men, to fight
in foreign lands, no dissensions arose either among
them or against the prince, whether in his bad
or in his good fortune. This arose from nothing
less than his inhuman cruelty, which, with his
boundless valour, made him revered and terrible
in the sight of his soldiers, but without that cruelty,
his other virtues were not sufficient to produce
this effect.[2]

Two chapters before this, Machiavelli has given us the general
rule of which this is a particular illustration:

Hence it is necessary for a prince wishing to
hold his own to know how to do wrong, and to
make use of it or not according to necessity.[3]

---

[1] *Jno.* 12, 7–8.
[2] *The Prince*, Cruelty and Clemency. See also his essay on
Castruccio Castracani.
[3] Concerning Praise or Blame.

Plate 17

Daitô Kokushi   Hakuin

When a village dog barked at him on the way home, Taigi said,

犬を打つ石のさてなし冬の月   太　祇

> Not a single stone
> To throw at the dog,—
> The wintry moon.

This is poetry, however inhumane it may also be. The point lies in the fact that Christ and Engo were not hindered by their morality from doing the will of God. Eckhart says the same thing, gladly contradicting what he says elsewhere:

> Wer aber Gott nicht allein sucht, liebt und im Sinne hat den hindert nicht nur schlechte Gesellschaft, sondern auch gute, und nicht allein die Strasse, sondern auch die Kirche und auch nicht nur böse Worte und Werke, sondern ich behaupte: auch gute Worte und Werke. Denn das Hindernis liegt in ihm.

This is the theme of *St. Mawr*, in which Lawrence speaks of

> people performing outward acts of loyalty, piety, self-sacrifice. But inwardly bent on undermining, betraying. Directing all their subtle, evil will against any positive living thing. Masquerading as the ideal, in order to poison the real.

A subtle example of this, Lawrence gives in *The Man Who Died:*

> For the flicker of triumph had gleamed in her eyes: *the greed of giving.*

It is not a merely superficial view which considers this something which is above morality as destructive. Life is only possible through death.

> Unless a grain of corn fall into the ground and die . . .

But the positive side of the matter is in life itself.

> Try to hold fast to the living thing which destroys as it goes, but remains sweet.[1]

The strange thing is that, because of, or in spite of, or irrespective of morality, all things work together for good, all that we behold is full of blessings:

> We aim at a petty end, quite aside from the public good, but our act arranges itself by irresistible magnetism in a line with the poles of the world.[2]

The final word rests with Spinoza, who in his conversations with Blyenburg explains as well as he may his conviction that good and evil are both human distinctions:

> ......the absence of good exists only in respect of man's understanding, not in respect of God's.

" God's understanding " is what we have at moments of enlightenment, of inspiration. What follows, gives man's understanding (that is, mine), of the problem of evil, and the practical problem of how to adjust oneself to it.

If anything is to exist at all, if the universe is to be, there must be activity:

> Im Anfang war die Tat.

For activity there must be time, one thing must follow another; there must be change. Comparisons thus arise in our minds between what is good and what is bad, the simple

[1] *St. Mawr*.
[2] Emerson.

and the complicated, here and there, then and now. In a sense, all things are equal, undifferentiated. In another sense, more easily perceived, things are different, unequal; one is long, the other is short, one black, the other white. If we like one colour and dislike another, the one we dislike is painful to us, we wish it out of the universe, we strive to explain it, to explain away its presence.

> Still standing for some false, impossible shore.[1]

So with moral judgements. What is distressing morally is thought away as an illusion, or dismissed as a holy mystery. What of course we should do is to get into the state in which we wish to happen all that does happen. But pain and grief for ourselves, for those we love, . . . how can they be desired as happiness and joy are desired? The answer is that they are not, cannot be, should not be so desired.

There are two kinds of desiring,[2] one with our superficial, temporal minds, another with our deepest self, which, because it is originally, in essence, one with the nature of all things, desires that that which was, which is, and which shall be, should be thus. On the one hand we desire that we should be able to over-eat without paying the penalty; on the other, we desire (with our body) what must happen, the consequent discom-

---

[1] Matthew Arnold, *A Summer Night*.

[2] Compare the two meanings of " enjoyment ". When Schiller says,

> All art is dedicated to enjoyment,

he means something quite different from the ordinary enjoyment, rather what Wordsworth expressed in

> Thought was not; in enjoyment it expired,

and Spinoza in

> Beatitudo non est virtutis pretium sed ipsa virtus.

fort and ill-health. This importance of the body is realized
in Christian dogma. Froude says, in *The Philosophy of Christianity*:

> The carnal doctrine of the sacraments ... has
> long been the stumbling-block to the Protestants.
> It was the very essence of Christianity itself.
> Unless the body could be purified, the soul could
> not be saved, or rather, as from the beginning soul
> and flesh were one man and inseparable, without
> his flesh, man was lost or would cease to be.

Spinoza emphasizes the body in a way quite unexpected in
such a purely intellectual philosopher:

> We do not yet know what body can or cannot
> do, or what would naturally follow from the struc-
> ture of it ... The fabric of the body exceeds infinite-
> ly any contrivance of human skill, and an infinity
> of things, as I have proved, ought to follow from it.

The desire of the body is the real desire, what God desires,
and this desire must seep through, break through from the
body into the reluctant mind.

The flesh is willing, but the spirit is weak.

The only way to get into the state of willing acceptance
of all things is through suffering. This suffering may be
voluntary or involuntary; it may be the cause of illumination
or not. Profound suffering may be the pedagogue " that leads
us to Christ," may bring us to the acceptance of the will of
God, by which we become ourselves Buddha, and know the
truth of the universe by mere introspection.

If, however, life has not yet racked us with such pain
that enlightenment is thrust upon us, we must by some means

or other undergo that vicarious suffering that is symbolized in the *Yuimakyô* by the sickness of Yuima, who is sick because, and only because the world is sick.

Why should suffering be the one indispensable qualification for enlightenment? Such questions cannot be asked, because they concern the universe as a whole. We can only ask and be answered concerning the relation of the parts. A question "Why?" concerning the universe would imply something outside it. It is so, because it is so. This is why Christ hangs contorted on the cross, and must hang there forever. Either in the flesh, in time, or in the compassionate spirit, in eternity, man must suffer.

> Hell hath no limits, nor is circumscribed
> In one self place; for where we are is Hell,
> And where Hell is, there must we ever be.[1]

If man must suffer, God must suffer; this deepest suffering is the divinity of things. So Saigyô says,

> 心なき身にもあわれは知られけり、
>   しぎ立つ澤の秋の夕ぐれ

> Even in the mind
> Of the mindless one
>   Arises grief,
> When the snipe wings up
> In the autumn evening over the marshes.

It is in this sense that we say, Zen is non-moral. It lives a deeper life than morality as such, not cast down by sin or elated by virtuous action, a life of painful joy without ceasing.

[1] Marlowe, *Faustus*.

X
Simplicity

Zen has an extreme *simplicity*, and the volubility of the Japanese language has been completely overcome in haiku. When we say "Eastern Thought", meaning the manner of apprehending the world by Japanese, Chinese, Koreans and Indians, we refer to a unity of Chinese practicality, Japanese simplicity and plainness, Korean independence, and Indian non-ego-ness. Such a simplicity, however, implies an extraordinary acuteness, such as we find, for example, in the following:

The best of all is, God is with us.[1]

Whatever interests, is interesting.[2]

Ist Gottes Gottheit mir nicht inniglich gemein,
Wie kann ich dann sein Sohn und er mein Vater
    sein?[3]

  People all over the world try to know what they do not know, instead of trying to know what they already know.[4]

天下皆知求其所不知。
而莫知求其所已知者。（莊子、外篇、胠篋、第十）

    Was Gott liebt das ist; was Gott nicht liebt,
das ist nicht.[5]

[1] Wesley.
[2] Hazlitt.
[3] Silesius.
[4] Sôshi.
[5] Eckhart.

Go out, and you meet Shakamuni;
Go home, and you meet Miroku.

出門逢釋迦、 入門逢彌勒。　　　（禪林句集）

Go where he will, the wise man is at home.[1]

Gott ist namenlos.[2]

And if God dieth not for men, and giveth not
himself Eternally for man, man could not exist.[3]

There is nothing mysterious, nothing subtle and complicated,
nothing " poetical " in the world:

There was never mystery,
　　　But 'tis figured in the flowers;
Was never secret history,
　　　But birds tell it in the bowers.[4]

One of Bashô's recorded sayings is:

俳諧は三尺の童にさせよ

Get a three-foot child to write haikai.

As an example of this we may take one of Bashô's own
verses:

道のべの木槿は馬にくはれけり

The Rose of Sharon
　　By the roadside,
　　　　Was eaten by the horse.

What Bashô means is something that belongs to Zen, namely,
that we must not wish to do something clever, write a fine
poem, but do it as naturally, as freely, as unselfconsciously as

[1] Emerson, *Woodnotes 1.*
[2] Eckhart.
[3] Blake, *Jerusalem.*
[4] Emerson, *The Apology.*

a child does everything. Take, for instance, the verse Bashô
composed one snowy day when Sora called on him:

君火たけ好き物見せん雪まろげ

You light the fire;
I'll show you something nice,—
A great ball of snow!

Compare this simplicity with that of Issa;

うまさうな雪がふはりふうはりと

I could eat it!—
This snow that falls
So softly, so softly.

An example of *ne plus ultra*:

時雨れけり走り入りけり晴れにけり　惟　然

A shower came;
Running inside,
It cleared up.　　　　　　　　　　Yuinen

Spengler quotes Goethe as follows:

> The highest to which man can attain is wonder;
> and if the prime phenomenon (the shower, run-
> ning inside, and clearing up) makes him wonder,
> let him be content, nothing higher can it give
> him, and nothing further should he seek for be-
> hind it; here is the limit.

Spengler explains this "prime phenomenon", as

> that in which the idea of becoming is presented
> net.[1]

The life of Zen is that in which the idea of becoming is
presented in activity, activity of mind or body or both. The

---

[1] Physiognomic and Systematic.

Plate 18

Pine Tree

Ryôto

Pine Tree

Gijôen

aim of haiku is to express the prime phenomena in words. The idea of becoming is presented with as little material as possible. This paucity of material is the cause of the deceptive simplicity of haiku, and this simplicity is in itself an appeal to the reader for all his delicacy and depth of poetic feeling. As an example of this, we make take the following;

櫻散る日さへ夕となりにけり　　　　　　樗　良

    This day on which
  The cherry blossoms fell,
      Has drawn to its close.　　　Chora

All day long the cherry blossoms have been sifting down, and this faint sense of inevitable loss and dejection is deepened as the day begins to darken into night. In the twilight, the branches are almost bare; the ground is covered with the glimmering petals that once were so fair.

名月や只美しく澄み渡る　　　　　　　　樗　良

    The full moon,
  Only lovely,
      Flawlessly clear.　　　Chora

見れば曇り見ねば晴れゆく月見かな　樗　良

    Moon-gazing:
  Looking at it, it clouds over;
      Not looking, it becomes clear.　Chora

A well known example by Bashô, in praise of the most beautiful place in Japan:

松島や、あゝ松島や松島や　　　　　　　芭　蕉

    Matsushima !
  Ah, Matsushima, ah !
      Matsushima, ah !　　　Bashô

Bashô and Chora are the greatest poets of simplicity:

初秋や海も青田の一みどり　　　　　芭　蕉

> The beginning of autumn;
> The sea and fields,
> All one same green.　　　Bashô

このあたり目に見ゆるものは皆涼し　芭　蕉

> All around
> That meets the eye
> Is cool and fresh.　　　Bashô

Where there seems to be least Zen, there may be most.

Simplicity is the philosophic background of all Asiatic poetry as it is of all European science. Shiki says:

汽車すぎて煙うづまく若葉かな

> The train passes;
> How the smoke
> Swirls round the young leaves!

This simplicity in the realm of thought and feeling appears as brevity in that of form. Silence is deeper than speaking; from silence springs speaking, and returns to it. How indeed should any symbol represent the activity which is beyond speech and silence? The brevity of haiku has its origin in the endeavour to appeal from the unconscious in one human being to the unconscious in others. Spengler gives for once a practical illustration of this in an old couple sitting in the evening sunshine in a complete harmony of silence:

> The deeper and more intimate a spiritual
> communion, the more readily it dispenses with
> signs and linkages through waking consciousness.
> A real comradeship makes itself understood with

few words, *a real faith is silent altogether*. The
purest example of an understanding that has
again got beyond language is the old peasant
couple sitting in the evening in front of their
cottage and entertaining each other without a
word being passed, each knowing what the other
is thinking and feeling. Words would only disturb
the harmony. From such a state of reciprocal
understanding, something or other reaches back
far beyond the collective existence of the higher
animal world, deep in the primeval history of
free-moving life. Here deliverance from the
waking consciousness is, at moments, very nearly
achieved.[1]

Walter de la Mare has a verse which repeats this thought:

When all at peace, two friends at ease alone
Talk out their hearts, yet still
Between the grace-notes of
The voice of love
From each to each
Trembles a rarer speech,
And with its presence every pause doth fill.[2]

Simplicity of subject, which is one of the marked characteristics of haiku, the choice of the peaceful and temperate
aspects of nature, the avoidance of all confused and violent
things both in man and in nature, is due to a delicate sensi-
tiveness that cannot bear the dramatic and hyperbolic. It is
in no wise due to shallowness:

The sea is as deepe in a calme as in a storme.[3]

1 Peoples, Races, Tongues, IV.
2 *Silence.*
3 Donne, *Sermons*, Mundus Mari

As Johnson says, (what might be taken as the motto of all haiku),

> Nothing is little to him who feels it with great sensibility.

XI
Materiality

Zen, like haiku, emphasizes the *material*, as against the so-called spiritual. There is no abstract arguing, no general principles. Everything is concrete. If we glance through a number of haiku we find they are entirely about *things*, snow, cherry blossoms, people dancing, frogs, the wind. *Walden* is the same. Speaking of himself, Thoreau says

> I felt that some berries which I had eaten on
> a hill-side had fed my genius.

Lawrence tells us, in *The Man that Died*, that Christ realised, after his death, with regard to Mary Magdalene, that his teaching, his life itself, had been too spiritual.

> I asked them all to serve me with the corpse
> of their love. And in the end I offered them only
> the corpse of my love.

It seems a far call from these words to those in which Chora describes himself, but there is a deep affinity between them:

> 夜はうれしく晝は靜かや春の雨
> > At night, happiness;
> > In the day-time, quietness,—
> > Spring rain.

> 冷水にせんべい二枚樗良が夏
> > Cold water,
> > Two biscuits,—
> > Chora's summer.

The second of these two poems reminds us of the words of reproof to Martha,

> But one thing is enough.

It is a mistake to suppose that in poetry we are to perceive the absolute in the relative, the eternal, the infinite in the finite, the spiritual in the material. If there is any antithesis to Zen, it is this kind of Zoroastrianism, so easy to fall into, because it is of the very nature of the intellect to function dichotomously. Our poetic life, our religious life is one long, never-ending struggle against this tendency. The nature of the soul, however, is simple; the eye of the soul is single. Eckhart says:

> Ein Meister spricht: "Die Seele ist ein Punkt oder eine Ecke, wo sich Zeit und Ewigkeit treffen. Die Seele aber ist weder von Zeit noch von Ewigkeit gemacht, sondern sie hat eine Natur aus Nichts geschaffen zwischen beiden." Wäre sie von Zeit gemacht, so wäre sie vergänglich; ware sie dagegen von Ewigkeit geschaffen, so wäre sie unwandelbar.

The materiality of Zen comes out in the fact that the religious life is at its lowest ebb in church, where everything is arranged to incline the mind to some other place, Heaven or Hell, some other time, the past or the future. There is more religion in the public-house, on the battle-field. It is for this reason that, as Christ says,

> the publicans and the harlots go into the Kingdom of God before you.

Men live by Zen. All they desire is to see it and feel it. They go to the cinema for it. The cowboy romances are full

of failures to attain it. When the "killer" advances into the
dance-hall with his hands ready for the draw, it is his Zen
alone that our eyes are fixed on. But this so-called "Zen,"
does not exist, as a thing. Nothing is symbolical of it.
Goethe says,

> Alles Vergängliche ist nur ein Gleichnis.

But he does not tell us of what it is a symbol, because he
cannot. It is 'a symbol proper," as Carlyle calls it, which
means, as Rinzai would say, a no-symbol. In this sense we
may remind ourselves of Keats' lines:

> It is a flaw
> In happiness to see beyond our bourne,
> It forces us in summer skies to mourn,
> It spoils the singing of the nightingale.

In poetry, at least as the haiku poets understand it, we
simply cannot manage to do without things. Contrast the
first of the following verses with the other three, all on the
subject of the change of servants, which in olden times took
place on the fifth day of the third month of the lunar
calendar:

出がはりや幼心に物あはれ　　　嵐雪

The change of servants;
The pathos
Of her childish heart.　　Ransetsu

出がはりや傘提げて夕ながめ　　　許六

The departing servant;
Umbrella in hand,
She gazes out at the evening.
Kyoroku

出代や疊へ落す涙かな　　　　　　太　祇

> The change of servants;
> 　　Her tears
> 　　　　Splash on the tatami.　　　Taigi

紙屑や出代のあとの物淋し　　　　千　那

> 　　Some scraps of paper,
> After she had gone;
> 　　　　A feeling of lonesomeness.　　Senna

Poetry is greatly concerned with umbrellas, tatami, scraps of paper. Goethe, with characteristic courage, seems to contradict his own words concerning the "symbolical" nature of all things:

> Do not, I beg you, look for anything behind phenomena. They are themselves their own lesson.
> (Sie selbst sind die Lehre.)

In the following well-known American poem, *Little Boy Blue*, by Eugene Field. we are told the lesson that things have for us, but the things, (the toys), are so strong they are able to overcome the dead weight of their lesson and speak for themselves:

> The little toy dog is covered with dust,
> But sturdy and staunch he stands.
> The little tin soldier is red with rust,
> And his musket molds in his hands.
> Time was when the little toy dog was new,
> And the soldier was passing fair,
> And that was the time when our Little Boy Blue,
> Kissed them and put them there.
> "Now don't you go till I come," he said,
> "And don't you make any noise."
> So, toddling off to his trundle bed,

He dreamed of his pretty toys.
And while he was dreaming, an angel's song,
Awakened our Little Boy Blue.
Ah, the years are many, the years are long,
But our little toy friends are true.
Ay, faithful to Little Boy Blue they stand,
Each in the same old place,
Awaiting the touch of a little hand,
And the smile of a little face.
And they wonder, as waiting these long years
    through,
In the dust of that little chair,
"What has become of our Little Boy Blue,"
Since he kissed them and put them there.

(Puzzle; point to the line where the Zen is.) This is the
faithfulness of things, that which the Psalmist refers to so
indirectly in the often-quoted lines:

The Lord is my shepherd;
I shall not want.

It is seen in the following;

おろし置く笈に地震る夏野哉　　　　蕪　村
      The travelling altar just set down,
    Swayed with an earthquake,
       On the summer moor.　　Buson

夕風や水青鷺の脛をうつ　　　　　　蕪　村
      With the evening breeze,
    The water laps against
      The heron's legs.　　Buson

蠅打に花さく草も打たれけり　　　　一　茶

Striking the fly,
I hit also
A flowering plant.   Issa

Another American poet gives us a list of things that a poet,
and preëminently a haiku poet, prizes most:

shadows, colors, clouds,
Grass-buds and caterpillars' shrouds,
Boughs on which the wild bees settle,
Tints that spot the violet's petal.[1]

This is the practicality of haiku. The practicality of Zen
results from the constitution of the world we live in. Whatever beliefs we have are meaningless except in so far as they
motivate our inner life, with the necessary expression in
manner and act:

But indeed conviction, were it never so excellent,
is worthless, till it convert itself into conduct.[2]

This "felt indubitable certainty of experience" must be
felt in and through the body:

And he took the cup and gave thanks, and
gave it to them, saying, Drink ye all of it.[3]

In the Tea Ceremony, it is the smell, the taste of the
tea, the sound of the boiling water, the touch of the tea-bowl
which give to the devotee the meaning which no abstract
thought, no watching of the tea ceremony will ever convey.

[1] Emerson, *Woodnotes, 1*.
[2] *Sartor Resartus*.
[3] *Matt,* 26, 27.

> Doubt of any sort cannot be removed except
> action.[1]

What kind of action is this? It is the physical activity of
listening to the higurashi as the shadows fall across the sky.
It was the smelling of the scent of the flower which Buddha
held up before the congregation of monks. It is the taste of
the tear that falls, we know not why, the touch of the dentist's
drill, the sight of ugly people whom we love.

We suppose that the body is a machine and that the soul
drives it at will hither or thither, but the reverse is the case.
Our boasted self-control, confession and penance, reformation,
conversion, salvation,—all are determined physically, in our
bodies. These have the true dark life. It is the root which
in the cold and silent earth decides what flowers are to
bloom in the wind and sun. This Spengler has portrayed in
his own way, with his characteristic, almost physical thinking,
his intellectual violence:

> The plant-like cosmic being, heavy with
> destiny, blood, sex, possesses an immemorial
> mastery and keep it. They are life. The other
> only serves life. But this other wills, not to
> serve, but to rule; moreover it believes that it
> does rule, for one of the most determined claims
> put forward by the human spirit is its claim to
> possess power over the body, over "nature."
> But the question is: is not this very belief a
> service to life? Why does our thought think
> just so? Perhaps because the cosmic "it" wills
> that it shall. Thought shows off its power when
> it calls the body a motion, when it establishes

[1] *Sartor Resartus.*

the pitifulness of the body, and commands the voices of the blood to be silent. But in truth the blood rules, in that silently it commands the activity of thought to begin and cease.[1]

Even when the subject does not admit of very gross or earthy treatment it is well to return to the material if only for a moment, lest we should lose touch with solid ground:

> "Then tell me," I said, "Whence do you believe these moments come? And will you give me half your onion?"
>
> "With pleasure," he replied, "for no man can eat a whole onion; and as for that other matter; why, I think the door of heaven is ajar from time to time, and that light shines out upon us for a moment between its opening and its closing."[2]

雷晴れて一樹の夕日蟬の聲　　　　　子 規

> The thunderstorm having cleared up,
> The evening sun shines on a tree
> Where a cicada is chirping.
>
> Shiki

By this materiality of aspect, animate and inanimate things lose much of their difference, as do also human and non-human. Man loses his dignity as lord of creation, things are seen with their Buddha nature fully displayed:

> It was so large that she couldn't help feeling a little shy with it, as she had been with the mutton; however she conquered her shyness by a

---

[1] The Cosmic and the Microcosm.
[2] Belloc, *The Onion Eater*.

great effort, and cut a slice and handed it to the
Red Queen.

"What impertinence!" said the Pudding.
"I wonder how you'd like it, if I were to cut a
slice out of *you*, you creature!"

This equality of things and ourselves, our common nature,
is reciprocal. We exist only if they do. They will not be
lorded over and treated with contempt. We are equals and
can live together harmoniously only if our independence and
dependence, our separateness and continuity is recognized.
Things have done their part; it is for us to do ours:

"Well, now that we have seen each other,"
said the Unicorn, "if you'll believe in me, I'll
believe in you. Is that a bargain?" "Yes, if
you like," said Alice.

XII
Love

Zen is *love* of the universe. Without this "love," joy is uncertain, pain is inevitable, all is meaningless. Othello says,

When I love thee not,
Chaos is come again.[1]

This love must be complete, ...not that it aims at the universe as a whole, but that the personality as a whole is to be concentrated on the thing; the thing is to be suffused with the personality. Then we have the state, describe abstractly by Dr. Suzuki in the following words:

When an object is picked up, everything else,
One and All, comes along with it, not in the way
of suggestion, but all-inclusively, in the sense that
the object is complete in itself.

Dickens gives us the same thing, but alive and palpitating:

'Orses and dogs is some men's fancy. They're wittles and drink to me...... lodging, wife and children...... reading, writing and rithmetic...... snuff, tobacker and sleep.

We get the same complete, self-abandoning love of the universe, concentrated in one thing described in the 19th Case of the *Hekiganroku:*

俱胝和尚凡有所問只竪一旨。

Whatever question Gutei was asked, he simply held up one finger.

It must be without qualifications and reservations, taking the universe in good health and in bad health, for better and for worse, without fear of death.

> If I must die,
> I will encounter darkness as a bride,
> And hug it in my arms.[1]

It must be without attachment to life. The classical example of this in English literature is the scene of the death of Old Euclio, by Pope:

> "Your money, sir?"—"My money, sir, what, all?
> Why—if I must—(then wept) I give it Paul"—
> "The manor, sir?"—"The manor! hold!
> Not that—I cannot part with that,"—and died.

In so far as we doubt the "fatherhood" of God, his love of the sparrow, the maggots and germs of disease, we have no peace of mind, for we cannot help loving Him for his beauty of leaf and flower, falling rain and misty mountains, and

> Oh what damned minutes tells he o'er
> Who dotes, yet doubts, suspects, yet strongly loves![2]

The relation of love to poetry may be easy to make out, but that to Zen is much more difficult. Look at it like this. If we are without self-love, greediness, without desire of gain, of happiness, of life itself, all this energy must overflow somewhere. It overflows into all things, including oneself, so that now no actions are selfish or unselfish, good or bad, but are like the sunshine or the rain, but with mind instead of mindlessness. We say that we see the beauty of the fine drops of rain, the glittering of the leaves in the sun, the stars in their calm,—but what we really see is the mind of man,

---

[1] *Measure for Measure, III, 1.*
[2] *Othello, 3, 3.*

our own mind, in all these things. Through our activity and coöperation, these inanimate things acquire mind and affection. The waves drown the shipwrecked sailor regretfully, the sun scorches the weary traveller with remorse,

> Holding their pocket handkerchief
> Before their streaming eyes.

In return, we become windy, rainy, starry, sunny creatures living in all things, in all times and places. A man who exists thus, helps his neighbour as he helps himself; because it gives him the same pleasure. Asked to walk one mile he gladly walks two, yet also, as Goldsmith says,

> The naked hè clothes every day
> That he puts on his clothes.

The fact is, as Bernard Shaw pointed out once, that we cannot persuade ourselves to love the unlovely, the inimical, those who injure us, whether they be things or persons. Here Christianity and Buddhism both fail. But what we can do is to empty our minds of self-love by the realization of a fact, the fact that there is no self to love, no lover to love. No one is praising us, no one is blaming, no one killing, no one killed. It is only countless Buddhas all bowing to one another, men and creatures and things all praising God with one accord.

This kind of "love," then, is not the means, the first step, but the end and aim and consummation of our pilgrimage here. It is expressed in quite other ways than altruism and self-denial. It is effortless and continuous, unconscious and nameless, but we feel it and know it in ourselves and others as the health of the soul.

澁いとこ母が喰ひけり山の柿   一 茶

> Mountain persimmons;
> The mother is eating
> The astringent parts.   Issa

Zen cannot change a man's inborn character. (What we call "inborn character" is the universal and identical Buddha-nature in its physically limited and specific outworking). Nothing can do this. It cannot turn a cold, selfish heart into a warm loving one. What it does do is to change the direction of the inner energy, to bring out all the latent power, to show things to be interesting that were not noticed at all, or thought to be meaningless or repulsive:

山門をぎいと鎖すや秋の暮   子 規

> Shutting the great temple gate,
> Creak! it goes:
> An autumn evening.   Shiki

吾行けば共に歩みぬ遠案山子   三 允

> It walked with me
> As I walked,
> The scarecrow in the distance.
>   Sanin

This love is of One who is as free as we could be ourselves, if only we wished it. We ask our solemn, futile questions, and get our replies, but they are hardly to our liking, but

I am not bound to please thee with my answers.[1]

Yet in our secret heart we love the universe as it is, the short things so short, the long things so long, and inwardly

[1] *The Merchant of Venice, IV, 1, 65.*

detest that falsely fair and superficially perfect world we pretend to hope for or claim to believe in.

Just as Zen is love, haiku may be called love-poems, and the *Chushingura* a love-story. Passionate love between the sexes is not implied here, and it must be admitted as a fundamental weakness of both Buddhism and Christianity that they have never dealt with the love of men and women, but ignored the whole matter, as if we all came into the world by spontaneous generation, instead of as the result of the love of our parents.

Haiku are an expression of the joy of our reunion with things from which we have been parted by self-consciousness, so strong and tender in the sexual act, more diffused, yet equally powerful and delicate in our poetic moments. Though our love of things is so feeble, we all desire to be loved ardently in the wrong, the unbuddhistic, the unchristian way. Keats says,

> Yourself—your soul—in pity give me all,
> Withold no atom's atom, or I die,

and it is hard here as always to avoid throwing out the baby with the bath water, especially because from the Zen point of view, the baby *is* the bath-water; no baby, no bath-water; no bath-water, no baby. Difficult indeed it is to love as God loves the just and the unjust, the raper and the raped, the slug and the lettuce.

XIII
Courage

The last of these manifestations of Zen is in the form of *courage*. Though not one of the virtues especially emphasized by the moralist, it nevertheless includes all the other twelve characteristics mentioned above, selflessness, loneliness, grateful acceptance, wordlessness, non-intellectuality, contradictoriness, humour, freedom, non-morality, materiality and love. All these elements are in some way present when an act of courage is performed. It may be difficult, however, to see how courage is an essential, even the most essential part of a poet. We may look at the matter in the following way.

When we hear of some calamity that affects ourselves, our parents or families, the mind instantly endeavours to find some cheap compensation, some profit in the loss, something to console us for the inevitable grief. This is not in itself wrong. It is a necessary element in a universe that while it constantly supports us is nevertheless attacking and threatening us without a moment's respite; the world, the flesh and the devil are at us all the time. But this division into profit and loss must be understood, must be known as a superficial one; strongly and deeply superficial it may be, yet it is only the waves on the surface of a profound abyss of waters. In our timidity and selfishness we ask with misgiving, "Suppose I could and did take upon myself all the woes and joys of the entire creation, how am I to know whether that is a blessed state or not?" In other words; is the universe good or not; would it be better that it had never come into existence? Or to put it in another way, would

you rather be a clod, a pebble on the roadside, or will you
take the bitter with the sweet, will you be a man of sorrows
and acquainted with grief, as well as rejoicing always in the
presence of God?

It is in answer to this question that the courage of the
poet is shown, and courage is thus the greatest of the virtues,
for without it the true poetic life, the true religious life is
impossible:

> God will not have his work made manifest
> by cowards.[1]

Without courage, you cannot even get to first base, as the
Americans say. This courage is of two kinds, corresponding
roughly to the popular division into physical and mental
courage. Both are important; lack of either is fatal to the
life of perfection. By physical courage is meant courage in
relation to physical pain and death. By mental courage,
willingness to look facts in the face, ability to grasp the uselessness, the meaninglessness of things,[2] power to perceive one's
own egolessness, lack of any rights whatever, absence of the
so-called "love of God" for us,[3] that is, the "indifference"
of the universe. Without the courage to do all these things,
the activity of the poet or saint is restricted to poetical cant
and religious humbug. Spengler says,

> By understanding the world, I mean being
> equal to the world.

---

[1] Emerson, *Self-reliance*.
[2] Goethe says: What is important in life is life, not a result
of life.
[3] Nor does being weary prove that he has where to rest.
Arnold, *Empedocles*.

Courage is life, living. Life is change; change is suffering; the will to suffer is courage. The world is on the one hand a world of law, and

Nature is written in mathematical language,

but life is incalculable.

> When Raleigh sailed into Cadiz, and all the forts and ships opened fire on him at once, he scorned to shoot again, and made answer with a flourish of insulting trumpets. I like this bravado better than the wisest dispositions to ensure victory; it comes from the heart[1] and goes to it.[2]

Goethe once said to Eckermann,

> The Godhead is effective in the living and not in the dead, in the becoming and changing, not in the become and set-fast, and therefore, similarly, the reason (Vernunft) is concerned only to strive to the divine through the becoming and the living, and the understanding (Verstand) only to make use of the become and the set-fast.

This "striving to the divine" is life, is courage. Every animal and plant, in so far as it has this striving, has this courage. It is a light that however low it sinks, burns to the end, and is extinguished only in death. Not only men, but all things are

> Made weak by time and fate, but strong in will
> To strive, to seek, to find, and not to yield.[3]

---

[1] The Buddha nature.
[2] Stevenson, *The English Admirals*.
[3] Tennyson, *Ulysses*.

It is the will to live which in inanimate things is the *will to exist*. In Buddhism it is called the "thusness of things" which again is the "becoming" of things of Goethe.

It requires courage to wind up one's watch before being executed. It requires courage to discard all the mind-colouring and emotion-colouring of a thing, to disdain all that passes for poetry but which is superfluous ornament, soul-clogging words. Religious and poetical courage are one and the same thing in their highest manifestations. In the following quotation from Spengler we can apply his words with ease to either:

> With the soul's awakening, direction, too, first reaches living expression,—Classical expression in steady adherence to the near-present and exclusion of the distant and future, Faustian in direction-energy which has an eye only for the most distant horizons; Chinese in free, hither and thither wandering that nevertheless goes to the goal; Egyptian in resolute march down the path once entered.[1]

Another quotation from Spengler will bring out still more clearly what is meant when we say that *poetry is courage.*

> Consider his (Hebbel's) treatment of the Judith story—Shakespeare would have taken it as it was and scented a world-secret in the physiognomic charm of the pure adventure.[2]

This "world secret" is in Shakespeare's own mind. He must take the skeletons out of his own cupboard, and when this is

---

[1] Symbolism and Space, IV.
[2] Destiny and Causality, XI.

done, all the grimness and horror appears as "physiognomic charm," what Schiller calls "enjoyment;" the sordid, brutal story becomes "pure" adventure. It is the courage of the poet which effects this transformation. Emerson says,

> Heroism feels and never reasons, and therefore is always right.

It is the heroism of the poet which makes every poetical word that Christ uttered perfectly true and eternally valid.

From courage comes wordlessness and silence:

> If thou hast a woe, tell it not to the enemy,
> Tell it to thy saddle-bow, and ride singing forth[1].

Selflessness derives from it:

> I had a singular feeling at being in his company. For I could hardly believe that I was present at the death of a friend, and therefore I did not pity him.[2]

It gives freedom:

> 格に入りて、格を出て始めて自在を得べし。
>
> 　　　　　　　　　　　芭蕉
>
> Abide by the rules, then throw them overboard, and for the first time you will achieve freedom.[3]

Simplicity is its invariable accompaniment:

> 道のほとりのあだごとの中に我が
> 　一念の發心を樂しむ。
>
> 　　　　　　　　　　　鴨長明

[1] Proverbs of Alfred, 1246–50.
[2] *Phaedo*, 58.
[3] Bashô.

Trivial things said by the wayside gladden
the faith of my awakened heart[1].

It enables us to accept contradictions and absurdities without
question:

萬山重からず君恩重し。
　　一髪輕からず、我が命輕し。

大石良雄

Ten thousand mountains are not heavy, but
my lord's benevolence is.　A single hair is not
light, but my life is.[2]

Courage gives that " loneliness " that defies definition:

人を相手にせず、天を相手にせよ。

西鄉隆盛

Do not deal with men; deal with Heaven.[3]

It makes us intimate with material things:

糞水を汲まざれば善農となること能はず。

大宰春臺

Unless a man ladles out ordure, he cannot
be a good farmer.[4]

It is entirely non-intellectual:

あしはらの, みずほの國はかんながら
　　ことあげせぬ國。

人麻呂

Japan is a country where people do not argue
against the will of the gods.[4]

[1] Kamô Chomei, 12–13th Cy.
[2] Oishi Yoshio, 1659–1703.
[3] Saigô Takamori, 1827–1877.
[4] Dazai Shuntai, 1680–1747.

Courage it is that endows us with the power to accept gratefully all that happens; Bashô says:

見るところ花にあらずと云ふことなし、
思ふところ月にあらずと云ふことなし。

> There is nothing you see that is not a flower;
> there is nothing you can think of which is not
> the moon.

We must have that boldness which will not quail at the ab-
surd.

> The Red Queen said, "That's a poor thin
> way of doing things. Now here, we mostly have
> days and nights two or three at a time, and
> sometimes in the winter we take as many as five
> nights together—for warmth, you know."
> "Are five nights warmer than one night,
> then?" Alice ventured to ask.
> "Five times as warm, of course."
> "But they should be five times as *cold*, by
> the same rule—."
> "Just so!" cried the Red Queen.
> "Five times as warm, *and* five times as cold,
> just as I'm five times as rich as you are, and
> five times as clever!"

Without courage we shall never be able truly to grasp
the fact that all things, all events are vehicles of something
that is far above and beyond the rules of morality:

> The setting sun is reflected from the windows
> of the almshouses as from the rich man's abode.

Last, love and courage are one thing in the following
lines from the end of Emerson's *Woodnotes* I:

When the forest shall mislead me,
When the night and morning lie,
When sea and land refuse to feed me,
' Twill be time enough to die:
Then will yet my mother yield
A pillow in her greenest field,
Nor the June flowers scorn to cover
The clay of their departed lover.

SECTION III

HAIKU AND POETRY

HAIKU AND POETRY

In *Biographia Litteraria* (Chapter XIV) Coleridge gives us a definition of poetry that will hardly fit haiku, though it may apply to other forms of verse:

> A poem is that species of composition which is opposed to works of science, by purposing for its *immediate* object pleasure, not truth.

It is strange that a critic who was also a poet, should not have realized that poetry is something which of its nature cannot be defined. When we have the experience of poetry we feel,

> Through all this fleshly dress,
> Bright shoots of everlastingness.

It is not pleasure; or if it is, it is poetic pleasure, and we are in the same difficulty as before.

> Life is a pure flame, and we live by an invisible sun within us.[1]

It is invisible, but we know the flame is there. We do not see the light; we see by it.

A haiku is the expression of a temporary enlightenment, in which we see into the life of things.

稲妻にこぼるゝ音や竹の露　　　蕪 村

> A flash of lightning!
> The sound of drops
>   Falling among the bamboos. Buson

---

[1] Browne, *Hydriotaphia*.

Plate 19

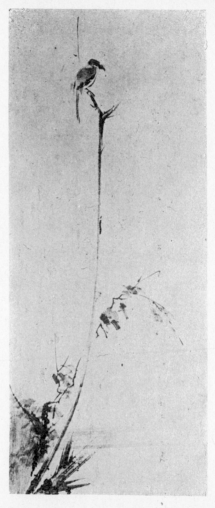

Shrike Screeching on a Dead Branch

Miyamoto Musashi

There is no distinction, at the moment of composition or appreciation, between inner and outer. Life runs so freely between them that we perceive things by introspection, and our experiences of the outer world have the same immediacy, validity and certainty as have states of pure self-consciousness. As Hôjô, 法常, lay dying, a flying squirrel, 鼯鼠, screeched. He thereupon said,

> 即物、非他物。汝等諸人善護持之。吾今逝
> 矣。　　　　　　　　　　　　　　　　　（傳　七）

>   It is immediately this thing; it is not that.
> All you monks, hold fast to this (immediacy).
> Now I shall depart.

In the same way Confucius says:

> 二三子以我爲隱乎、吾無隱乎。
> 　　　　　　　　　　（論語七、二十三）

>   My friends, do you think I conceal anything
> from you? I conceal nothing from you.

This is the work of a poet, to hide nothing from us. When he does so, the Buddha nature of a thing is clearly seen.

Each thing is preaching the law incessantly, but this law is not something different from the thing itself. Haiku is the revealing of this preaching by presenting us with the thing devoid of all our mental twisting and emotional discoloration; or rather, it shows the thing as it exists at one and the same time outside and inside the mind, perfectly subjective, ourselves undivided from the object, the object in its original unity with ourselves.

　傘におしもどさるゝしぐれ哉　　　　紫青女

> Walking in the winter rain,
> The umbrella
>   Pushes me back.   Shiseijo

Haiku thus make the greatest demand upon our internal poverty. Shakespeare pours out his universal soul, and we are abased before his omniscience and overflowing power. Haiku require of us that our soul should find its own infinity within the limits of some finite thing It is in this sense that nothing is hidden from us. Haiku is the result of the wish, the effort, not to speak, not to write poetry, not to obscure further the truth and suchness of a thing with words, with thoughts and feelings. Of things be it said with Emerson,

> What you are speaks so loudly, I cannot hear
> what you say.

Things must speak to us so loudly that we cannot hear what the poets have said about them.

A haiku is not a poem, it is not literature; it is a hand beckoning, a door half-opened, a mirror wiped clean. It is a way of returning to nature, to our moon nature, our cherry blossom nature, our falling leaf nature, in short, to our Buddha nature. It is a way in which the cold winter rain, the swallows of evening, even the very day in its hotness, and the length of the night become truly alive, share in our humanity, speak their own silent and expressive language.

> 舟と岸と話してゐる日永かな   子規
> How long the day:
> The boat is talking
>   With the shore.   Shiki

It is a silent language because it only beckons to a certain region and does not explain why and where and how. In the above verse by Shiki, the simple meaning that the man in the boat is talking to the man in the shore, is not, for all its poetic brevity, the really significant point of the verse. This lies in quite another realm, where boats and shores speak freely to each other and continue their eternal conversations, indifferent to our prosaic and intellectual expostulation.

What is a poet? A poet is a spirit speaking to spirits.

相見呵呵笑
園林落葉多　　　　　（禪林句集）

Meeting, the two friends laugh aloud:
In the grove, fallen leaves are many.

Confucius is not thinking of a poet, but his words apply:

唯天下至誠、爲能盡其性、能盡其性、則
能盡人之性、能盡人之性、則能盡、物之
性、能盡物之性、則可以贊天地之化育、
可以贊天地之化育、則可以與、天地參矣。
（中庸廿二）

Only he who has attained to (perfect) sincerity under Heaven can exhaust (the infinite potentialities of) his nature. He who does this, can exhaust the nature of man, and thereby, the nature of (all other) things, thus attaining (the power of) taking part in the transforming and life-giving (activity) of Heaven and Earth, and as Man, making a third with them.

In what language do poets speak to one another?

It is expressed neither by words nor by silence. In that condition that is neither words nor silence, its nature is grasped.　　　*Sôshi*, 25.

What do poets say of those who are not poets?

道即大煞道
只道得八成。　　　（碧、八十九）

When you speak, you speak well,
But your speaking is incomplete.

This is why poetry is so exhausting to read, why we instinctively avoid it. To come closely into contact with things or persons is often a painful business. Even with God this is so.

God loves all things equally.

> Gott ist in allen Dingen und an allen Orten gleich, und ist uberall gleich bereit sich dem Menschen zu schenken, so weit es an ihm liegt.

Eckhart's intuition is expressed in a typically Zen way:

虛空無脊面
鳥道絕東西　　　（禪林句集）

In the vast inane, there is no back or front;
The path of the bird annihilates East and West.

But all things do not and cannot receive that love equally. God is in all things equally, but things do not manifest him in the same degree. Eckhart says,

> Nun habe ich schon oft gesagt: wenn ich von Gleichheit spreche, so meine ich nicht, dass man alle Werke und alle Orte und alle Leute fur gleich halten soll. Das wäre unrecht; denn Beten ist ein besser werk als Spinnen, und die Kirche ist ein edlere Stätte als die Strasse. Aber du sollst in den Werken ein gleiches Gemut und ein gleiches Zutrauen und einen gleichen Ernst zu deinem Gott haben.

And these differences in things, these limitations are, in a most astounding way, the very qualities that manifest God. It is *in virtue* of its lack of something that a thing has value.

樹呈風體態
波弄月精神　　　　　（禪林句集）

The tree manifests the bodily power of the wind;
The wave exhibits the spiritual nature of the moon.

If the tree were strong enough it would manifest nothing. If the wave were rigid, the moon's nature could not be expressed in it. This strength made perfect in weakness is what Eckhart calls becoming a son, one who rejects nothing, who lays aside all that obstructs perfect union with all things, good and bad, profitable and unprofitable, pure and impure.

Sollt ihr also ein Sohn sein, so müsst ihr ablegen und von euch scheiden alles, was eine Besonderheit an euch ausmacht.

A poet sees things as they are in proportion as he is selfless.

My judgement is just *because* I seek not my own will, but the will of Him that sent me.

In relation to every circumstance, we are to be like the servants at the Feast of Cana:

Whatever he saith unto you, do it.

The flowers say "Bloom!" and we bloom in them. The wind blows and we sway in the leaves. Lawrence describes the poet in the following words:

A pure animal man would be as lovely as a deer or a leopard, burning like a flame fed

> straight from underneath. And he'd be part of
> the unseen, like a mouse is, even. And he'd never
> cease to wonder, he'd breathe silence and unseen
> wonder, as the partridges do, running in the
> stubble. He'd be all the animals in turn, instead
> of one fixed automatic thing which he is now,
> grinding on the nerves.[1]

We may reach the same conclusion from the other end of
the scale. In so far as a tomato exists, God exists. When
a tomato rots, God rots. God blooms in the summer flowers,
falls in the autumn leaves, lies quiet and cold in the snow
and ice of winter.

青山元不動
白雲自去來 　　　　（禪林句集）

The blue hills are by their nature immovable;
The white clouds of themselves come and go.

Again we say, God loves all things equally, the mouse that
the cat catches, the water that engulfs the mariner, the man
who beats his mother to death. Replace the word "God"
by the word "poet", and the above statements are equally
true. If you think the universe is inimical to you, that is
simply a reflection of your enmity to the universe. If you
think

I am so glad that Jesus loves me,

that is a reflection of your friendliness towards it. It is in
fact neither inimical nor friendly nor indifferent. It is you,
your real self. The poetical, the religious life is that of the
angels

St. Mawr.

Who *always* behold the face of your Father
in Heaven.

Thus, though the poet's life is one of pain, it is also one of
peace. The interpenetration of life with life is an agonizing
business, yet it is like the lancing of a boil, like the birth of
a child, in Dante's language,

> com' acqua recepe
> Raggio di luce, permanendo unita.[1]

> as water receives
> A ray of light, remaining whole.

The following account is given of the creation of Bashô's

古池や蛙飛び込む水の音
The old pond;
A frog jumps in,—
The sound of the water.

It is of very doubtful authenticity, and in a way spoils the
simplicity and apparent spontaneity of the original. In fact,
one feels a tendency towards dragging out of the unconscious
and instinctive what should be left there, a certain artificiality
and esoteric conventionality that is repugnant to the poetic
mind. Nevertheless, it is an illustration of one of the ways
in which Zen and haiku are related, and further, shows a
certain kind of trend of poetic thinking that has accompanied
haiku since the advent of Bashô.

Bucchô, 佛頂, of Komponji Temple, (帝州鹿島
根本寺), a monk of wide reading and profound
enlightenment, became the teacher of Bashô.
Moving to Chôkeiji Temple, 長慶寺, at Fukagawa

[1] *Paradiso, 2, 85–56.*

near Edo, he one day visited the poet, accompanied by a man called Rokusô Gohei, 六祖五兵衞. The latter first entering into the hermitage, cried out, "How is it, the Buddhist Law in this quiet garden with its trees and grasses?"

如何なるか是れ閑庭草木中の佛法。

Bashô replied, "Large leaves are large, little ones are little."

葉に大底は大、小底は小なり。

Bucchô then entering said, "Recently, what is your attainment?"

近日何の有る所ぞ。

Bashô replied, "The rain over, the green moss is fresh."

雨過ぎて青苔を洗ふ。

Bucchô further asked him, "What is this Buddhist Law, *before* the green moss began to grow?"

如何なるか是れ青苔未生前の佛法。

At this moment, hearing the sound of a frog that leapt into the water, Basho exclaimed, "The sound of the frog jumping into the water."

蛙飛び込む水の音

Bucchô was full of admiration at this answer, considering it as evidence of Bashô's state of enlightenment...... At this time Sampû, 杉風, respectfully congratulated Bashô on having composed this verse, acknowledged by Bucchô, adding to art the glory of religion; Ransetsu, 嵐雪, said, "This sentence of the sound of the water may be said to represent fully the meaning of haiku, yet the first part of the verse is missing. Please complete it." Bashô answered, "I was thinking about it myself, but I would like to hear your opinions first and then I will decide." Several of his pupils tried their hands at it; Sampû suggested

宵闇や　　The evening twilight;
as the first five syllables;

Ransetsu,
淋しさに　　In the loneliness,

Kikaku,
山吹や　　The mountain rose;

Bashô, looking at these said, "You have each and all in your first line expressed an aspect of the matter and composed a verse above the ordinary; especially Kikaku's is brilliant and strong. However, not following the conventional mode, just for this evening I will make it,

古池や　　The old pond;

All were struck with profound awe. In this verse, the Eye of Haiku is fully opened. It moves Heaven and Earth and all the Gods and Demons therein to admiration. This is indeed the way of Shikishima, equal to the creation of a Buddha. The Dharani of Hitomaru, 人丸, Saigyô's Praising the Coming of the Buddha, 讚佛來, are contained in these seventeen syllables.

Somehow or other I do not care for all this. Haiku and the practice of Zen should be kept apart, in my opinion. Zen as an exercise leading towards enlightenment is a matter of life and death for the soul. Haiku is concerned only with life. It is the flower of living. It is true enough that in Zen

we endeavour to see the world as a poet sees a flowering
tree, but to get into that state needs violent exertions, extremely unpoetical spiritual convulsions, quite different from
that

> emotion recollected in tranquility,

which is the inflow and outflow of object and mind in moments
of poetic insight. A better example of the relation between
Zen and haiku is the following. When Sotôba, 蘇東坡, the
great Chinese poet of the Sung dynasty, was studying the
problem of Insentient Preaching, 無情說法, at Ryukôji Temple,
龍興寺, in Rozan, 盧山, under Jôchô, 常聰, leaving the temple
at dawn, he suddenly became enlightened and expressed his
realization in the following well-known verse;

> 溪聲便是廣長舌、 山色豈非淸淨身。
> 夜來八萬四千偈、 他日如何舉示人。
>
> The mountain torrent is the broad, long tongue
>   of Buddha;
> The colours of the mountains,—are they not His
>   Pure Body?
> All night,—eighty four thousand Buddhist verses,
> But in after days, how shall I show this to others?

This is also the problem of the poet, to convey something of
what he has seen, to convey rather, *the power of seeing,* the
creative life that forms the essential part of what appears in
words and rhyme and rhythm.

We have this same identity of poet and saint in the
verse of Sotôba in which he describes his experience of the
mountains of Ro, 盧:

> 盧山烟雨浙江潮、 不到千般恨未消、
> 到得歸來無別事、 盧山烟雨浙江潮。

Misty rain on Mount Ro, the incoming tide at
  Sekkô,—
Before you have been there, you have many
  regrets;
When you have been there and come back,
It is just simply misty rain on Mt. Ro, the in-
  coming tide at Sekkô.

This experience of Sotôba, the man, is deeper than a
reader would suppose, but so is that of Sotôba the poet. The
difference between the two is that the poetic experience may
be, and usually is, confined to that area of the mind concerned with the particular things, whereas that of the illuminated
man spreads itself willy-nilly throughout the whole personality,
the whole activity. In Sotôba we have the combination of
man and poet in one, and from either point of view, his total
experience may be surmised. The peaks seen through the
smoke-like rain,—these the poet perceives as the manifest
deity; the swelling water of the creek is God himself, but
only if *immediately* so perceived; when there is a hair's
breadth of separation between them, between the thing and
God, between himself and God, we have an intellectual cleav-
age which no passion can join again. When we *think* this
is that, it is not so, and no intensity of thought will make it
so, because it is as a result of our immediacy of perception
that it is so. Further, when, this *thusness* of things is perceived, it is with ecstasy, but as soon as it has become a
daily experience, and lost its first shock of surprise, that
newly-created world becames the every-day world that we
live in, but this world is not that of the matter-of-fact, unpoetical, unillumined man devoid of religion or poetry. This
is what Sotôba means when he says it is nothing special,

nothing out of the ordinary, these misty mountains and surging waves. People who live in Heaven, those who have a desireless peace, who look at things without reference to the profit and loss to themselves, such people find their lives quite ordinary and unexciting.

For the reader, every haiku is a *kôan*, a question in Zen, an open door that looks shut, leading into—? Into nothing and nowhere, for the door is what it leads into and what it leads out of. It is not even different from him who passes through it, him who has no real existence whatever. Everything that confronts us is a *kôan*, an examination which we duly fail in or pass, things of the past, present, and future, things near and things far away, real and unreal, abstract and concrete. And all these things are in themselves poems like those dried up artificial water-flowers, 水造花, which open when they are plunged into the water of the mind. We give things their life, they give us our life.

We must be neither the slaves nor the masters of things. Today is New Year's Day, and when we go out to the well in the early morning and see the rays of the sun glistening on the water as we pour it into the bucket, we say:

汲上る水に春たつ光りかな　　　　　林　外

> In the water I draw up,
> Glitters the beginning
> Of spring.　　　　　　　　　　**Ringai**

But

Every day is a Good Day, 日々是好日,

or as the poet expresses it:

やつと來た元旦も只ひと日哉　　　　　鳳　朗

> This New Year's Day
> That has come at last,—
> It is just a day. Hôrô

The light in the water is no different from that of any other morning. We wabble between the feeling that it is specially bright and meaningful, and the knowledge that it is not. Hold fast to both; do not divide what is given from what we give. Everything is as it is, but everything is wonderful. All is law, but we are free. On the one hand, things are what they are:

> The sea was wet as wet could be,
> The sands were dry as dry.
> You could not see a cloud, because
> No cloud was in the sky:
> No birds were flying overhead—
> There were no birds to fly.

On the other hand, nothing is as it seems to be, all is wildly improbable and contradictory. We feel our deep spiritual kinship with the White Knight:

> He said, "I hunt for haddocks' eyes
> Among the heather bright,
> And work them into waist-coat buttons
> In the silent night.

> I sometimes dig for buttered rolls,
> Or set limed twigs for crabs,
> I sometimes search the grassy knolls
> For wheels of Hansom-cabs."

We feel with Puck,

> And those things do best please me
> That befall preposterously.

That is to say, things are unpredictable, unique, lawless. Yet things are simply what they are, of no ulterior meaning. Things are infinite in significance; but also, they are disappointing, they are finite and limited. But at bottom, at the ground of our existence we ask for nothing, not even that things should be as they are. For all our desiring and loathing, our deepest instinct is:

元旦や何ももとめぬ宿のさま　　　　南 枝

New Year's Day;
The hut just as it is,
Nothing to ask for.   Nanshi

Moments of vision come when least expected, unbidden, and in most men, pass into oblivion, unnoticed and unremembered:

> Sometimes, when the soul least thinks of it, and when it least desires it, God touches it divinely, causing certain recollections of Himself. Sometimes, too, the divine touches are sudden, occurring even while the soul is occupied with something else, and that occasionally of trifling moment.

白菊にしばしたゆたふはさみかな　　　蕪 村

The scissors hesitate
Before the white chrysanthemums,
A moment.

かなしさや釣の糸ふく秋の風　　　　蕪 村

Ah, grief and sadness!
The fishing-line trembles
In the autumn breeze.   Buson

This seeing into the life of things may come from the slightest of physical causes, for example, a mere touch, a faint sensation of warmth and resilience:

She paused, as if thinking, while her hand
rested on the horse's sun-arched neck. Dimly, in
her weary, young-woman's soul, an ancient understanding seemed to flood in.[1]

畑を打つ翁が頭巾ゆがみけり   几 董

> The old man
> Hoeing the field,
> Has his hat on crooked.   Kitô

盗んだる案山子の笠に雨急なり   盧 子

> How heavy the rain
> On the *kasa*[2] stolen
> From the scarecrow.   Kyoshi

It comes from some primitive realm of sound, that calls us
back to something we have lost, some recollections that have
intimations of immortality in them:

> When he reared his head and neighed from
> his deep chest, like deep wind-bells resounding,
> she seemed to hear the echoes of another, darker,
> more spacious, more dangerous, more splendid
> world than ours, that was beyond her, and there
> she wanted to go.[1]

The English poet *says* this, but all this is taken for granted
in the haiku:

村々の寐こころ更けぬ落し水   蕪 村

> Night deepens,
> And sleep in the villages;
> Sounds of falling water.   Buson

To hear these overtones of meaning, not only selflessness but

---

[1] *St. Mawr.*
[2] An umbrella-like hat.

extreme sensitivity is required. In truth it means

> On the torture of the minde to lye
> In restlesse extasie.[1]

This is the condition of the extravert; the introvert expresses it with more moderation;

> Silent unobtrusive sympathies
> And gentle agitations of the mind
> From manifold distinctions, differences
> Perceived in things, where to the unwatchful eye
> No difference is.[2]

An example of the Japanese poets' extreme delicacy of perception:

白菊の高う見えけり朝ぼらけ   野　泉

> The white chrysanthemums
> Seem higher than they are,
> In the morning twilight.   Yasen

What most people do not realise is that poetry like religion and morality is a continuous thing; this poetic sensitivity never ceases as long as life lasts. Emerson says,

> We pass for what we are. Character teaches
> above our wills. Men imagine that they com-
> municate their virtue or their vice only by overt
> actions, and do not see that virtue or vice emits
> a breath every moment.

The one thing that a haiku poet is instinctively and consciously on his guard against is "explanatory" poetry. What Spengler says of himself as a historian might be taken as a manifesto of the haiku poet, the Way of Haiku:

---

[1] *Macbeth, 3, 2.*
[2] *Prelude, I, 400.*

We are sceptics in regard to any and every mode of thought which "explains" things causally. *We let things speak for themselves,* and confine ourselves to sensing the Destiny immanent in them and *contemplating the form of manifestations we shall never penetrate.* The extreme to which we can attain is the discovery of causeless, purposeless, purely existent forms underlying the changeful picture of nature.[1]

The haiku poet not only makes no effort to understand anything he hears and sees, he sternly checks the fatal tendency for the intellect to pass judgement on the wholeness of things.

> Matto è chi spera che nostra ragione
>   Possa trascorrer la infinita via
>   Che tiene una sustanza in tre persone.
> State contenti, umana gente al *quia.*[2]

> Mad is he who hopes that our intellect
>   Can compass the infinite way
>   Which three persons in one substance hold;
> Be content, O human kind, that *It is so.*

おのづから頭が下るなり神路山　　　一 茶

> Kamiji Yama:
>   My head bent
>   Of itself.   Issa

Mount Kamiji is the hill consecrated in the Inner Precincts of the Shrine of Ise. Issa no doubt believed that this place

---

[1] Group of the Higher Cultures, 3.
[2] *Purgatorio,* 3, 34–37. Goethe versifies this:

> Wie? Warum? Und Wo?
> Die Götter bleiben stumm!—
> Du halte dich an's Weil,
> Und frage nicht Warum.

was intrinsically sacred, but for poets, any place that is felt
to be, or has been felt to be a holy spot, is also sacred to
them, for it is thinking that makes it so, the "thinking" of
mankind yet done for them by the poets.

The aim of haiku is to bestow on things the poetic life
which already they possess in their own right. As with
moral coduct, the material is indifferent; any time, any place,
any thing will do.

> What matters whether such stuff be of this
> sort or that, so the form thou give it be heroic,
> be poetic?[1]

This poetry of things is not something superimposed on them,
but brought out of them as the sun and rain bring the tender
leaf out of the hard buds. There is a poetry independent of
rhyme and rhythm, of onomatopoeia and poetic brevity, of
cadence and parallelism, of all form whatsoever. It is wordless and thoughtless even when expressed in words and notions,
and lives a life separate from that of so-called poetry. It is
the seeing we do when a white butterfly flutters by us down
the valley, never to return:

> Behold, I make all things new.

But not only the beautiful things of life, not even the beauty
of beautiful things, but their significance, the part they play
in the whole, their flowing activity, whether of lightning or
of seemingly eternal rocks, are to be the subjects of haiku.
Marcus Aurelius says,

> So too the ears of corn bending towards their
> mother earth, the shaggy eyebrows of the lion,

[1] *Sartor Resartus.*

the foam dripping from the jaws of the boar,
and objects innumerable of the same type, considered by themselves are far enough removed
from beauty, but being sequels to the operations
of nature, serve to deck her out, and gladden
the heart of the onlooker.

The progress of poetry must be in two extreme directions,
widening its scope into the remote, and into the near; into
the infinite, and into the finite.

江月照松風

The moon in the creek shines upon the breeze
in the pine-trees.

This requires a certain Shelleyan vagueness of vision to com-
prehend it in its really concrete sense.

白馬入蘆花

The white horse enters the white flowers of
the reeds.

Whiteness always leads us towards the absolute.

草むらや名も知らぬ花の白き咲　　子規

Among the grasses,
A flower blooms white,
Its name unknown.　　Shiki

On the other hand, poetry must give speech to the most inarticulate things:

Hal. Via Goodman Dull; thou hast spoken no word all
this while.
Dull. Nor understood none neither, sir.
Hal. Allons, we will employ thee.
Dull. I ll make one in a dance or so, or I will play on

> the tabor to the worthies, and let them dance the
> hay.
> Hal. Most dull, honest Dull, to our sport away.

In his short stories, O. Henry, and still further Ring
Lardner,[1] have rendered the inarticulate individuals that make
up the " many-headed multitude " as expressive of their inner
life as Hamlet or Macbeth. However, the endeavour to widen
the scope of haiku has often been made, not so much from
any consciously-felt need to include all things, even the most
recalcitrant, beneath the sway of poetry, or the desire to see
everything in time *sub specie aeternitatis*, but because poets
grew weary of saying the same thing about the same limited
range of subjects. One way of reviving poetry is to widen
the relations of the subject. In a letter to his pupil Kitô,
Buson says that in regard to plum-blossoms, poets have ex-
hausted their conventional aspects, and fresh efforts must be
made to get new meanings from them. He then quotes his
own verses to show what he means by the old and the newer
style of poetic thinking.

Poems of the ordinary way of thinking (よのつねにおもひ
よる句):

かはほりのふためき飛ぶや梅の月
> The bat flits and flutters
> In the moon
> Over the plum-blossoms.

梅散るや螺鈿こぼるゝ卓の上
> The plum-blossoms falling,
> Mother of pearl
> Is spilt on the table.

[1] Died 1933.

Plate 20

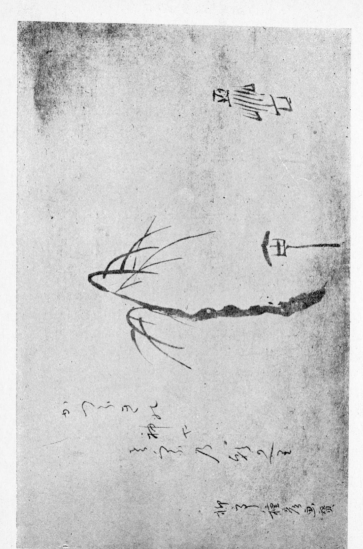

Willow at Dawn   Tanehiko

Poems seeking a different approach （別に趣向をもとむる
句）：

しら梅や北野の茶店にすまひ取

> White plum-blossoms;
> In a tea-house of Kitano,
> A wrestler.

梅咲て帶買ふ室の遊女かな

> Courtezans
> Buying sashes in their room,
> Plum-blossoms blooming.

The latter two verses bring man and nature together.

大門の重き扉や春の暮　　　　　　　蕪　村

> How heavy
> The doors of the Great Gate,—
> An evening of spring.　　Buson

What is the relation between the end of spring and the
heaviness of the door? The cherry-blossoms are falling;
leaves are filling the skies that now are darkening. The
ponderous, iron-studded doors that must be dragged along
the ground to open and shut them, have left ruts in their
track. The whole world is brooding and heavy with the
coming of summer.

We may take an example of the same kind, secretly
harmonious things brought together:

肴屋が入つた門は柳かな　　　　　浪化上人

> By the gate
> The fishmonger entered,
> A willow tree.　　Rôka Shônin

A pair of verses by Shiki may be put side by side to illustrate two kinds of harmony:

雲の峰白帆南に群がれり

> Billowing clouds;
> White sails
> Crowding in the south.

雲の峰硯に蟻の上りけり

> Billowing clouds;
> An ant climbs
> Onto the ink-stone.

We can say that there are three kinds of haiku, just as there are three ways of combining the obi (or sash) with the kimono. First, concord of colour or feeling or form. Second, discord and contrast of colour or sentiment. These two are illustrated by Shiki's verses above. The third is quite inexplicable yet unmistakable, an inner, secret harmony which intuition creates, and recreates in appreciation. For example, by Buson:

菜の花や鯨もよらず海暮れぬ

> Flowers of rape;
> No whale approaches,
> The sea darkens.

What we call " harmony " as the object of the poetic and the religious life, the man of broad and deep culture calls " uniformities ":

> Who amongst the historians realises that
> between the Differential Calculus and the dynastic
> principle of politics in the age of Louis XIV,
> between the Classical city state and the Euclidean

geometry, between the space perspective of western oil-painting and the conquest of space by railroad, telephone and long-range weapons, between contrapuntal music and credit economics, there are deep uniformities?[1]

The spirit of haiku is one which seeks to perceive clearly and deeply such uniformities wherever they may be found, and they are found everywhere. We may say, then, that the aim of haiku is to

> assert Eternal Providence,
> And justify the ways of God to man.

Below are given some examples of concord:

牛部屋の牛のうなりや朧月　　　　　　子 規

> A cow is lowing
> In the cow-shed,
> Under the hazy moon.　　　　　Shiki

蟬なくやつくづく赤い風車　　　　　　一 茶

> A cicada is chirping:
> The toy wind-mill
> Is bright red.　　　　　Issa

遠山の目玉にうつる蜻蛉かな　　　　　一 茶

> Reflected
> In the eye of the dragon-fly,
> The distant hills.　　　　　Issa

---

[1] *The Decline of the West*, Introduction.

雉子立つて人驚かす枯野かな　　　　一茶

> A pheasant flew up
> And startled us,
>> Over the withered moor.　　　Issa

六道の辻に立ちけり枯野かな　　　　一茶

>> Standing at the cross-roads
> Of the Six Ways,[1]
>> The withered moor!　　　Issa

豊年の聲を舉げけり門の蠅　　　　一茶

>> The flies at the gate
> Raise the sound
>> Of a fruitful year.　　　Issa

脊の低き馬に乘る日の霞かな　　　蕪村

> One day
> Riding on a short-legged horse,
>> In the haze.　　　Buson

山寺や撞きぞこなひの鐘霞む　　　蕪村

>> A mountain temple;
> The sound of the bell struck fumblingly,
>> Vanishing in the haze.　　　Buson

低き木に鶯鳴くや晝さがり　　　蕪村

>> Noon is past;
> The *uguisu*
>> Sings on a low tree.　　　Buson

風鈴の鳴りつゝ葱をそよぎけり　　初犀

> The wind-bells ringing,
> While the leeks
>> Sway.　　　Shosei

---

[1] The Six Ways are the six conditions of sentient life, hell, that
of the hungry ghosts, animals, nature spirits, human beings, gods.

わら葺の法華の寺や鶏頭花 　　　子 規

    In the straw-thatched temple
Of the Saddharma Pundarika,[1]
      Cockscombs are abloom.   Shiki

人形をきざむ小店や菊の花 　　　子 規

    A small shop
Carving dolls,—
      Chrysanthemums.   Shiki

寺見えて小道の曲る野菊哉 　　　子 規

    At the bend of the road,
The temple in sight,—
      Wild chrysanthemums.   Shiki

鰯雲天にひろごり萩咲けり 　　　秋櫻子

    Mackerel clouds
Spread over the sky:
      Bush-clover is blooming.   Shûôshi

Examples of Discord or Contrast are various, but in all, the collision of thoughts or images supplies the stimulus by which the mind is encouraged to make the effort to overcome the difficulty of uniting what God has put asunder.

居酒屋の喧嘩むしだす朧月 　　　子 規

    The quarrel
In the ale-house,
      Revived by the hazy moon.   Shiki

市中は物の匂ひや夏の月 　　　凡 兆

    In the market place,
The smell of something or other,—
      The summer moon.   Bonchô

[1] The Dharma-flower, i.e. the Lotus Sutra.

猫の戀やむ時ねやの朧月　　　　　芭 蕉

> The loves of the cats;
> When it was over, the hazy moon
> Over the bed-chamber.　　　　Bashô

投げ出した足の先より雲の峰　　　　一 茶

> Over my legs,
> Stretched out at ease,
> The billowing clouds.　　　　Issa

鶯や竹の子籔に老を鳴く　　　　　芭 蕉

> The *uguisu*
> In the bamboo-sprout thicket,
> Sings of old age.　　　　Bashô

廢館に鶏遊ぶ芙蓉かな　　　　　子 規

> By the ruined mansion,
> Fowls roaming
> Among the hibiscus.　　　　Shiki

雷に小家は燒かれて瓜の花　　　　蕪 村

> Round the small house
> Struck by lightning,
> Melon-flowers.　　　　Buson

The third kind of haiku is that in which the concord and discord are hidden from our eyes, yet the mind perceives them the more; no examples are given here, for they form the greater part of the verses of succeeding volumes.

HAIKU IN ENGLISH POETRY

In *Zen in English Literature* examples were given from the whole range of English literature of the spirit of Zen which infuses it. Wherever there is the spirit of haiku, there is Zen, but the reverse is not true, for Zen may be diffused throughout long passages, or on the other hand, be contained in a single word or phrase that in its brevity of utterance and length of context transcends the power of the seventeen syllables of haiku.

Proverbs, in poetry certain phrases, in prose a stray sentence here and there,—these correspond to haiku in the sense of being the peaks of poetic feeling and insight. Coleridge says in *Biographia Litteraria,*

> A Poem of any length neither can be, nor ought to be, all poetry.

Pater, in his essay on *Wordsworth*, after pointing out the neccessity of a selection of the poems of Wordsworth, speaks of his many prosaic poems, which yet contain

> the few perfect lines, the phrase, the single word, perhaps,

which represents the moment of enthusiasm, of divine possession. Besides the question of length, there is that of aim, and we find something about a great deal of English poetry that is faintly repulsive to a delicate feeling. Especially where there is a striving after effect, the exquisite epithet, the bowel-stirring last line, we feel a desire to give up all literature and return to things themselves, things which never say more

than they are, which are never understatements with an
ulterior motive.

> Only we'll sit upon the dasied grass,
> And hear the larks and see the swallows pass;
> Only we'll live awhile, as children play,
> Without tomorrow, without yesterday.[1]

Haiku are not these peaks of strenuous poetic effort;
they are not the cream of a western verse. There is something spontaneous, effortless, something even flat about them;
but this flatness also comes unsought for. It is emotion recol-
lected in moments of *tranquillity*—this is what is overlooked
by so many poets. This tranquillity of the poet is an essential
element, for it corresponds to the tranquillity, the point of
rest, of all living things. The haiku poet also

> remembers
> The beauty of fire from the beauty of embers.[2]

The following are haiku taken from various forms of
literature. There has been no change in the words or their
order; only a three-line division has been made to approxi-
mate it to a haiku form. For many of them, the ascription
of season is quite arbitrary, or in accordance with the mood
of the verse. It does not follow that these, if translated into
Japanese verse, would all be acceptable by the standards of
haiku; much would be omitted as redundant and unnecessary, as too intellectual or abstract. The origins are given
in Appendix 3.

---

[1] A. Mary P. Robinson, *Let us Forget*.
[2] Masefield, *On Growing Old*.

SPRING

The sun shines warm,
And the babe leaps up
On his Mother's arm.

The budding twigs
Spread out their leafy fan,
To catch the breezy air.

The Lark

All nature listens to him,
And the awful sun
Stands still upon the mountain.

The lark begins his flight,
And singing, startles the dull night
From his watch-tower in the skies.

Thou dost float and run
Like an unbodied joy,
Whose race is just begun.

The lark now leaves her wat'ry
nest,
And climbing,
Shakes her dewy wings.

The lark at break of day arising
From sullen earth,
Sings hymns at heaven's gate.

The lark's shrill fife
May come
From the fallow.

In the broad daylight
Thou art unseen,
But yet I hear thy shrill delight.

The Cock

On his toos he rometh up and
  doun;
Hym deyned not
  To sette his foot to grounde.

Father of lights!
What sunnie seed, what glance of day
  Hast thou confined into this bird!

The cock with lively din,
Scatters the rear
  Of darkness thin.

Butterflies will make side-leaps,
As though escaped from Nature's hand
  Ere perfect quite.

A young beech tree
On the edge of the forest
  Stands still in the evening.

A lonely pool,
And let a tree
  Sigh with her bosom over me

Loveliest of trees,
The cherry now is hung with bloom
  Along the bough,

My heart leaps up
When I behold
  A rainbow in the sky.

I will touch
A hundred flowers,
  And not pick one.

The pliant harebell,
Swinging in the breeze
On some gray rock.

Tender blue-bells,
At whose birth
The sod scarce heaved.

Daffodils,
With the green world
They live in.

The cattle are grazing,
Their heads never raising,
There are forty feeding like one.

As words of air,
Life makes of starry earth,
Sweet soul-delighted faces.

Whither,
O splendid ship,
Thy white sails crowding?

In him was life,
And the life
Was the life of men.

Three Men of Gotham;
Whither in your bowl so free?
To rake the moon from out the sea.

My heart was full;
I made no vows,
But vows were made for me.

SUMMER

We passed in silence,
And the lake
        Was left without a name.

Soft sunshine,
And the sound of old forests
        Echoing around.

The blue noon is over us,
And the multitudinous billows
        Murmur at our feet.

The top of the hill,
Where the sky grows wide,
        And where the sun grows red.

In the meadows and the lower
        grounds,
Was all the sweetness
        Of a common dawn.

That uncertain heaven
Received into the bosom
        Of the steady lake.

You fade—
As if the last of days were fading,
        And all wars were done.

The tinkle of the thirsty rill,
Unheard all day,
        Ascends again.

These as they change,
Almighty Father!
        These are but the varied God.

Give me the splendid silent sun,
With all his beams
Full-dazzling.

The gods are happy;
They turn on all sides
Their shining eyes.

To bend once more
Upon the mountains high
The quiet of a loving eye.

Love me still but know not why,—
So hast thou the same reason still
To dote upon me ever.

Annihilating all that's made,
To a green thought
In a green shade.

A rainbow and a cuckoo, Lord!
How great and rich
The times are now.

O cuckoo!
Shall I call thee bird,
Or but a wandering voice?

Over his own sweet voice
The stock-dove
Broods.

The weak-eyed bat,
With short shrill shriek,
Flits by on leathern wing.

O happy living things!
No tongue
Their beauty might declare.

The bittern
Sounds his drum, booming
From the sedgy shallow.

Some sang high,
And some sang low,
Yet all their song made one accord.

Let my deep silence speak for me
More than for them
Their sweetest notes.

How can ye chant,
Ye little birds,
And I sae weary, fu' o' care!

Up the tall mast
Runs
The woodpecker.

The busy woodpecker
Made stiller with her sound
The inviolable quietness.

Some bird from out the brakes
Starts into voice a moment,
Then is still.

I like the pheasants
And feeding things
Of the unsuspicious morn.

The meadows
Were drinking at their leisure;
The frogs sat meditating.

Far in the stillness,
A cat
Languishes loudly.

The summer's flower
Is to the summer sweet,
 Though to itself it only live and die.

I could sit down here
Alone,
 And count the oak-trees one by one.

Every leaf and every flower,
Pearled
 With the self-same shower.

In shades the orange bright,
Like golden lamps
 In a green night.

A violet
By a mossy stone,
 Half-hidden from the eye.

AUTUMN

The moon doth with delight
Look round her
 When the heavens are bare.

The moonlight steeped
In silentness
 The steady weathercock.

The innocent moon,
That nothing does
 But shine.

By the sea,
Under the yellow
 And sagging moon.

Greatly shining,
The autumn moon
Floats in the thin sky.

The deep burnished foliage overhead
Splintered
The silver arrows of the moon.

The long day wanes;
The slow moon climbs;
The deep moans round with many voices.

With how sad steps,
O moon,
Thou clim'st the skies!

Alone the sun rises,
And alone
Spring the great streams.

Coldly,
Sadly descends
The autumn evening.

Over the old wooden bridge
No traveller
Crossed.

Twilight was dimming the day;
Another night
For the living and the dead.

Look thy last
On all things lovely,
Every hour.

The railroad bridge
Is a sad song
In de air.

Plate 21

Hakuin

A Wren

I loved him not,
And yet now he is gone,
    I feel that I am alone.

You are too young to fall asleep for ever,
And when you sleep,
    You remind me of the dead.

The light extinguished of her lonely hut,
The hut itself abandoned to decay,
    And she forgotten in the quiet grave.

The heavy elms wait,
And restless and cold,
    The uneasy wind rises.

The Waterfowl

The desert and illimitable air—
Lone wandering,
    But not lost.

WINTER

The frozen wind
Crept on above,
    The freezing stream below.

The immeasurable height
Of woods decaying,
    Never to be decayed.

Ivy serpentine,
With its dark buds and leaves,
    Wandering astray.

The one blasted tree,
And the bleak music
From that old stone wall.

The most ancient heavens
Through thee
Are fresh and strong.

Turn to the old;
Things do not change,
We change.

I warmed both hands before the fire of life;
It sinks,
And I am ready to depart.

It was because
You did not weep,
I wept for you.

Strange power!
I trust thy might;
Trust thou my constancy.

I see around me here,
Things
You cannot see.

The old men know
When an old man
Dies.

And then the clock collected in the tower
Its strength,
And struck.

Come, come, the bells do cry;
I am sick, I must die,
Lord, have mercy upon us!

Minute by minute,
The clock
Ticks to the heart.

A distant engine whistles,
Or the floor
Creaks.

The wandering night-wind
Bangs
A door.

The large and gentle furniture has stood
In sympathetic silence
All the day.

So let the boat carry me;
Tomorrow
Is another day.

Haiku, or something like them, may be found scattered throughout English prose, perhaps more frequently than in poetry, where the tension and intention are so much greater. Here follow some examples from Thoreau's *A Week on the Concord and Merrimack Rivers*. Less known than *Walden*, it reminds one of the short pieces of poetic writing by haiku poets, known as *haibun*.

We see men haying far in the meadow, their heads waving like the grass they cut. In the distance, the wind seemed to bend all alike.

As the night stole over, such a freshness was wafted across the meadow that every blade of cut grass seemed to teem with life.

All day fireflies husbanded their light under the grass and leaves against the night.

The barking of the house-dogs, from the loudest and hoarsest bark, to the faintest aerial palpitation under the eaves of heaven.

Various species of brake, whose downy stems stood closely grouped and ranked as in a vase, while their heads spread several feet on either side.

The stillness was intense and almost conscious, as if it were a natural sabbath.

Our thoughts too begin to rustle.

The storks, bound to some northern meadow, held on their stately, stationary flight.

POETRY

Poetry is one of the four "ways," or values, religious, moral, aesthetic and intellectual. Every man walks to some extent upon all of them, though predominantly upon one, but it often happens that a man supposes himself to be proceeding along one when in his secret heart he walks another. Many a tragedy comes from this mistake. The problem then is not which of the four is the best, but which of them is the way upon which most men walk in fact, whatever they may suppose and assert of themselves.

Of all of them, the way of beauty, the way of poetry seems at first sight to be the least common. It must be remembered, however, that biologically speaking it is by far the oldest. Ages before the idea of a universe entered the mind of man, long before his lips had formed the words to think with, when his relations even to his mates and offspring were almost entirely selfish, already form, colour, and sound set him atremble with their significance to him. In Darwinian language, sexual selection was already at work.

Again, in the way of beauty alone, there is little hypocrisy, and no self-deceiving. As for the moral life, the Stoics and the Christians have told us what to do, but we pretend not to understand what they say; we allegorize it, or say that it is out-dated. Their commands are clear and unequivocal:

Sell all thou hast and give to the poor.

A good man; one who accepts with cheerfulness

his lot in the sum of things, and deems it bliss
enough if his own deeds be just and his nature
kindly.[1]

Love mankind, and follow in God's footsteps.[2]

Our religion and intellectual problems, though really distinct, are confused in a reciprocal way. In our youth we are
given so-called religious, but actually intellectual problems,
that of their nature have no religious answers. Who made
the universe? Are our souls immortal? What is the nature
of evil? How could God become a man? As we grow older,
we get the answers to questions that can never be asked.
The mystery that rises and falls in waves within and without
us, our individual-universal life, our spaceless and timeless
existence in time and space, these are realized more or less
by every one of us, but since we can never express them in
words, (we do indirectly, in music and pottery, for example)
our unspoken answers lack questions, our self-imposed questions lack answers, and we struggle in double confusion of
mind and spirit.

The way of beauty, the way of poetry, Wordsworth said,
is nothing tangible or definable; it is the *expression* on the
face of mankind searching for truth. Poetry is that excess,
that over-abundance which makes morality bearable and
virtue alive:

> Whoso shall compel thee to go one mile, go
> with him twain.

It is what makes true the untruth of that which was said
by a man far away and long ago:

[1] Marcus Aurelius, IV, 25.
[2] Marcus Aurelius, VII, 31.

> Come unto me, all ye that labour and are
> heavy laden, and I will give you rest.

It makes true the untruth of that which was said of what is
above space or being,

> Our Father which art in heaven.

Poetry is a *saikeirei*, a kowtow so deep and complete that
there is no one bowing and nothing bowed to, a state that is
nearly attained to in the following famous waka of Saigyô:

何事のおはしますかは知らねども
かたじけなさに涙こぼるゝ

> What it is
> I know not;
> But with the gratitude,
> My tears fall.

It is a feeling of our separateness, of our unity, our
identity with the Godhead. We are both God and not God;
sometimes we feel the one, sometimes the other. On the one
hand,

> All creatures are God in God.[1]

On the other hand,

> No created essence can become one with God's
> Essence and pass away from its own substance.[2]

Poetry is thus not only the spirit of wonder but is that self-
sufficient state beyond it.

[1] Suso, *The Book of Truth.*
[2] *Adornment of the Spiritual Marriage.*

Poetry is sympathy.

> Whoever walks a furlong without sympathy,
> walks to his own funeral, drest in his shroud.

What Whitman says here in his vast, world-embracing manner, repeats what Saigyô felt about the cherry-blossoms of
Mt. Yoshino:

身を分けて見ぬ梢なくつくさばや
萬の山の花の盛りを

> Could I but divide myself up,
> And see every spray
> On the countless hills
> Of flowers abloom!

There is another of Saigyô's waka where the sympathy is so
deep that the poet becomes himself the old tree:

わきて見む老木は花もあはれなり
今幾度か春に逢ふべき

> Looking above all on this old tree,
> The flowers also are full of pathos;
> How many more times
> Are they to greet the spring?

Poetry is a return to nature: to our own nature, to that
of each thing, and to that of all things. Of these three, the
first is the most difficult to modern man. To go back to the
unreasoning, superstitious past, to feel as an animal or plant
feels, to become unselfconscious and selfless—this needs a
strong will, imagination, a delicate and sensitive organism.
In the following verse by Bashô, the poetic life is in a
strange realm:

故郷や臍の緒に泣く年の暮

In my old home,
Weeping over the umbilical cord,[1]
At the end of the year.

The love and gratitude to his mother goes back to ages
when all the parts of a man's body, hair, skin and even
faeces were seen to be as *he*, as the body of impermanence
that stands before us. Just as a so-called savage thinks that
burning an enemy's finger-nails will cause him pain, so Bashô
grieves over the physical cord that once bound him to his
mother and feels virtue to flow through it to him as it did
long ago.

Poetry is interpenetration. Marcus Aurelius says:

All things are interwoven each with other;
the tie is sacred, and nothing, or next to nothing
is alien to aught else.

"The tie is sacred." Poetry is that tie, poetry in the sense
of the life of its poet. He it is and he alone that creates the
world out of chaos and it is his life in things that binds
them together. Marcus Aurelius again:

All things that participate in a common element hasten to rejoin their kin...... In proportion
to its superiority over the rest is its readiness to
mingle with whatever comes of a common stock
and to be fused with it.

The intellectual element in this passage keeps the life
cold and dormant. In the following passage, from Willa

[1] Japanese people still preserve their children's umbilical cord.
Bashô is speaking of his own, that his mother, now dead,
had preserved.

Cather's *My Antonia*, the rational function is absorbed into the physical experience;

> The earth was warm under me, and warm as I crumbled it through my fingers. Free little red bugs came out and moved in slow squadrons around me. Their backs were polished vermilion, with black spots. I kept as still as I could. Nothing happened. I did not expect anything to happen. I was something that lay under the sun and felt it, like the pumpkins, and I did not want to be anything more. I was entirely happy. Perhaps we feel like that when we die and become part of something entire, whether it is sun and air or goodness and knowledge. At any rate, that is happiness, to be dissolved into something complete and great. When it comes to one, it comes as naturally as sleep.

Poetry is not thé words written in a book, but the mode of activity of the mind of the poet. In the same way, the scriptures are not dead thoughts fossilized in writing, but the working of the Buddha-mind, the Buddha nature. Ikkyu says:

> Something merely expressed in words or written in letters, cannot be called *Shingyô*;[1] it is something pointing to one's mind. What is written in words is a *Hannya*[2] in words. We seek for a sutra of words outside ourselves, and this is the height of folly, a rejection of the wisdom of *Hannya*. Each thought is the Hannya Sutra.

---

[1] 心經, Heart Sutra, that is Hannya Shingyô.
[2] 磐若, Prajna, Wisdom.

Plate 22

The Slope of Osaka

Senna

何にあらはし文字に書きうつしたるを心
經といふに非ず。此の經は則ち自心を指
していふなり。文字に書きたるは文字磐
若なり、自心をはなれて外に文字にて書
きたる經を求めなば、是即ち愚痴の心な
り。はんにやの知慧にそむくなり。念々
皆磐若經なり。　　　（一休の磐若經提唱）

Poetry is beauty. However much we may free ourselves
from all things, some of them have a charm over and beyond
their purely poetical significance, — in other words, some
things are so poetical in the ordinary, rather shallower sense
of the word, that they drag us, resist as we may, to heaven.
So Saigyô says, thinking of his priestly vows of renunciation:

花に染む心のいかで殘りけむ
　　捨てはてゝきと思ふ我が身に

With all renounced as I had thought,
　　There still remains a heart
　　　Dyed with the flowers.

Poetry is Zen. It is our living. When we are really
alive, when we are really seeing, when the thing seen sees
itself with our eyes, sees itself in the mirror of our minds,
whatever comes before it, vice or virtue, beauty or ugliness,
glory or squalour, all has that meaning which is a no-mean-
ing, for it can never be expressed but only experienced. Haiku
is poetry, but there is poetry that is not haiku. Haiku is
concerned with the ordinary, the everyday. It has nothing
to do with exceptional things, evenings of extraordinary
magnificence and splendour. It turns inwards, towards the
infinitely small and subtle, not to the vast and sublime. It
does not seek movement, but the movement that is in rest,
the rest that is in movement.

The old pond;
A frog jumps in,—
The sound of the water.

This was seen at once to epitomise the aim of haiku. There is
the movement of the frog and the disturbance of the water, but
the point is in something that the sound of the water conveys,
the silence that is behind it and within it. Moreover, it is
not the sound of a million frogs, but of one only, although all
the frogs, all the creatures of the world, all the world itself
is contained in this one frog. The vastness of the Indian
imagination has shrunk to a small particle, a grain of sand,
but has gained, and not lost, in profundity and breadth of
spiritual significance.

Poetry, or rather, haiku is a perception and expression of
unity, even though it is at its highest, particular, concrete;
an enumeration of differences, the slightest of infinite importance. The differences must be expressed directly, with no
vagueness or ambiguity. The unity, on the other hand, must
never be expressed: it must be overheard, seen in a glass
darkly, felt like a breath of wandering air. So it is well said,

此の一致を観じて後に多くの不一致を観
ず、是詩人なり

The unity is to be seen: afterwards, all the
differences. This is the function of a poet.[1]

The plum blossoms and the peach blossoms are equally and
indifferently the spring in its most intense manifestation. But
the plum blossoms and the peach blossoms are entirely different from each other in every respect, and these differences

[1] 北村透谷。

cannot be too strongly emphasized. The identity of the two, however, can be revealed only by silence,

> with a look sidelong and half-reverted.[1]

Let us conclude this section with a statement of the nature and function of poetry from the haiku point of view, and a short account of "sabi".

When a Nô actor goes about the stage or a Tea-man comes in and out of the room, there are two qualities of his walking that belong to the deepest thought of Mahayana Buddhism. First, he is unconscious of his walking, he walks like a child or an animal. Second, he walks as if he were not walking. There is movement, but its activity is that of perfect repose. The nature of poetry also includes in itself a double function. It expresses what is, and what is not, the particular and the universal, the minute and the vague. Almost always we have in poetry one of these pairs (for the absolute also exists because of the relative), and the poet implies the other; the reader supplies the implicit. Time and space are respectively and mutually telescoped, but nevertheless, the specific time, the particular object retain all their meaning and value. The reader is to do again what the poet has done once for all, unite and fill out by his energy of mind these contradictory fragments of life. So in the haiku of Onitsura:

> 大旦昔吹きにし松の風
> > The Great Morning:
> Winds of long ago
> > Blow through the pine tree.

---

[1] *The Old Cumberland Beggar.*

On New Year's Day, when we hear the wind in the pine trees, we hear the winds of a thousand years ago, all the winds that have ever blown or that will ever blow. And yet it is only this wind of this moment that sighs above us.

In religion we say, "unconsciously,"

God is love.

God is a person, but when he is equated to love, an abstraction, he is to some extent depersonalized. Love is a principle, but when we are told that God is love, it becomes personalized. So Wordsworth says:

The moon doth with delight
Look round her when the heavens are bare.

If we take this as meaning that the poet is delighted at the moon in a cloudless sky, we are denying the existence of poetry. The moon is a dead world, and feels nothing; but it also feels grief and joy just as we do, and because we do.

Thoreau says in *A Week on the Concord and Merrimac Rivers*,

Over the old wooden bridge,
No traveller
Crossed.

This "no traveller" is very different from nothing at all. It is not that there is a bridge and nothing else. The bridge is crossed by this ghostly no-traveller. Shelley, in the first verse of the *Skylark*, says of it,

Bird thou never wert.

The skylark is a bird, but it is also not a bird. Hardy says of a man who was superlatively good at tree-planting,

He had the green hand.

His hand was brown or red. In *Bliss*, Katherine Mansfield says of the tulips,

> They seemed to lean upon the dusk.

"Seemed" is inserted because it is a short story,—but how can a flower lean on the darkness?

Very often in poetry or great literature of any kind, we are presented by the writer with one half, one aspect of the truth, and we are required to add, unconsciously, with our fluid and dynamic minds, the other half, the other aspect. For example, Macbeth says of life,

> it is a tale
> Told by an idiot, full of sound and fury,
> Signifying nothing.

This is true; life is quite meaningless. It has no object, no purpose, no guiding principle. But it is equally true to say that it is deeply significant, brimming over with purpose, with meaning in the smallest incident. This latter truth is what we add, *unconsciously*, as we read it, and then our walking through life is as if we did not walk; from this comes the elation we feel instead of the dejection we are supposed to. It is common to explain this odd feeling of increase of power and life, by saying that we are inspirited by the skill with which the pessimism is expressed. This is only a more superficial way of saying the same thing, namely, that when life is seen in the particular, it manifests the universal; the universal has meaning, has existence only when it blossoms forth in the particular, and it is the "energy" (that is, the "skill") which enables the poet and us to complete

the whole which alone can satisfy us. To recapitulate, our
composition and appreciation of poetry (and indeed, all art
and religion) is like the walking of the Tea man and the Nô
actor,—it is unconscious, and it is a supplying of all that is
unsaid, unpainted, uncarved, unlived, to what is given us in
the outward and partial expression of poem or act. Haiku
are the recording of experiences of what seem to be particular things and sensations, but which demand from us
a universalization that nevertheless does not relinquish an
atom of the uniqueness and differential of the thing. In order
to achieve the complete fusion of example and law, creation
and the appreciation must be instantaneous, in the sense that
no rational elements, no logical thinking as such, is to inter-
fere or come between us and the thing that is at one and the
same time itself alone, and yet includes all other things.   In
the *Lankavatara Sutra* it says, in praise of the Buddha:

> As thou reviewest the world with thy trans-
> cendental knowledge and compassion, it is to thee
> like an etherial flower, of which one cannot say
> whether it is born or destroyed, as the category
> of being and non-being is inapplicable to it.

To the poet, the world is like this etherial flower. The cate-
gory of being and non-being does not apply,—and yet he
asserts that this *is*, and that is not. The artist paints the
bamboos black, because he knows they are not green.

芋を煮る鍋の中まで月夜かな   許 六

Even to the saucepan
Where potatoes are boiling,—
A moonlit night.   Kyoroku

It is only when we realize that the moon is in the saucepan with the potatoes that we know the grandeur of the moon in highest heaven. It is only when we see a part that we know the whole.

Sabi is little written about among Bashô and his school, not because of its unimportance, but for precisely the opposite reason; we do not readily speak of what is all in all to us. In the *Saga Nikki*, 嵯峨日記, Bashô says:

寂しさなくば憂からましと西上人の詠み
侍るは寂しさをあるじなるべし。

"Where there is no *sabishisa* there will be sadness." This is what Saigyô Hôshi says in a waka. *Sabishisa*, "loneliness," must be Lord of All.

This *sabishisa* has some deep and (historically) distant connection with Nirvana, which is the state of freedom in which all things are seen as "empty," as they really are. An example of Bashô's sabi is the following:

秋深き隣は何をする人ぞ

It is deep autumn:
My neighbour,—
How does he live?

In this verse, self is entirely gone, the self that still lingers in

この道やゆく人なしに秋のくれ

Along this road
Goes no one;
Autumn eve is falling.

From the Middle Ages there came to Bashô a certain conception of wabi or sabi, expressed in waka, renga, and the Art of Tea, deriving ultimately from Zen and allied forms of Buddhism. That is to say, the aim of waka may be said to be the same as that of haiku; the form alone, however, apart from the indistinctness and vagueness of the aim of the waka poets, made it impossible for them to attain to the sabi of Bashô and his followers. We look in vain through the *Shinkokinshû* for what we find in every verse of *Oku no Hosomichi*. Indeed there is more freshness and energy and freedom in the *Manyôshû* than in succeeding anthologies of waka. It lacks, however, depth; for instance, in an anonymous poem we have the *sabishisa* that was later to become sabi:

> さゞれ波たぎちて流る泊瀬川
> 　　よるべなき磯のさきがさぶしさ

> Rippling waves
> Flow seething down the River Tomase;
> 　　Lonely is the shore
> Which they approach.

Then we come, for example, to the waka of Saigyô quoted before:

> こゝろなき身にもあはれはしられけり
> 　　鴫立つ澤の秋の夕ぐれ

> Even in the mind of the mind-less one
> Arises grief,
> 　　When the snipe wings up
> From the marsh
> In the autumn evening.

We have here what is called 物の哀れ, *mono no aware*, lachrimae rerum. This for Bashô's sabi is too explicit. What can be said, is not sabi. The reng poets added nothing to this *mono no aware* of the later waka poets, and have rather less than they. This is true also of the predecessors of Bashô, Sôkan, Moritake, Teitoku, Sôin. They seem to be marking time or going backwards. No one could have told what an extraordinary thing was going to happen at the hands of Bashô and Onitsura, how that from this *mono no aware* would come sabi. It was the flowering in poetry of what had already appeared in renga (Sôgi), painting (Sesshû) the Art of Tea (Rikyû), Nô (Seami), and this occurred first in Bashô's own life, his daily life from morning to night. Into it he put the meaning of things, their " loneliness ", their sabi.

SECTION IV

THE FOUR GREAT HAIKU
POETS

BASHÔ

There are three great names in the history of haiku, Bashô, Buson and Issa; we may include a fourth, Shiki. Bashô is the religious man, Buson the artist, Issa the humanist. Bashô is concerned with God as he sees himself in the mind of the poet before flowers and fields. Buson deals with things as they exist by and for themselves, in their own right. Issa is concerned with man, man the weak angel; with birds and beasts as they struggle like us to make a living and keep their heads above water. If we do not begin with Bashô, our interpretation of haiku is bound to lack depth. The objectivity of Buson and the subjectivity of Issa both spring from the homely little man with long eyebrows and a bad digestion.

It is truer in Japanese poetry than in any other, that for the understanding of it we need to understand the poet. Itô Jinsai[1] said,

> 師は道のあるところ、師を崇むるは
> すなはち道を崇むる所以なり

Where the teacher is, there is truth; respect
for the teacher is respect for truth.

When therefore we come to Bashô, we do so because he is the Way, the Truth and the Life. Apart from human beings, there is no Buddha. Nevertheless, there is to be no imitation of Christ or any other person, no imitation of any teacher. In Bashô's own words,

> 古人の跡を求めず、
> 古人の求めたるところを求めよ

---

[1] 伊藤仁齊, 1627–1705, Confucianist scholar.

> Do not follow in the footsteps of the Ancients;
> seek what they sought.

As with Wordsworth, piety was the foundation of both Bashô's character and of his literary work. To him more than to any other oriental poet do Gensei's[1] words apply;

> 忠孝を以て根底となし、文学を以て
> 　　枝葉となさば詩も亦深邃なり

> By making faithfulness and filial piety the fundamental, and giving literary work a secondary place, poetry is profound.

We may compare what Wordsworth says:

> To be incapable of a feeling of poetry, in my sense of the word, is to be without love of human nature and reverence for God.

Bashô felt that life was not deep enough, not continuous enough, and he wanted to give every action, every moment the value that it potentially had. He wanted the little life we lead to be at the same time the greater life. Every flower was to be the spring, every pain a birth pang, every man a haiku poet, walking in the Way of Haiku.

> It was the life of the little day, the life of little people. And the man who had died said to himself, "Unless we encompass it in the greater day, and set the little life in the circle of the greater life, all is disaster."[2]

What is this greater life, and how is the little life to be related to it? Or, to put the question in a more prosaic but

---

[1] 元政, 1623–96; priest and waka poet.
[2] Lawrence, *The Man Who Died.*

more pertinent form, what is the social value of haiku?
When we compare the life of Bashô especially, or of any other
great haiku poet, with those of Wordsworth, Milton, Shelley,
Keats, and so on, we are struck by one fact of seemingly
little importance, that the Japanese haiku poets all had disciples; the English poets none. This is a matter of the greatest
significance, for it is just here, in this religious attitude, that
the little, prosaic life of little people may be set in the greater,
the poetic life.

冬籠り又寄添はんこの柱   芭 蕉

> Winter seclusion:
> Once again I will lean against
> This post.   Bashô

Here, and here only, is the little life set in the circle of the
greater, the ordinary in the extraordinary, the commonplace
in the miraculous, the material in the spiritual, the human
in the divine. To sit on the floor and lean one's back against
a post may not seen the acme of comfort, but this is the
pleasure Bashô is promising himself. During the winter, while
the snow is silently falling, he will lean against the post as
he did last year, reading and writing poetry, thinking

> Thoughts that wander through eternity,

through *our* eternity, through the greater life. This post,
rubbed smooth with countless vigils, black where his head
rested against it, is all he asks for.

The Way of Haiku requires not only a Franciscan poverty,
but this concentration of all the energies of mind and body,
a perpetual sinking of oneself into things. Bashô tells us,
and it is to be noted, we believe him:

名月や池をめぐりて夜もすがら

The autumn full moon:
All night long
I paced round the lake.

All night gazing at the moon, and only this poor verse to
show for it? But it must be remembered that Bashô was
a teacher. And thus we too, when we look at the moon, look
at it with the eyes of Bashô, those eyes that gazed at that
moon and its reflection in the placid water of the lake. Buson
says,

さむしろを畠に敷て梅見かな

Spreading a straw mat in the field,
I sat and gazed
At the plum blossoms.

This sitting and looking at a flowering tree is not quite so
simple and easy as it appears. Buson, besides being a poet,
was an artist, and was expressing in silence and motion-
lessness the poetic and artistic meaning of this plum tree
(for this is the meaning of " gazing ").

One of Bashô's haiku which illustrates both this plain
severity of life and his tender affection for his pupils is the
following:

春立つや新年ふるき米五升

The beginning of spring:
For the new year,
Five shô of rice from last year.

At Fukagawa, Bashô's disciples, especially Sampu, brought
him all the necessities of life. He had in the house a large
gourd which would hold five shô (1 shô=3.18 pints=1.8 litres).

The happiness of the New Year is the remembrance of the
fidelity and affection of his pupils, symbolized in the rice
remaining over from the year before. A similar verse is:

嵐雪が送りし正月小袖を着て
誰やらか姿に似たり今朝の春

> Putting on a silk garment that Ransetsu gave
> me for the New Year
>
> > The first morning of spring.
> I feel like
> > Someone else.

Literally, " Whom do I look like?" Bashô's lack of affectation
is shown also in the following:

和角蓼螢句

朝顔に我は飯食ふ男かな

> Answering Kikaku's poem about *tade* (smart-
> weed) and the firefly.
>
> > I am one
> Who eats his breakfast,
> > Gazing at the morning-glories.

This was Bashô's reply to:

草の戸に我は蓼くふ螢哉　　　　　　　　　其角
> > A firefly;
> I partake of the smart-weed,
> > In my hermitage.　　　Kikaku

Kikaku means that, like the firefly, he prefers the night, and
has eccentric tastes, enjoying the bitter flavour of the smart-
weed that other people dislike. Bashô says that the true
poetic life is not here, but in eating one's rice and pickles

for breakfast and gazing at whatever nature and the seasons bring us.

It would be just as hard to thing of Bashô living in affluence or as even moderately well-off, as it would to imagine St. Francis a rich man. Bashô lived a life very similar to that of Meg Merrilies:

> No breakfast had she many a morn,
> No dinner had she many a noon,
> And 'stead of supper she would stare
> Full hard against the moon.

Chora gives us a picture of Bashô,—how different from that of the average European poet:

旅姿時雨の鶴よ芭蕉翁　　　　　樗　良

> In travelling attire,
> A stork in late autumn rain:
> The old master Bashô.

The first poem in the *Nozarashi Diary* shows us Bashô's idea of the normal state of the poet, little different from that of the ascetic. The end proposed is not different from that ideal which Keats held up before himself, but the means are poles apart:

野ざらしを心に風のしむ身かな

> Resigned to death by exposure,
> How the wind
> Cuts through me!

Prepared to die by the roadside, he sets out on his journey. Why did he not stop at home, if not in comfort, at least out of the wind and rain? For several reasons. Without contact with things, with cold and hunger, real poetry is impossible.

Further, Bashô was a missionary spirit and knew that all over Japan were people capable of treading the Way of Haiku. But beyond this, just as with Christ, Bashô's heart was turned towards poverty and simplicity; it was his fate, his lot, his destiny as a poet.

年の市線香買ひに出でばやな

The year-end fair:
I would like to go out and buy
Some incense-sticks.

The modesty of Bashô's desires is evident in this verse. Nothing could be cheaper, or more cheerless, by ordinary standards.

Bashô's sympathy with animate things did not arise from any theory of the unity of life, nor from an innate love of living things. It was strictly poetic, and for this reason we find it partial and limited, but sincere. It springs, as is seen in the individual cases where it is expressed, from a deep experience of a particular case. Bashô was once returning from Ise, the home of the gods, to his native place of sad memories. Passing through the lonely forest, the cold rain pattering on the fallen leaves, he saw a small monkey sitting huddled on a bough, with that submissive pathos which human beings can hardly attain to. Animals alone possess it. He said:

初時雨猿も小簑をほしげなり

First winter rain:
The monkey also seems
To want a small straw cloak.

He was preserved from any sentimentality about animals by

the fact that his own life was full of discomfort, which he
saw as inevitable, and, in a sense, desirable.

The gentleness of Bashô, (who was a samurai by birth)
is a very special quality. We may perhaps compare him to
Chaucer, of whom Thoreau says:

> We are tempted to say that his genius was
> feminine, not masculine. It was such a feminine-
> ness, however, as is rarest to find in woman,
> though not the appreciation of it; perhaps it is
> not to be found at all in woman, but is only the
> feminine in man.

Bashô was not a great poetical genius by birth. During
the first forty years of his life he wrote no verse that could
be called remarkable, or even good. Unlike his contemporary
Onitsura, who was mature at twenty five, Bashô made his
way into the deepest realm of poetry by sheer effort and
study, study here meaning not mere learning, but a concentration on the spiritual meaning of the culture he had inherited
in haikai. Indeed, we may say that few men have been so
really cultured as Bashô was, with his understanding of
Confucianism, Taoism, Chinese Poetry, Waka, Buddhism, Zen,
Painting, the Art of Tea. In *Oi no Kobumi*, 笈の小文, he
writes:

> 西行の和歌における，宗祇の連歌における，
> 雪舟の繪における，利休の茶における，
> 其の貫道する物は一なり。

> Saigyô's waka, Sôgi's renga, Sesshu's painting,
> Rikyu's Tea,—the spirit animating them is one.

Under Kigin, 季吟, 1623–1705, Bashô probably studied the
Manyôshu, the *Kokinshu*, the *Shin Kokinshu*, the *Genjimono-*

gatari, the *Tosa Diary*, the *Tsurezuregusa* and Saigyô's waka in his *Sankashu*, 山家集. Other haiku poets also studied Saigyô, e.g. the verse of Sôin, 宗因, written on a picture of Saigyô:

秋はこの法師すがたの夕かな

> This Hôshi's appearance,
>   In the evening,
>   Is that of autumn.

There are a great number of haiku concerning Saigyô, and not a few of Bashô's referring to or based on Saigyô's waka. Bashô's interest in these was due to their apparent objectivity but real subjectivity, their *yugen*, 幽玄, their painful feeling, artistry, purity. More than the Chinese poets, he admired Saigyô for his life of poverty and wandering, his deep fusion of poetry and religion.

With truly Japanese genius, he did not merely read and repeat the words and phrases of these men, but put their spirit into practice in his daily life. There is a far-off but deep resemblance here between Bashô and Johnson, two utterly different types of men, who yet both hold a position in the history of literature higher than their actual writings warrant, by virtue of their personal character.

When all is written that can be written, and all is done that can be done, it may be found that Bashô was not only the greatest of all the Japanese, but that he is to be numbered among those few human beings who lived, and taught us how to live by living.

BUSON

Buson was born in 1716, twenty two years after the death of Bashô, and died at the end of 1783. Comparatively little is known of the details of his life; he seems to have been a loving husband and devoted father.

When we compare Bashô and Buson, we are struck with the difference of the depth of their poetical life. Both use their eyes and ears, but in Buson, however sensitive, even supersensitive he may be, his sensations do not sink down into the very recesses of his soul, as with Bashô. Speaking first of sounds, we may say that in Bashô the thing, its nature, is expressed in a kind of onomatopoeia, which may be deeply spiritual. Voiceless things speak in the cadence of his verse:

秋深き隣は何をする人ぞ

    It is deep autumn
My neighbour,—
    How does he live?

Let us compare the following verses:

五月雨を集めて早し最上川   芭蕉

    Collecting all
The rains of May,
    The swift Mogami River.   Bashô

五月雨や名もなき川の恐ろしき   蕪村

    The May rains:
Even a nameless stream
    Is a thing of dread.   Buson

In Bashô's verse, though it does not speak of sound, we hear within ourselves the turbid water rushing down to the sea. Buson's verse tells us something poetic which he felt about the river, but the river does not echo through our whole body. Bashô has some few verses which are simple records of audible sounds, but not many:

烏賊うりの聲まぎれはしほととぎす

   The cuttle-fish seller's voice
  Mingles with the voice
   Of the *hototogisu*.[1]

As examples of Buson's exquisiteness of ear, we may quote:

凉しさや鐘を離るゝかねの聲

   The coolness:
  The voice of the bell
   As it leaves the bell!

蚊の聲す忍冬の花散る毎に

   The voice of mosquitoes,
  Whenever the flower of the honeysuckle
   Falls.

But with few exceptions, Buson's perceptions of sounds, however delicate and subtle, stop there. This is no criticism of Buson, for it is good to stop, and good to go on.

 Buson is primarily a poet of the eye, and Buson was an artist, a far greater artist in words than he was in indian ink or colour. Sometimes the description is so pictorial as to be unsuitable for poetry:

 [1] A kind of cuckoo.

若葉して水白し麥黄みたり

> Young green leaves,
> Water white,
> Barley yellowing.

Buson has almost a greediness for colour;

夕顔や黄に咲いたるもあるべかり

> Evening-glories;
> There should be also
> One blooming yellow.

A great many examples could be given; here are a few:

月に遠くおぼゆる藤の色香かな

> In the moonlight,
> The colour and scent of the wistaria blossoms
> Seem far away.

つゝじ咲いて片山里の飯白し

> Azaleas are blooming;
> In this remote mountain village
> The boiled rice is white.

公達に狐ばけたり宵の春

> The fox
> Changes himself into a young prince;
> The spring evening.

貌白き子のうれしさよ枕がや

> Happiness,
> At the white face of the child
> In the small mosquito net.

高樓の灯影にしづむ若葉かな

> The young leaves,
> Drenched in the lights
> Of the tall tower.

牡丹散つて打ち重なりぬ二三片

> The peony scattering,
> Two or three petals
> Lie one on another.

きりぎりす自在をのぼる夜寒かな

> The cricket
> Climbs up the pot-hanger;
> The night is cold.

金屏の羅は誰れかあきの風

> Over the gold screen,
> Whose silk gauze dress?
> The autumn wind.

To put it in a word, Buson lived in the world of phenomena, and his inner life was thin compared to that of Bashô. Look at the two following verses:

古池や蛙飛びこむ水の音　　　　　　芭蕉

> The old pond:
> A frog jumps in,—
> The sound of the water.　　Bashô

古池に草履沈みてみぞれかな　　　　蕪村

> The old pond,
> A straw sandal sunk to the bottom;
> Sleet falling.　　Buson

Bashô's verse has a life within it, it has Life, whereas Buson's verse is dead, in this sense. The dreariness of the scene with the straw sandal is not superficial, but it does not involve within itself all the dreariness of the world; it is the thing-as-it-is, but not the Thing-as-It-is. We choose one or the other, according to our character and mood.

One other fundamental contrast between Bashô and Buson is this: in Bashô, his understanding of Zen, the influence of Chinese poetry, the work of the waka poets,—all these and many other things are melted in his mind, in his experience of life; the same can be said, with even greater truth perhaps, of Issa. With Buson, and Shiki also, these things are used and imitated, but never form part of the man himself. Buson follows Bashô, Shiki follows Buson, but Bashô and Issa imitate no one; their life is their own.

ISSA

As Bashô is the poet of life, and Buson the poet of the studio, Issa is the poet of destiny. Bashô, though his mind is tender and compassionate, has something resigned, something divine in him. Buson sees the world as a spectator. Issa is moved with the movement of fate. Life goes along joyfully and painfully, with ecstasy and anguish, and Issa goes with it. He does not praise or condemn, but he is not withdrawn from anything which exists. More than this, Issa has that Shakespearean quality of not telling things what they ought to be, of not knowing better than God himself how the universe should be run, of not opposing the predestined accidents of life, or its strange course to an unknown goal. We see this in the following passage from Issa's *Shichiban Nikki*, 七番日記, under February 12:

> I made a pilgrimage to the temple of Tokaiji in Fuse. Feeling sorry for the chickens that followed after me longingly, I bought some rice from a house in front of the temple gate and scattered it among the violets and dandelions. Soon they began to fight among themselves here and there. Meanwhile, pigeons and sparrows came flying down from the boughs and were quietly eating up the rice. The chickens coming back, they flew off to the branches again, sooner than they wanted, no doubt wishing that the kicking match had lasted longer. Samurai, farmers, artizans, merchants and all the rest are just like this in the way they live.

> Scattering rice,—　　．
This also is a sin,
> 　The fowls kicking one another!

布施東海寺に詣でけるに，雞どもの跡した
ひぬることの不便さに，門前の家によりて
米一合ばかり買ひて，菫たんぽゝのほとり
にちらしけるをやがて仲間喧嘩をいくとこ
ろにも初めたり。其のうち梢より鳩すゞめ
ばらばら飛び來りて，こゝろしづかにくら
ひつゝ，鶏來る時小ばやくもとの梢へ逃げ
去りぬ。鳩雀は蹴合の長かれかしとや思ふ
らん，士農工商その外さまざまのなりはひ
皆かくの通り。

米蒔も罪ぞよ鶏は蹴合ふぞよ

Issa's whole life was a tragedy. He was one of those
men who attract failure and misfortune, just as some men
succeed in all they attempt. Christ, by his own nature, was
destined for violent death, and Issa was marked for poverty
and suffering, but in both cases the distant result was indeed
different from what might have been expected. And there
is another parallel between the two men. Christ is our ideal
of what a human being should be, yet how Jewish he is in his
loves and hates, his rising above the particular into the
general. Issa also is the most Japanese of the haiku poets,
or it may be of all Japanese poets, yet in spite of this or
because of it, his work has universal appeal. This paradox
is true perhaps of all the greatest men.

Issa is often spoken of as having a somewhat warped
view of life. This mistaken idea comes from not realizing
that Issa, unlike most of us, said what he thought. He told
not only the truth, but the whole truth. Ikkyû, the famous

Zen eccentric of the fifteenth century, suffers from the same
cause. Even in sexual matters he was perfectly frank to
anyone and everyone, and his reputation has suffered accor-
dingly. Issa, like Bashô, was an exceedingly moral man, but
not quite so "stuffy" perhaps. Bashô was born and educated
as a samurai, but Issa has a broader view of life, one that
can hardly be put into any rules or maxims. The following
passage will show his world-view, and the "standards" by
which he judged.

> Instead of the artistic pleasure of flowery
> gardens, bend yourself to the cultivation of the rice
> field at the back of the house. Take a hoe in your
> hand and use it; be exceedingly careful of the
> lives of your parents and what you have received
> from your ancestors. Be happy in your work
> rather than in the cherry blosssoms of Yoshino
> or the moon of Sarashina.
>
> More than the mountain roses of Ide, love
> the flowers of rape, and look after them sedulously.
> The green ears of the barly are more moving
> than the peonies.

風流をたのしむ花園ならで後の畑前の田の
物作りに志し，自ら鋤を探つて耕し，先祖
の賜と親の命に懇を盡し，吉野の櫻，更級
の月よりもおのが業こそ樂しけれ。朝夕心
をとゞめて打むか小菜種の花は井出の山吹
よりも好もしく，麥の穗の色は，牡丹芍藥
より腹ごたへありと覺ゆ。

In other words, life is more important than art; our art and
poetry are to be put into our living. Beauty is to be found
in our daily life; it is then created naturally and sponta-
neously.

Plate 23

Morning Glories   Issa

Issa is like Heine, he has the power of saying lightly and humorously what others have only been able to say in the grand manner. St. Paul's words are,

> The whole creation groaneth and travaileth
> together until now, waiting for the manifestation
> of the sons of God.

How different Issa sounds:

蚤ども〻夜永だらうぞ淋しかろ

> For you fleas too,
> The night must be long,
> It must be lonely.

SHIKI

Shiki, 1869–1902, in opposition to the prevailing trend
of the times, rather depreciated Bashô and affirmed the superiority of Buson. What appealed to him in Buson was
his objectivity, his attitude as painter-poet looking with
clear, fresh eyes upon the various world. This is no place
to discourse upon objectivity and subjectivity, but we may
say this, that at their best Bashô and Issa have an objective-
subjectivity in which the thing is suffused with the poetic
life of the poet, and suffers no distortion or discoloration but
rather reveals vividly its own intrinsic nature.

よの中は稲かる頃か草の庵　　　　芭 蕉

My thatched hut;
In the world outside
It is harvest time?　　　Bashô

In Shiki and Buson, their objectivity has something cool and
delightful in it; we feel restful before it, for it makes no
demands upon us. When Bashô or Issa fail, we fall into
sentimentality. or something worse. When Buson and Shiki
fail, the landscape is made of cardboard, and things belong
to a two-dimensional world, without life or depth.

The personality of Shiki is not perhaps a very attractive
one, but when we read his haiku we are struck with the
large number of excellent, perfect verses which he wrote.
He was a great believer in nature, "still life," the avoidance
of all intellectual elements in poetry. His strength and his
weakness lay in his lack of religion. This is brought out in
a letter sent to his uncle while lying ill in bed:

When I die, it is needless to advertise the
funeral etc. The house is small and the street
narrow, and if twenty or thirty people crowd in,
the coffin won't be able to move. Whatever sect
the funeral service may be held by, *funeral
speeches and reading accounts of my life are
unnecessary. A posthumous Buddhist name I don't
want—nor a tombstone made of a natural stone.
It is not necessary to hold a wake before the coffin.
If a wake is held, do it in turns. No crocodile
tears, please; talk and laugh in the ordinary
way.

我等亡くなり候とも葬式の廣告など無用
に候　家も町も狹き故二三十人もつめか
け候はゞ、柩の動きもとれまじく候。何
派の葬式をなすとも、柩の前に弔詞、傳
記の類讀み上げ候事無用に候。戒名とい
ふもの用ひ候事無用に候。……。自然石の
石碑もいやな事に候。柩の前に通夜する
こと無用に候。通夜するとも代りあひて
可致候。柩の前にて空涙は無用に候。談
笑平生の如くあるべく候。

From his lack of religion comes his clearness of eye and
mind, lack of sentimentality, love of truth, and devotion to
literature. But we feel some want of depth: the baby has
been thrown out with the bath-water. Shiki is not in touch
with much that is human, though its form be superstitious
and irrational. As Whitman says,

Only what proves itself to every man and woman
　　is so,
Only what nobody denies is so.

Shiki is a humanist, but we feel something a little hard, superficial, unloving in him.

Bashô laid the foundations of haiku, Buson broadened its scope; Issa raised it above art, above poetry, above all aesthetic value, into the realm of life. It is in this sense also that Issa is *the* Japanese poet, in that he is nearest to Heaven when when closest to earth. Shiki, though strongly realistic, takes haiku back to Buson; he sees things under the aspect of beauty, as an artist.

We may compare the four poets in the following verses on the same subject, with one added from Kikaku, whom we may regard as a counterfoil to Bashô:

一家に遊女も寝たり萩と月　　　芭　蕉

> Lodging in one inn,
> Together with courtezans:
> Lespedeza flowers and the moon.

Bashô

傾　　廊

時鳥あかつき傘を買はせけり　　　其　角

> A Courtezan Enclosure
> A *hototogisu* sings;
> In the dawn,
> I am made to buy an umbrella.

Kikaku

わかたけや橋本の遊女ありやなし

蕪　村

> Young bamboos;
> Courtezans of Hashimoto,
> Not there still?

Buson

凩や二十四文の遊女小屋　　　一　茶

The autumn storm;
A prostitute shack,
　　At 24 cents a time.　　　　Issa

船着きの小き廓や綿の花　　　子規

Near the boat-landing,
A small licensed enclosure;
　　Cotton-plant flowers.　　　Shiki

Bashô's verse does not express directly the compassion he felt for the unfortunate creatures with whom he chanced to lodge in the same inn at the barrier-town of Ichifuri. They were on a pilgrimage to the Great Shrines of Ise. By comparing them to the lespedeza flowers, and himself or his way of poetry to the moon, Bashô has glorified both, and lifted them out of this world into the world of poetry.

Kikaku treats the subject with nonchalance. In the morning, when about to leave the Yoshiwara, a shower of rain forces him to buy an umbrella outside, or (more probably) inside the enclosure. At this moment, a *hototogisu* sings. Kikaku is the poet devoid of religion, of true Zen.

Buson is so engrossed in the picture, the associations, so carried back into the distance, the historical past, that the courtezans are symbols of the flourishing hey-day of Hashimoto. Are not those women still there, plying their trade, by the young bamboos that grow in profusion as of old? The things of long ago seem as if they had never passed away.

In contrast to these, Issa gives us a picture of life, in which the only artistic element is the selection of his material. The useless, meaningless, wild, wanton wind of autumn is blowing. The shabby, flimsy building, the hard-eyed, soft-faced women, even the very price for which they earn their daily bread, all are put before us, with no comments added. Issa does this and yet brings out more meaning than the most careful art.

Shiki goes back to Buson. In reaction to the feeble, pointless poets of his time who supposed themselves to be followers of Bashô, Shiki affirms in theory and practice that we must follow nature, in its outward manifestations. So Shiki's verse above shows the small wharf, the enclosure with its indefinable but unmistakable atmosphere, the white flowers of a field of cotton plants. This is a picture of life, but has it any life in it, any depth?

SECTION V

THE TECHNIQUE OF HAIKU

THE TECHNIQUE OF HAIKU

In this last section, a brief account is given of the following subjects:—

1. Humour, and the meaning of the original punning nature of haiku.
2. Their brevity.
3. The nature of the Japanese language as related to haiku.
4. Onomatopoeia.
5. The 5, 7 form.
6. Kireji.
7. Haiku Sequences.
8. The seasons, and seasonal classification.
9. Methods of translation and interpretation.

I
HUMOUR AND PUNS

The humour of haiku is hardly part of their technique, for it is not something detachable, but belongs to the spirit rather than to the form. It is some indispensable element without which haiku can hardly exist, some poise of the mind, some balance of conflicting elements from which arises that pleasure whose peculiar quality causes us to give it the name of humour. The historical origin has been explained above.[1] It should be remarked, perhaps, that Bashô's serious and rather humourless character could not, fortunately, remove the comic element from haiku. Instead, receiving its inestimable benefit, Bashô gave haiku a depth and moral strength that, because of its inheritance of inalienable humour, never fell into philosophizing or didacticism.

The spiritual origin is in the paradoxical nature of things which it is the aim of haiku to express. In many haiku it is obvious; it can be faintly felt in most. It can be unearthed even in those that seem devoid of any humorous element, but it is a painful and thankless task to drag forth into the light what can only exist in the darkness of the elemental nature of things. In any case, humour can only be written about, if at all, humorously, and it is better to leave the subject here.

Puns are supposed to be a form of humour, but in one sense they have not the surface-shattering effect of a good

[1] Page 214.

joke. On the other hand, they loosen the fixed connotations of words and soften their hard lines, they telescope ideas that are in thought irreconcilable, and induce a willing suspension of disbelief, by what is often a mechanical and verbal trick, but which is sometimes a kind of linguistic gaiety of mind.

In renga and earlier haiku, as in the literature of Nô, puns and word-play were used, not so much as jokes, and not only for mere delight in word-conjuring or as verbal ornament and language-music, but as carrying on meanings where grammar and syntax separate, uniting the most distant ideas that language divides, thus breaking down the barriers that the intellect incessantly raises;

> And custom lie upon thee with a weight
> Heavy as frost, and deep almost as life.

The following haiku was composed on Bashô's parting from his friends when setting out for Ise; it concludes *Oku no Hosomichi*:

蛤 の　　　　二見に 別れ　　　行く秋ぞ
Hamaguri no　　futami ni wakare　　yuku aki zo

Autumn
Parting we go, clams opening,
To Futami.

This verse has no poetical value beyond the puns in it. "Futami" means "two looks." It is the name of a place near Ise. The clams with their two shells like *futa*, 蓋, lids, are symbols of two friends divided. Goes, 行, applies both to Bashô's own departure and to that of autumn. Such a haiku is nowadays considered as having but little value; nevertheless, the intention is admirable. This Euphuism with its etymological and verbal pleasure in unity, in uniting, is significant of a deep-seated desire for harmony. In English poetry, a rather different method was popular at almost the same period. Richard Crashaw, who died when Bashô was five years old, has the following well-known verse in *In the Holy Nativity of Our Lord:*

> She sings Thy tears asleep and dips
> Her kisses in Thy weeping eye:
> She spreads the red leaves of Thy lips
> That in their buds yet blushing lie;
> She 'gainst those mother-diamonds tries
> The points of her young eagle's eyes.

This means: Mary sings the infant Jesus asleep, and he stops weeping. She kisses his tears away, and then kisses his parted lips. She tests the eyes of the young child, their rays, "points," against her own diamond-bright eyes, just as the eagle tests its eyes against the sun. Another and simpler example from Donne's *Daybreak:*

> Stay O sweet, and do not rise!
> The light that shines comes from thine eyes:
> The day breaks not: it is my heart,
> Because that you and I must part.

Puns are part of the poetical life of Nô. Since they are by nature untranslatable, we may quote just one, from *Sotoba Komachi*. Komachi herself is speaking:

> 我は此の時力を得。猶ほ戯れの歌を詠む。
> 極樂の内ならばこそ惡しからぬ。そとは
> 何かは苦しかるべき。

Now emboldened, I will intone a jesting song:

Were I in Paradise,
It would indeed be bad;
Outside,
What is grievous about it?

The pun is on a *sotoba*, stupa[1], and *soto wa*, outside. It is feeble enough, but expresses Komachi's joy in triumphing over the two priests in theological argument. They say that the stupa is the symbol of the incarnation of Buddha; she says, so is man, and that she is therefore not wrong to sit on the stupa.

The first lines of this *Sotoba Komachi*, the greatest of the Nô plays, have a more poetical pun:

山は浅きに隠れがの、山は浅きに穏れがの、
深きや心なるらん

Our hidden home is on shallow hills, on shallow hills, but deep in the heart.

But as said before, the point of these puns is not the separate play on words, but the way in which continuity is achieved through them, linking one passage with the next. This is of course helped by the text itself, which in its cursive form often joins words together.

[1] A repository of a relic of the Buddha.

II
BREVITY

Brevity is called the soul of wit. To what extent is it also the soul of poetry? Beyond the merely mechanical brevity of haiku it is almost impossible to go, since form and rhythm must also be taken into account. Nevertheless, true brevity is not a matter of quantity but of quality. Many a haiku is a failure because, in spite of its simplicity and brevity, it is reality still clobbered up with unessential material, reality minus art. More must be taken away, less must be said. If we take the well-known Zen aphorism

> The willow is green; flowers are red,

we see what the haiku poet wants to convey, but the angle of approach is different. "The willow is green, the flowers are red" takes the universe in its suchness, dynamically, absolute-relative-ly. But the poet should see the universe under the aspect of harmony, as rhythm and symphony; in the deepest sense of the word, *musically*. The relation of the elements of the haiku is that of the phrases of a melody, and this melody, is in counterpoint to, is a variation of, the music of the spheres.

An example of almost telegraphic brevity, if translated literally, is the following:

我が事と鰌の逃げし根芹哉　　　文草
> Myself, and loach fled, root-parsley, ah!

We may paraphrase it:

> While gathering parsley,
> Thinking I am after him,
> The loach slips off.　　　Jôsô

Even here, of course, meditation on the poem is necessary to get down to the poetic root of the matter. It lies in the fear of the loach, the unity and yet disunity of the poet with it, the fact that though there is sameness, there is difference; though there is difference there is sameness, and there cannot be one without the other. This last sentence does not demonstrate what is meant by "meditation on the poem," which means looking steadily at the object, keeping one's eye on the ball, dissolving one's personality into the poet and parsley waving in the stream, and the loach slipping off through the clear water into hiding. The brevity of the haiku is such that

it velo è ora ben tanto sottile
Certo, che il trapassar dentro è leggiero.

the veil is now so thin
That entering within is easy.

Another aspect of brevity, the omission of the personal pronoun, is a point of great importance. In itself, by itself, it unconsciously teaches the ego-lessness of things. The subjective and the objective are fused without a word being uttered. The matter is further dealt with in the section on Methods of Translation.

III

The Japanese Language

Chinese, that is, ancient Chinese was the ideal language for Zen, clear and brief, really monosyllabic (modern Chinese is disyllabic), and, to express it in a rather Irish way, it is entirely unambiguous when you know what it means. For example:

入林不動草
入水不立波

Entering the forest, he does not disturb a blade
of grass;
Entering the water, he does not cause a ripple.

This describes the self-less activity of the poet or sage in his relation to nature. There are ten syllables, words, in all, three times less than in the translation. Literally it is:

Enter forest not move grass;
Enter water not raise ripple.

Another, also from the *Zenrinkushû*, is the following:

梅瘦占春少。
庭寬得月多。

The plum-tree dwindling (with age) contains less
of the spring;
But the garden is wider, and holds more of the
moon.

The genius of the Japanese language (that is, until recently,) was quite different from that of the Chinese. Not only were subject, predicate and object to some extent indistinguishable, and punctuation non-existent, but the edges of the words themselves are blurred. We may compare English, Chinese, and Japanese, in the translations of the Bible. The English and the Chinese correspond in their definiteness and majesty; the Japanese seems weak and pettifogging by comparison. But in actual fact this vagueness of the Japanese corresponds to something in life that Hebrew thought, that is, the Hebrew language, and the English and Chinese languages, miss. There is in life no fixed subject and predicate, cause and effect; no important and unimportant, such as we deceive ourselves into supposing, and such as is implicit in these languages. Things do not begin with a capital letter and end with a full stop; there is simply ceaseless becoming. The English language does not recognise this; hence the chief difficulty of the translator.

As an example of Japanese poetry in prose, we may take the following from the *Collected Works of Kashizono*, 橿園文集, or Nakajima Hirotari, who died in 1864:

木々紅葉むらむら染めわたして尾花が袖
も人待ち顔に打ちまねく山路のいとおも
しろきに女郎花蘭などのやうやうらが
れ行く中より今咲きはじめたる菊の露も
とをたなびき出でたる物よりことに目に
立ちていとなつかしうおぼゆ。

　　Here and there the leaves of the trees are
deeply dyed with yellow and crimson, the pampas-
grass waving as though beckoning someone, with
long sleeves,—in such a mountain-path of beauty,
from the gradually withering midst of maiden-
flower and orchid, the chrysanthemums now beginning to bloom, their branches bowed with dew,

Plate 24

Landscape

Isshô

sway out, and, more than all else, touch us with
their grace and loveliness.

This is far vaguer, more shadowy and flowing away from
the reader in the original than in the translation; it is also
more difficult. The beauty of the style of the original has
something of the poetry of the best of Ruskin, when he is
describing nature; for example, when in *Modern Painters*, he
speaks of sunrise in the Alps, how the mists

> float in level bays and winding gulfs about
> the islanded summits of the lower hills, untouched
> yet by that dawn, colder and more quiet than
> a windless sea under the moon of midnight;
> watch when the first sunbeam is sent upon the
> silver channels, how the foam of their undulating
> surface parts and passes away, and down under
> their depths the glittering city and green pasture
> lie like Atlantis, between the white paths of wind-
> ing rivers; the flakes of light falling every
> moment faster and broader among the starry
> spires, as the wreathed surges break and vanish
> above them, and the confused crests and ridges
> of the dark hills shorten their gray shadows upon
> the plain.

Haiku has been remarkably free in the matter of language, colloquial, dialectical, literary or Chinese expressions
being to some extent used from the earliest times, and
gradually increasing. Here are some examples:

べたべたと物につきたる春の雪　　　一　茶

> It sticks like butter
> To everything,—
> This spring snow.

Issa

The clammy nature of spring snow is brought out by this colloquial expression,. *beta-beta*.

桐の木やてきぱき散つてつんと立つ　一　茶

The paulownia tree,
Quickly stripped clean of its leaves,
Stands prim.   Issa

てきぱき, *tekipaki* is a colloquial phrase that expresses the quickness of the fall of the paulownia leaves; つんと, *tsun to*, often translated "prime", implies the peculiarly formal aspect of the tree.

春の風柳が無くば吹くまいぞ　　　如　帛

If the willows are leafless,
Do not blow,
Winds of spring!   Johaku

Nakuba is a literary form of *nakattara*, "If there were not".

蕭條と石に日の入る枯野かな　　　蕪　村

Desolately,
The sun sets in the rocks
On the withered moor.   Buson

Shôjô, solitary, lonesome, is a Chinese compound word, often used in *shi*, Chinese poems.

IV
ONOMATOPOEIA

Of all languages, Japanese is by far the richest in onomatopoeic elements, especially of the simpler variety, in which the sound of the word is directly an imitation of the thing. As one of the " figures of speech ", onomatopoeia is allowed a very small place in our books of grammar and rhetoric, but in its broadest sense, onomatopoeia represents not only the most important part of poetry, but of prose and of speech itself. How we say a thing is of more importance, of more significance, than what we say, the conscious meaning; for through the tones of the voice, the words chosen, their combination, the sounds echoing and reëchoing one another, their concords suspended and reëstablished, their discords sustained and resolved, through all this there is a music as free and yet as law-abiding as is that of the flute, the oboe, and the violin. Too obvious examples have something approaching the ludicrous in them, for example, Tennyson's:

> The moan of doves in immemorial elms,
> And murmuring of innumerable bees.

This fact may be taken advantage of, as it is in the following:

> Rend with tremendous sound your ears asunder,
> With gun, drum, trumpet, blunderbuss and thunder.

And in Buson's

> 日は日くれよ　夜は夜明けよと　　鳴蛙
> Hi wa hi kure yo yo wa yo ake yo to naku kaeru.

> " Day, ah, darken day !
> Night, ah, dawn away ! "
> Chant the frogs.

In the last example also there is a representation of the humorous aspect of the thing.

Haiku, by its nature, cannot show us such examples as the following, meaning given or intensified by regular, repeated rhythm:

> Most friendship is feigning,
> Most loving mere folly.
> Then heigho the holly,
> This life is most jolly.

Here the amphibrachs dance as featly as

> the slythy toves
> Did gyre and gimble in the wabe.

Japanese rhythmical effects are more in the style of the lines of Pope in which he represents length by the emphasizing and lengthening of unaccented syllables:

> When Ajax strives *some* rock's *vast* weight to
> move,
> The line *too* labours and the words *move* slow.

In the following well-known verse of Buson the sounds of the sea strike on the ear more truly in the sound of his seventeen syllables than through the sound of the actual waves on the physical ear:

> 春の海　ひねもすのたり　のたりかな　蕪村
> Haru no umi　hinemosu notari　　notari kana

> The spring sea,
> Gently rising and falling,
> The whole day long.　　　　　　Buson

Plate 25

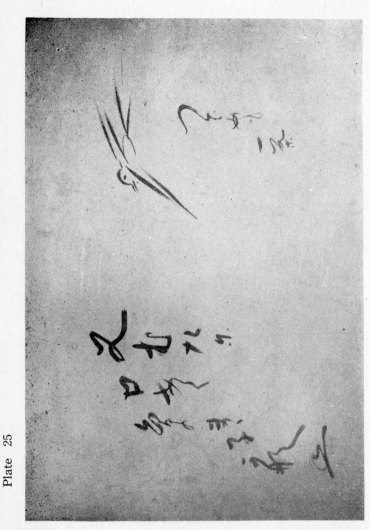

The Swallow

Issa

The sounds of *hinemosu* almost reverse the sounds of *haru no umi*. The repetition of *notari, notari*, the *kana* which echoes the *a* sounds of *haru* and *notari*,—all this represents, for some unknown reason, not so much the sound of waves, but rather the meaning of the long spring day by the shore. What *is* the meaning of this? It is

> Haru no umi
> hinemosu notari
> notari kana.

Compare this to the meaning of the rhythm in the following poem of Freeman. The tears fairly gush out, again, beyond all reason:

CHILDHOOD CALLS

Come over, come over the deepening river,
Come over again the dark torrent of years,
Come over, come back where the green leaves
quiver,
And lilac still blooms and the grey sky clears.

Come, come back to the enchanting garden,
To that green heaven, and the blue heaven above,
Come back to the time when time brought no
burden,
And love was unconscious, not knowing love.

But however spontaneous such poems may seem, we know that a great many of them were the result of arduous toil. Some never attain perfection and betray all through the working of the selective process. Of this class, Dante Gabriel Rossetti's *The Blessed Damozel* is an example. Issa is well known, in spite of his fluency and the large number of verses

he produced, to have revised his poems over months and
years, for instance, the following:

大螢　ゆらりゆらりと　通りけり　一茶

Ô botaru　yurari yurari to　tôri keri.

> Waveringly,
> A huge firefly
> Passes by.   Issa

This verse is the result of many revisions, but the final version appears artless and the work of a moment. This revision
of verse is a revision of experience. The experience had
matured in the words of the haiku so that *he came to know
what he should have wanted to say.*

We may summarize the function of onomatopoeia in the
following way:

(a) The direct representation of the sounds of the outside
world by the sounds of the voice.

をちこちをちこちと打つ砧かな　蕪村

> Ochikochi
> ochikochi to utsu
> kinuta kana.

> Here and there,
> There and here,
> Beating fulling-blocks.   Buson

一僕とぽくぽくあるく花見かな　季吟

> Ichiboku to
> poku poku aruku
> hanami kana.

> He ambles along
> With his man-servant:
> Cherry-blossom viewing.   Kigin

佛壇にほんぞんかけたか時鳥   宗鑑

Butsudan ni
honzon kaketa ka
hototogisu.

"Is the main image
Set on the altar?"
Cries the hototogisu.   Sôkan

Compare Tennyson's *The Throstle*:

"Summer is coming, summer is coming,
I know it, I know it, I know it.
Light again, leaf again, life again, love again!"
Yes, my wild little Poet.

(b) The representation of movement, or physical sensations
other than that of sound.

石川は   くわらり稲妻 さらりかな 一 茶
Ishikawa wa kuwarari inazuma sarari kana.

The Stony River rippling,
The lightning
Flickering—   Issa

ゆさゆさと   春が行くぞよ   野邊の草 一 茶
Yusa-yusa to haru ga yuku zo yo nobe no kusa.

Spring departs,
Trembling, in the grasses
Of the fields.   Issa

Yea, slimy things did crawl with legs
Upon the slimy sea.[1]

A cuff neglectful, and thereby
Ribbons to flow confusedly.[2]

[1] Coleridge.
[2] Herrick.

(c) The representation of soul states. This is always indirect, unconscious, spontaneous. Great poetry depends chiefly for its effect upon this factor. It cannot be imitated or artificially produced.

> Fear no more the heat o' the sun,
> Nor the winter's furious rages.

My heart's in the Highlands, my heart is not here;
My heart's in the Highlands, a-chasing the deer.

人ちらり　木の葉もちらり　ほらりかな　一茶
Hito chirari　konoha mo chirari　horari kana.

> People are few,
> Leaves also fall
> Now and then.　　　　　**Issa**

うたがうな　潮の花も　　浦の春　芭蕉
Utagauna　ushio no hana mo　ura no haru[1]

> Do not doubt it,
> The bay has its spring too,—
> The flowers of the tide.　　**Bashô**

We saw Thee in Thy balmy nest,
Bright dawn of our eternal Day;
We saw Thine eyes break from their east,
And chase the trembling shades away.[2]

遅き日の　つもりて遠き　　昔かな　蕪村
Osoki hi no　tsumorite tôki　mukashi kana.

> Slow days passing, accumulating,—
> How distant they are,
> The things of the past!　　**Buson**

---

[1] Notice the u's, and a's.
[2] Crashaw, *In the Holy Nativity of Our Lord God.*

The k sound is used again by Buson to portray the bitterness
of the passing of time:

遅き日や　　谺聞ゆる　　京のすみ
Osoki hi ya　kodama kikoyuru　kyô no sumi.

> The slow day;
> Echoes heard
> In a corner of Kyôto.

An example of onomatopoeia from waka is the following by
Saigyô:

何處にも　住まれずばたゞ　住まであらん
Izuko ni mo　sumarezuba tada　sumade aran

柴の庵の　　しばしなる世に
shiba no iori no　shibashi naru yo ni.

> If I feel I cannot live anywhere,
> I just will not,—
> In this thatched cottage
> Of a fleeting world.

We should remind ourselves once more of Bashô's advice to
his disciples:

舌頭に千轉せよ

> Repeat (your verses) a thousand times on
> your lips.

Haiku, no less than waka, are songs; they are meant to be
read aloud, and repeated aloud. Onomatopoeia is not a
matter of the eye, though it may help; the full and perfect
meaning of a haiku is not realized until it is heard by the
physical ear.

Five examples of onomatopoeia taken from Seisensui:

らつぱふいて麓のみちがこゝろよく
のびる馬車屋さん　　　　　　　　秋兎死

Rappa fuite
Fumoto no michi ga kokoro yoku
Nobiru bashaya san.

Blowing his horn,—
The road at the foot of the mountain
stretches out peacefully,—
The driver!　　　　　　　Akitoshi

This is 3,3,4; 3,3,2; which gives both the sound of the horn
and the rhythm of the horse's hoofs.

とんぼとぶ　とんぼのうへも　とんぼとぶ空　保流
Tombo tobu　tombo no ue mo　tombo tobu sora.

Dragonflies fly,—
Above them too fly dragonflies,—
In the dragonfly sky.　　　　Horyu

This is not a imitation of sounds like Tennyson's, it is an
endeavour to express the height of the sky through the repetition of the same sound.　It corresponds to Bach's use of the
step motif in suggesting destiny; here it represents infinity.

わらうつ　つきよの好い音　しだした　益雄
Wara utsu　tsukiyo no yoi oto　shidashita.

The beating of the straw,—
What a beautiful sound it has become,
This moonlit night!　　　　Masuo

The four-unit foot represents the striking of the straw.

をちこち　をちこちとうつ　砧かな　蕪村
Ochikochi　ochikochi to utsu　kinuta kana.

Here and there,
There and here,
Beating fulling-blocks.　　　Buson

あざみ　あざやかな　あさの　あめあがり　　山頭火
Azami　azayaka na　asa no　ame agari.

> The thistle is bright,
>> In the morning,
>>> After the rain.　　　　Santôka

3, 5, 5, 3, The open sound of *a* here represents the cheerful mood of the poet. The assonance of the beginning and the end of the verse, *azami*, *agari*, gives it a completeness of form.

V
THE FORM OF HAIKU

From earliest times in Japan, there seems to have been a delight in the alternation of five and seven syllables, the foundation of all Japanese verse. The long poems continued 5, 7; 5, 7; 5, 7;——ending with a 7. As an expression of the inherent Japanese love of the plain and short rather than the florid and long, the form of the waka or tanka, (which means "Short Poem") was obtained by reducing the series to 5, 7; 5, 7; 7. Later, the origin of the form being forgotten, it was taken as 5,7,5; 7,7; and the two parts named _Kami no ku_, 上の句, Upper Strophe; and _Shimo no ku_, 下の句, Lower Strophe. One poet composed the first, another the second, the two combined making one verse. This double form was suited to the poetic conversations of lovers, the sending and receiving of gifts, the setting and solving of riddles, in fact, all the duets and dialogues of ready wit. In the Heian Era, 794–858, it was common not only among the court ladies of the palace, and noblemen and noblewomen, but in the middle ranks of society. The continuous waka were called _renga_, chain poems, those in which wit was predominant being known as haikai[1] renga, witty chain poems. The first of the chain, that is, the Upper Strophe of 5,7,5 which began the series, and which was the only strophe which could stand by itself, was called the hokku, 發句, or First Strophe. In the history of haiku it is therefore noteworthy that it was the

---

[1] Haikai is written with two characters, 俳諧, both of which mean "sporting," "pleasantry."

beginning of a chain of poetical thoughts and images, and that its origins are inextricably mingled with those of humour and pleasant thought.

The 5,7,5 sequence was a method of obtaining unity of form, corresponding to rhyme and accent in Modern European poetry; rhyme, tone and and number of syllables in Chinese; long and short syllables in Latin and Greek; alliteration in Old English. Formally, haiku and waka have the feeblest method of making a verse into a whole. Nevertheless, this form is of a peculiar potency. This 5, 7, 5 has a wave-like character of flow, suspense and ebb, it is symmetrical, yet in odd numbers. Further, there is a kind of syllogistic nature about the form which gives it the utmost clarity while actually containing no logical elements, often no intellectual connections between the parts:

> The old pond;
> A frog jumps in,—
> The sound of the water.

Compare this to:

> All men are mortal;
> A negro is a man,
> Therefore a negro is mortal.

The haiku has no logical connection of premise and conclusion, but there is some subtle similarity between it and the syllogism. The "sound of the water" is contained, by implication, in "the old pond," just as "a negro is mortal" is contained in "all men are mortal." There is a rise, suspense, and fall of poetical meaning in the one as there is of intellectual purport in the other. There is nothing new in either, but ratiocinative satisfaction in the one, and poetical significance in the other.

The 5, 7, 5 form was kept fairly strictly up to modern times. Some haiku, however, were extremely irregular. The following, by Kikaku, one of Bashô's pupils, is 8, 8, 5:

猫に食はれしを　　　蟋の妻は　　　すだくらん

Neko ni kuwareshi wo　kôrogi no tsuma wa　sudakuran.

> Eaten by a cat,
> The wife of the cricket
> Will chirp his dirge.

The next verses, by Bashô himself, are very irregular:

8, 7, 5:　芭蕉野分して　　　盥に雨を　　　きく夜かな

Bashô nowake shite　tarai ni ame wo　kiku yo kana.

> The banana-plant in the autumn storm,
> Rain dripping in the tub,—
> Listening that night.

10, 7, 5:　櫓の聲波をうつて　　　腸氷る　　　夜や涙

Ro no koe nami wo utte　harawata kôru　yo ya namida.

> A bowel-freezing night;
> The sound of the oar striking the wave,—
> Tears.

5, 10, 5:　枯枝に烏のとまりたるや秋の暮

Kare-eda ni　karasu no tomaritaruya　aki no kure.[1]

> On a withered branch
> A crow is perched;
> An autumn evening.

6, 8, 5:　つゝじいけて其蔭に干鱈さく女

Tsutsuji ikete　sono kage ni hidara　saku onna.

---

[1] The original form of this famous verse.

> Behind a pot of azaleas,
> A woman tearing up
> Dried codfish.

Verses of more than seventeen syllables have been very common from earliest times, but verses of less than seventeen are rare. One example from Buson, given before, sixteen syllables:

をちこち	をちこちと打つ	砧かな
Ochi kochi	ochi kochi to utsu	kinuta kana.

> Here and there,
> Here and there,
> Beating fulling-blocks.

The strange thing about this verse is that it gives a feeling of length, of an infinity of sounds.

It may be mentioned that waka also show a similar irregularity of form, though not so great.

On the regular 5, 7, 5 is often superimposed a quite different rhythm-scheme or syllable division. For example, in the following, by Shiki, the three part form is two part rhetorically, being divided between *kite* and *haregi*:

初芝居見て來て	晴著未だ脱がず
Hatsu-shibai mite kite	haregi mada nugazu.

> In her best clothes,—
> Coming back from the first theatre this year,—
> Not yet taken off.[1]

In the following, by Bashô, the division is four-fold:

猿を聞く人	捨子に	秋の風	いかに
Saru o kiku hito	sutego ni	aki no kaze	ikani.

[1] Still talking excitedly of what she had seen.

Sad at the cry of the monkey,
Seeing the abandoned child in the autumn wind,
How would he feel?

The 5, 7 rhythm which ruled Japanese poetry for so many centuries, has lately been challenged. We now find such "haiku" as:

影も目高　　　　　　　　井泉水
Kage mo medaka.

The shadows too,
　　Killifish.　　　　　　　Seisensui.

小母さんのうぜんかつら咲きましたのうぜんかつら
　　　　　　　　　　　　　　　　一碧樓
Oba san nôzenkatsura sakimashita nôzenkatsura.

Auntie!
　A great trumpet-flower has bloomed,
　　　A great trumpet-flower!　Ippekiro

The conservatives ascribe this breaking with poetic conventions to foreign influences, and no doubt this is partly so. Hashi Maseki, 橋間石, in his book, *Lecture on the History of Haiku*, 俳史講話, also says that this change is caused by the loss of respect for and practice of renga, this being again due to the influence of Shiki, and ultimately to the same foreign influences.

VI
KIREJI

Kireji are a kind of poetical punctuation, or the marks piano, forte, cresc., con sordino, in music, by which the composer of the haiku expresses, or hints at, or emphasizes his mood and soul-state.

From at least the time of Sôgi, 宗祇, there were eighteen *kireji* fixed as marks of renga: these increased with the passing of time. The most important of them are the three *ya,* や, *kana,* かな, *keri,* けり. *Ya* corresponds to Ah! or Oh! in English, a sigh of admiration, as in:

荒海や　　佐渡によこたふ　　天の川　　芭蕉
Ara umi ya　sado ni yokotau　ama no gawa

> A wild sea!
> And stretching across to the Island of Sado
> The Galaxy.　　Bashô

櫓の聲波をうつて　　腸氷る　　夜や涙　芭蕉
Ro no koe nami o utte　harawata kôru　yo ya namida

> A bowel-freezing night!—
> The sound of the oar striking the wave,—
> Tears.　　Bashô

It may express doubt or uncertainty, or a question:

梅白し　　昨日や鶴を　　盜まれし　芭蕉
Ume shiroshi　kinô ya tsuru wo　nusumareshi.

> Plum blossoms are white;
> It was yesterday
> The crane was stolen?　　Bashô

君や蝶　　我や荘子の　　夢ごゝろ　　芭蕉
Kimi ya chô　ware ya Sôshi no　yume-gokoro

> You are the butterfly,
> And I the dreaming heart
> Of Sôshi?　　　　　　　Bashô

In this last example, the two ya's express the interpenetration of Sôshi and the butterfly, I and you.

It may show a kind of rhetorical question, or attitude of, "You think so, but you are wrong," as in:

箱を出る　　顔忘れめや　　雛二對　　蕪村
Hako o deru　kao wasureme ya　hina ni-tsui.

> Coming out of the box,
> This pair of dolls,—
> How could I forget their faces?
> 　　　　　　　　　　Buson

Keri, けり, shows that time has passed, something is finished, and that some kind of admiration or emotion is felt at it:

湖の　　水まさりけり　　五月雨　　去來
Mizuumi no　mizu masari keri　satsuki-ame

> The water of the lake
> Has increased,
> In the rains of June.　　Kyorai

A good example of the use of *kireji* is the following verse by Buson:

大雪と　　なりけり關の　　戸ざし時
Ôyuki to　nari keri seki no　tozashidoki.

> A great fall of snow,—
> Just as they are shutting
> The gates of the Barrier.

Here the *keri* divides the verse into two; the 5, 7, 5 form has a 9, 8 form superimposed upon it. The 3 beat together with the 2 beat reminds us of Brahms. The *keri* also has the effect of making the verse heavy, thus expressing the weight of snow and the ponderousness of the Barrier.

Kana is so common as to be sometimes almost meaningless, but usually it has a very similar effect to the *kana* and *kamo* of waka, that of an exclamation of an emotion that the verse implies. It also makes the word mentioned before it the centre of poetic interest and energy.

VII
HAIKU SEQUENCES

Shiki and others of his time, for instance, Natsume Sôseki, composed haiku sequences. Shiki wrote many groups of ten, for example:

ところどころ鹿の顔出す茂かな

> Here and there
> A deer shows its face
> Through the undergrowth.

釣床に入日洩りくる茂かな

> The evening sun
> Filters through the undergrowth
> Onto the hanging bed.

目じるしの喬木茂る小村かな

> The tall trees,
> Growing up together by the small village,
> A landmark.

山伏の法蝶吹きたつる茂りかな

> The *Yamabushi*[1]
> Blows his conch shell,
> Among the undergrowth.

植木屋は来らず庭の茂かな

> The gardener does not come;
> The garden
> Is all wild and untrimmed.

[1] Or *Shugenja*, 修験者, itinerant priests of a rather militant kind.

柱にもならで茂りぬ五百年

> Five hundred years
> They have flourished,—
> But have not become posts.

人住まぬ湖中の島の茂りかな

> On an island on the lake
> Where no one dwells,
> The foliage is dense.

一門はみな四位五位の茂りかな

> The family tree—
> All of the Fourth Rank, the Fifth Rank —
> Is flourishing.

墓の木は茂りぬたまや腐るらん

> Trees round the graves are rank;
> The spirits of the dead and their shrine
> May well rot here.

天狗住んで斧入らしめず木の茂

> No one may use the axe
> Where the trees are dense,—
> A long-nosed goblin dwells there.

These verses are very uneven, and united only by the *shigeri*. They are not so much a sequence, as ten variations on the theme of 茂り, " Growing in rank profusion."   Or better still, it is a kind of passacaglia, in which the theme is constantly repeated in some part of the ten variations that luxuriate around it.

VIII

The Seasons in Haiku

There is almost always a season word in haiku. This word may give the atmospheric background, it may be a kind of seed, a trigger which releases a whole world of emotion, of sounds and scents and colours. It is thus a form of brevity, so that when we say "the moon," we mean the full moon of autumn. If we wish to speak of any other time, we say *oborozuki*, the hazy moon (of spring), 朧月, *kangetsu*, 寒月, the cold moon (of winter) etc. If we say "flowers," we mean cherry blossoms only. When we see "The Festival of the Dolls," we think of spring; "sleeping in the daytime," of summer; "the fulling block," of autumn; "sowing barley," of winter. The season word has the additional function of unifying into a whole the scattered elements of the intuition. The season may be the actual subject of the poem, that which is to be apprehended through the thing which is the ostensible subject. For poets, it is a kind of poetic algebra or shorthand, enabling poets to speak to one another open secrets to which the unpoetical reader is not initiate. There are a few which have no season word, and these are called "Seasonless Haiku," 季無俳句. Occasionally a verse has two different season words, for example:

月花や四十九年のむだあるき　　　　一　茶

The moon and flowers:
　　Forty nine years
　　　　Walking about wasting time.

　　　　　　　　　　　　　　　　Issa

The following has no season word at all:

武藏野やさわるものなき君の笠　　芭蕉

> The Great Musashi Plain;
> There is nothing
> To touch your *kasa.*[1]   Bashô

Up to recent years, haiku was simply the poetry of the seasons. As stated above, in a sense we can say the season of each verse *is* the subject, the verse leading the mind to a vast aspect of the world in space and time. Thus every haiku is an aspect of one fourth of nature as we understand it in the Temperate Zones. The procession of the seasons finds its counterpart and mouthpiece in the poet as he changes in conformity with the moods of spring, summer, autumn and winter. The seasons, so well-marked in Japan, were already a distinct element in poetry by Manyô times. It is even more important however to notice once more the effect of renku on haiku. In renku, the first or starting verse, the hokku, always had a season word in it, and this had the effect of fixing the season ineffaceably upon haiku. In recent times, with ideas of freedom and spontaneity, the conventionality and artificiality of the seasonal classification has become apparent, and poems are written nowadays without any season word: the season is not expressed or implied. This is especially of value when a subject is of any season, e. g. the moon, pine trees, the various activities of human beings; or where the subject itself is above and beyond all seasonal significance. The following is an example:

[1] An umbrella-like hat made of strips of wood.

心澄ませば林の奥の雫なり　　　鳳　車

Quietening the mind,
Deep in the forest
Water drips down.　　　Hôsha

Deep in the forest, but clear and distinct, is the sound of
water dripping down after the shower. We seldom look or
listen or feel, almost always it is seeing, hearing, touching.
But now we listen, and the water drip-drips into the depths
of the mind. The season of the poem, however, is quite in-
definite. It may be a hot, summer shower, a cold rain of
winter, the heavy, deafening rain of spring that has just ceased. It is not the water of spring, but just *water* which is
beating away inflexible moments of time. For any place in
the world, at any moment, this verse is true and valid.

Haiku have been for long classified according to the
seasons and the subjects of the verse. There are, as it were,
five seasons: the New Year, Spring, Summer, Autumn and
Winter; there are also a few verses that will not go into
any particular season. The subjects of haiku were limited,
up to modern times, to a great number of set themes.
Nowadays no limit is admitted. A rough classification, however, serves as an index, and in this book such a plan has
been followed. It enables a reader to find a verse if he remembers the subject of it, and has the additional advantage
of grouping together all the verses on the same subject.
However, by putting the verses in seasonal order, we obscure
completely both the development of haiku historically and
that of each poet. In addition to this, there is the
danger of reading into the verse meanings which the age
had not attained to, or which the poet did not intend. But

there are several points to be noted here. The history of haiku is a comparatively short one, and further, it is only two hundred and fifty years since the death of Bashô. Thus the background against which we are to read haiku of any period, the general attitude, was more or less fixed long before this. It belongs to Mahayana Buddhism, the Kegon philosophy, the practicality and materiality of Zen, the innate simplicity of the Japanese mind. When therefore we distinguish Bashô the spiritual, Buson the artist, Issa the humanist, Shiki the universal, we are not wrong if we read Buson's haiku from Bashô's point of view. Indeed we may and should slightly de-moralize Bashô's haiku in our reading of them; we can deepen the meaning of Buson's still-lifes. The only danger is one which the present writer has consciously but unwillingly fallen into, that of over-subtilizing, over-refining, bringing out into the conscious what whould be left in the unconscious, philosophizing instead of expanding the poetical life,—in a word, talking where he should have been silent. In any case, whatever the differences of temperament and experience of life of the haiku poets may have been, what we are to give them is the poetical life we live in them and they in us.

Each season, (except the New Year, which is too short for such a purpose) is subdivided in the customary Japanese way:

1. THE SEASON

    The heat or cold, the shortness or length of the day.

2. THE SKY AND ELEMENTS

    This is called in Japanese 天文, astronomy. It includes snow, rain, wind, clouds, lightning, the stars, tempests.

3. FIELDS AND MOUNTAINS

This is called in Japanese 地理, geography. It comprises rivers, the sea, mountains, moors, paddy-fields.

4. TEMPLES AND SHRINES

This is called in Japanese 神佛, Gods and Buddhas. To this belong the Buddhist and Shintô festivals, pilgrimages, visiting graves.

5. HUMAN AFFAIRS

In Japanese 人事, "the things of men." It deals with the change of clothes, fishing, secular festivals, rice-planting, fireworks, scarecrows, etc.

6. BIRDS AND BEASTS

7. TREES AND FLOWERS

In Japanese, 植物, botany. It includes also turnips, leeks, mushrooms and so on.

IX
TRANSLATION

The general principle of translation has been, on the one hand to put nothing in the English version which is not in the original; on the other, to endeavour to imply in the translation what is meant to be inferred from the Japanese. The first is not difficult, but leads to dryness or incomprehensibility. The verbal implications are of course to a large extent untranslatable, but still more those that are purely grammatical. Take for example Kikaku's verse:

日 の 春 を さ す が に 鶴 の 歩 み 哉

A word for word translation is:

> The spring of day;
> Indeed, the crane's
> Walking, ah!

"The Spring of day" is New Year's Day, the first day of spring according to the lunar calendar. Kikaku was a rich man, and following an ancient Chinese practice, he kept tame cranes in his extensive garden. The cranes walk about every day in their stately yet graceful way, but on New Year's Day their manner of pacing here and there is peculiarly appropriate to the season. This is the point of さ す が に, *sasuga ni*, which as Bashô says in a criticism of this verse, is its very life and soul. We may therefore translate as follows:

> The cranes are pacing
> On the first day of spring,
> True to their nature.

But we miss here the connection between the nature of the crane, which is expressed more vaguely in the original, and the nature of New Year's Day, implied by putting " The Day of Spring" in the accusative with を, though it is not the object of anything else in the verse. Then again, the extremely common, not to say overdone use of *kana* is hardly to be reproduced in English. It expresses a sigh of admiration or grief or pure poetical feeling, much quieter and vaguer than Oh! or Ah! in English.

Another use of this same accusative without verb is the following:

蛸壼やはかなき夢を夏の月   芭 蕉

> The octopuses in the jars:
> Transient dreams
> Under the summer moon.   Bashô

The jar is attached to a float, *uki*, and then submerged. The octopus thinks the mouth of the jar is a hole, and entering it, is thus caught. Bashô saw these jars being submerged in the evening at Akashi, 明石, where he spent a night. They are still used there in this way. In the original, the sentence is incomplete, the verb being omitted after *yume wo*. This vagueness makes the life of the octopuses more shadowy; we feel all the more deeply, because indirectly, the transience of the short summer night, the life of the octopus, the life of all things.

In haiku, the form is often so elliptical that we are able, without effort of will, to experience the underlying, subterranean unity of ourselves and other things. The following is by Chora:

Plate 26

Tilling the Field   Shimada Tadao

すかし見て星に淋しき柳かな　　　樗良

This is literally,

> Peeping through with stars lonely willow ah!

"Lonely" applies to the stars and the willow, and to the peeping as well. Each word has the potency of being superimposed on every other word, the seventeen syllables thus being telescoped into one word. We may translate:

> Peeping through
> The willow, lonely
> With stars.

The poet also is present, impalpable as the loneliness itself. Another example, from Bashô:

吹きとばす石は淺間の野分哉

> Stones blowing,
> The autumn storm
> From Mt. Asama.

This really says "Stones which blow." Here the confusion of subject and object assists the mind to unify the various discrete phenomena. We would expect,

吹きとばさるゝ石は

> Blown stones,

or at least:

石を吹きとばすは

> Blowing of stones.

Take the well-known verse of Sodô:

目に青葉山郭公初松魚

> For the eye, the green leaves,
> 　The mountain *hototogisu,*
> 　The first bonito.

Here the ellipsis, the omission of " To the ear," " To the sense of taste," is not mere brevity; the *hototogisu* and the bonito also are faintly *seen.*

In translation, the question of singular and plural is important. A Japanese reading the original, instinctively makes his mental picture according to his poetical capacity, not always as distinct as the English version must be. In the following examples the reasons for the singular and plural should be clear:

雨蛙芭蕉にのりて戦ぎけり　　　　　　其　角

> 　The tree-frog,
> Riding the banana-leaf,
> 　Sways and quivers.　　　　Kikaku

暁や鵜籠に眠る鵜の病れ　　　　　　　子　規

> Morning twilight;
> In their basket, the cormorants
> 　Asleep, exhausted.　　　　Shiki

As a general rule, it is the singular that is intended in haiku. Single things are what catch the eye and move the poetic mind of the haiku poet, but there are certain exceptions, for example the cherry blossoms and other flowering trees, the young leaves of spring, wild geese, melons, mosquitoes, fireflies.

The question of the personal pronoun is also an important one. The avoidance, or rather, the lack of their use in Greek and Latin, in Chinese and Japanese, has a deep significance, and when we use the personal pronouns in translation, the whole life-feeling is changed. The opposition of ego and cosmos is there, and once there, ineradicable. In oriental feeling, in its poetry and art and music, the cosmos is suffused with "I," though not coloured by it. The "I" is interpenetrated with the cosmos, but not overwhelmed by it. In fact, it is difficult to see how Zen, as an independent body of ordered experience, could ever have come into existence or thriven, save in a country where the ego was systematically suppressed by language and custom. Wordsworth says, "We see into the life of things," but the fact is that it is our seeing which *is* the life of things.

The Romantic movement in English literature, as exemplified by Byron and Shelley, was a glorification of the ego in poetry such as had never been seen in the world before. In this sense, the Continental valuation of Byron is correct. In comparison with such a fire-brand, the candle light, the firefly glow of haiku must seem but a glimmer. Nevertheless, it is precisely by this Nirvana of self, this apparent self-annihilation, that everything else is given its meaning:

> When the half-gods go,
> The gods arrive.

When man by ceasing to be man becomes Man, then and then alone

> Not a worm is cloven in vain.

The author's interpretation of many of these poems may seem to be somewhat arbitrary, drawing out meanings never intended by the writers themselves. Within limits, this is not only excusable but necessary, and is justified not merely on general principles and analogy with other instances, for example Confucius' treatment of *The Odes*, but by the practice of the poets themselves, who often quarrelled about the meaning of their own poems or those of other poets. A very pertinent illustration is the contention that took place between Bashô and Kyorai concerning one of the latter's own poems, the following:

岩鼻やこゝにもひとり月の客

On the edge of this rock
Here is one more
Moon-viewer.

In 去來抄, *Records of Kyorai*, the following conversation is given:

Kyorai said, "Shadô[1] asserted that this must be a monkey, but what I intend is another person." Bashô retorted, "A monkey! What does he mean? What were you thinking when you composed the poem?" Kyorai answered, "As I was walking over the fields and mountains, singing under the light of the full moon, I found, on the edge of a rock, another man filled with poetical excitement." Bashô said, "In the phrase, 'There is one more person,' you announce yourself; in this there is poetry. I prize this verse and intend to include it in *Little Compositions of the Travelling Altar*."[2] My poetical taste is below the highest, but in Bashô's interpretation there is something fantastic, I think.

[1] Doctor of Osaka; Bashô's pupil.
[2] An anthology of his pupils' poetry that Bashô intended to publish, *Oi no Kobumi*.

去來曰、洒堂は此の句を月の猿とすべし
と申し侍れど、予は客まさりなんと申す。
先師曰、猿とは何事ぞ。汝此の句をいか
に思ひて作せるや。去來曰、明月に山野
を吟歩し侍るに岩頭亦一人の騷客を見付
けたりと申す。先師曰、「こゝにもひとり
月の客」と名乘り出でたらんこそ幾ばくの
風流ならぬ。たゞ自稱の句となすべし。
此の句は我も珍重して『笈の小文』に書入
れけるなん。予が趣向は一等下り侍りけ
り。先師の意をもて見れば少し狂者の感
もあるにや。

Quite apart from the question which of the two was right,
we have here the entertaining picture of Bashô telling Kyorai,
not what he ought to have said, but what he ought to have
meant by what he said.

APPENDICES

APPENDIX

I

WORK	AUTHOR
(A) HAIKU COMMENTARIES AND COLLECTIONS	
俳句辭典	大江圭虫
俳句大全	今井柏浦
古今名句評釋	矢田挿雲
俳諧名作集	穎原退藏
俳句讀本	高濱虚子
和歌選釋	松井博信
芭蕉講座（上）	｛穎原退藏　加藤楸邨
同　　　　（中）	｛同　上　　同　上
日本古典讀本芭蕉	穎原退藏
五元集全解	岩本梓石
蕪村句集講義	鳴雪、子規
（夏之部）	虚子、紅綠
蕪村夢物語（夏之部）	木村架空
蕪村俳句評釋	佐藤紅綠
蕪村名句評釋	河東碧梧桐

WORK	AUTHOR
一 茶 名 句 評 釋	勝 峯 晋 風
一 茶 俳 句 新 釋	川 島 露 石
一 茶 讀 本	荻 原 井 泉 水

(B) HAIKU: GENERAL	
新 選 俳 諧 辭 典	⎰岩 本 梓 石 ⎱宮 澤 朱 明
俳 諧 歳 時 記	小 島 伊 豆 海
俳 句 敎 程	荻 原 井 泉 水
芭 蕉 雜 纂	菊 山 當 年 男
俳 聖 芭 蕉	野 田 別 天 樓

(C) RELATED SUBJECTS	
和歌俳句の解釋と鑑賞	加 藤 一 郎
和 歌 選 釋	松 井 博 信
和 漢 朗 詠 集 新 釋	⎰金 子 元 臣 ⎱江 見 清 風
白 詩 新 釋	簡 野 道 明
唐 詩 選 詳 解	笠 松 彬 雄
菜 根 譚 講 話	釋 宗 演
老 子 の 新 研 究	井 上 秀 夫
莊 子 新 釋	坂 井 喚 三
日 本 の 生 花	西 川 一 草 亭

APPENDIX
II

THE HAIKU OF THIS VOLUME IN
ROMAN LETTERS

Preface

Page

viii Inu wo utsu   ishi no sate nashi   fuyu no tsuki.
Shizukasa ya   iwa ni shimiiru   semi no koe.
Sunahama ni   ashiato nagaki   haruhi kana.

x   Ochizama ni   mizu koboshikeri   hanatsubaki.
Akebono ya   mugi no hazue no   haru no shimo.
Ushi mô mô   mô to kiri kara   detari keri.
Ume ga ka no   tachinoborite ya   tsuki no kasa.

xi   Ezôshi ni   shizu oku mise no   haru no kaze.
xii   Ni-mon nagete   tera no en karu   suzumi kana.
Ni-mon nagete   tera no en karu   suzumi kana.

Section I The Spritual Origins of Haiku

Futa-mo to no   ume ni chisoku wo   aisu kana.

6   Samazuke ni   sodate-raretaru   kaiko kana.
6   Rusu no ma ni   aretaru kami no   ochiba kana.
7   Shira-uo ya   kuroki mewo aku   hô no ami.
8   Takotsubo ya   hakana i yume wo   natsu no tsuki.

Moro moro no   kokoro yanagi ni   makasu beshi.
Hasu-ike ya   orade sonomama   tamamatsuri.
Aki no iro   nukamiso-tsubo mo   nakari keri.
Ochiba eda ni   kaeru to mireba   kochô kana.

Page

11   Hana chitte   mata shizuka nari   enjyôji.
     Hana chiru ya   garan no hitsugi   otoshi yuku.
     Hana chiri te   ko no ma no tera to   nari ni keri.

12   Hana no kumo   kane wa ueno ka   asakusa ka.

23   Tei-zen ni   shiroku sakitaru   tsubaki kana.

24   Kitsutsuki mo   io wa yaburazu   natsu kodachi.

26   Saki midasu   mono no naka yori   hatsu-zakura.
     Kane kiete   hana no ka wa tsuku   yûbe kana.
     Hara naka ya   mono nimo tsukazu   naku hibari.
     Niwa haite   yuki wo wasururu   hôki kana.

27   Yama mo niwa mo   ugoki iruru ya   natsuzashiki.
     Hitoha chiru   totsu hitoha chiru   kaze no ue.

28   Minasoko no   iwa ni ochitsuku   ko-no-ha kana.
     No mo yama mo   yuki ni torarete   nani mo nashi.
     Minasoko wo   mite kita kao no   kogamo kana.

29   Tobikonda   chikarade ukabu   kawazu kana.

32   Umi kurete   kamo no koe honoka ni   shiroshi.

37   Yono naka ya   chôchô tomare   kaku mo are.

40   Kabe no mugi   yomogi sen-nen wo   warôto kaya.
     Kogarashi to   narinu katatsumuri no   utsusegai.

41   Sô asagao   iku shi ni kaeru   hô no matsu.

42   Morokoshi no   haikai towan   tobu kochô.
     Kimiya chô   ware ya sôshi no   yume-gokoro.

43   Okiyo okiyo   waga tomo ni sen   nuru kochô.

44   Yo mo sugara   arashi ni nami wo   hakobasete
     tsuki wo taretaru   shiogoshi no matsu.

Page

46 Horo horo to   yamabuki chiru ka   taki no oto.

47 Mizu-giwa mo   nakute furue no   shigure kana.

48 Yuku haru ya   tori naki uo no   me wa namida.

49 Saru wo kiku hito   sutego ni aki no   kaze ika ni.

50 Shôshô no   kari no namida ya   oboro-zuki.

51 Senzoku no   tarai mo morite   yuku haru ya.

52 Araumi ya   sado ni yokotô   ama no gawa.

63 Kufû shite   hana ni ranpu wo   tsurushi keri.

66 Sabishisa wo   toute kurenu ka   kiri hito-ha.

80 Tsuka mo ugoke   waga naku koe wa   aki no kaze.

Teni toraba   kien namida zo atsuki   aki no shimo.

Nadeshiko ni   kakaru namida ya   kusunoki no tsuyu.

Yagate shinu   keshiki mo miezu   semi no koe.

Ôkaze no   ashita mo akashi   tôgarashi.

81 Hatsu-yuki ya   suisen no ha no   tawamu made.

89 Kare-eda ni   karasu no tomarikeri   aki no kure.

94 Hatsushigure   saru mo komino wo   hoshige nari.

96 Uguisu ni   nari ga nita tote   misosazai.

98 Yoshi-ashi no   ha wo hisshiite   yûsuzumi.

Asagao ni   ware wa meshi kû   otoko kana.

Ôsaka no katamaru   koro ya   hatsuzakura.

Fuji hitotsu   uzumi nokoshite   wakaba kana.

Hi no hikari   kesa ya iwashi no   kashirayori.

99 Tomoshibi wo   mireba kaze ari   yoru no yuki.

Hane-oto sae   kikoete samushi   tsuki no yoru.

Asagao no   hana de fuitaru   iori kana.

100 Mata muda ni   kuchi aku tori no   manako kana.

Page
101　Katsuragi no　　kami ya sakura no　　asagaeri.
　　　Tô no yubi soroete　　matsu no　　midori kana.
　　　Matsuyani wo　　hanare kanete ya　　semi no koe.

102　Kuretake no　　yoyoni auhi no　　matsuri kana.

103　Ta ya mura ya　　hitogoe mo naki　　nochi no tsuki.

106　Omoi-kane　　imogari yukeba　　fuyu no yo no
　　　kawa-kaze samumi　　chidori naku nari.

107　Hana yorimo　　dango ya arite　　kaeru kari.

108　Haru-gasumi　　tatsu wo misutete　　yuku kari wa
　　　　hana naki sato ni　　sumi ya naraeru.

　　　Manmaru ni　　izuredo nagaki　　haruhi kana.

109　Atai araba　　nanika oshiman　　aki no kei.

111　Higekaze wo fuite　　boshû tanzuru wa　　tare ga ko zo.

112　Hito sumanu　　fuwa no sekiya no　　itabisashi
　　　arenishi nochi wa　　tada aki no kaze.

　　　Aki-kaze ya　　yabu mo hatake mo　　fuwa no seki.

113　Imo arau onna　　saigyô naraba　　uta yoman.

114　Musasabi no　　kotori hami-iru　　kare-no kana.
　　　Yo ni ireba　　naoshitaku naru　　tsugi-ho kana.
　　　Ômi no umi　　yûnami-chidori　　na ga nakeba
　　　kokoro mo shime ni　　inishie omôyu.

115　Negawaku wa　　hana no shita nite　　haru shinar
　　　　sono kisaragi no　　mochizuki no koro.
　　　Hotoke niwa　　sakura no hana wo　　tatematsure
　　　　waga nochi no yo wo　　hito toburawaba.
　　　Ura ura to　　nodokeki haru no　　kokoro yori
　　　　nihoi idetaru　　yamazakura kana.

Page

116   Kagiri naku   kanashiki mono wa   tomoshibi no
        kiete no nochi no   nezame nari keri.

        Shoku no hi wo   shoku ni utsusu ya   haru no yû.

117   Yamazato no   haru no yûgure   kitemireba
        iriai no kane ni   hana zo chiri keri.

        Honobono to   akashi no ura no   asagiri ni
        shima kakure yuku   fune wo shizo omou.

118   Hisakata no   ame no kaguyama   kono yûbe
        kasumi tanabiku   haru tatsurashi mo.

        Haru nare ya   namonaki yama no   usu-gasumi.

        Hingashi no   no ni kagerou no   tatsu miete
        kaeri misureba   tsuki katabuki nu.

119   Na-no-hana ya   tsuki wa higashi ni   hi wa nishi ni.

        Muragimo no   kokoro tanoshi mo   haru no hi ni
        tori no muragari   asobu o mireba.

120   Nabatake ni   hanami-gao naru   suzume kana.

        Rokugatsu ya   mine ni kumo oku   arashi-yama.

121   Ashibiki no   yamakawa nose no   naru nabe ni
        yuzuki gatake ni   kumo tachi wataru.

122   Sabishisa ni   yado o tachi idete   nagamureba
        izuko mo onaji   aki no yûgure.

        Yamazato no   inaha no kaze ni   nezameshite
        yofukaku shika no   koe o kiku kana.

        Omohoezu   kimaseru kimi a   sahogawa no
        kawazu kikasezu   kaeshitsuru kamo.

        Tazune kite   hana ni kuraseru   ko-no-ma yori
        matsutote mo naki   yamo no ha no tsuki.

123   Yamabe yori   kaeru wagami o   okuri-kite
        akureba mon o   tsuki mo iri keri.

Page

Hototogisu nakitsuru kata o nagamureba
tada ariake no tsuki zo nokoreru.

Hototogisu kieyuku kata ya shima hitotsu.

Kaze kaoru kure ya mariba no cha no kyûji.

124 Aoyagi ya waga ôkimi no kusa ka ki ka.

148 Nusubito wa nagabakama o ya kitaru ran
soba o torite zo hashiri sarinuru.

146 Hana no kage utai ni nitaru tabine kana.

147 Aoyagi ni kômori tsutau yûbae ya.

Michi no be ni shimizu nagaruru yanagi kage
shibashi tote koso tachidomari tsure.

149 U no mane wo u yori kôsha na kodomo kana.

152 Kome no naki toki wa hisago ni ominaeshi.

155 Shiragiku no me ni tatete miru chiri mo nashi.

Sôji shite hyôtan tataku ya sumi hokori.

156 Aki chikaki kokoro yosuru ya yojô han.

157 Matsumushi no rin tomo iwanu kuro chawan

159 Tomoshibi ni kôreru fude wo kogashi keri.

160 Ame ni orete homugi ni semaki komichi kana.

Section II Zen, The State of Mind for Haiku

163 Kiri-shigure fuji wo minu hi zo omoshiroku.

164 Chô kiete tamashii ware ni kaeri keri.

165 Koe bakari ochite ato naki hibari kana.

Page
166   Utaureba   ware mo hotoke mo   nakari keri
         namu amidabutsu   namu amidabutsu.

      Tatazumeba   tôku mo kikoyu   kawazu kana.

167   Aki fukaki   tonari wa nani wo   suru hito zo.

168   Honrai mo   naki inishie no   ware nareba
         shini-yuku kata mo   nani mo ka mo nashi.

      Go-roppon   yorite shidaruru   yanagi kana.

172   Uki ware wo   sabishi garaseyo   kankodori.

176   Ushi tsunde   wataru kobune ya   yû-shigure.

177   Nashi saku ya   ikusa no ato no   kuzure-ie.
      Na-no-hana ya   kujira mo yorazu   umi kurenu.

      Ku no shaba ya   sakura ga sakeba   saita tote.
      Aki no kure   hi ya tomosan to   toi ni kuru.

179   Ko no michi ya   iku hito nashi ni   aki no kure.

180   Nishi fukeba   higashi ni tamaru   ochiba kana.

182   Toshi kurenu   kasa kite waraji   hakinagara.
      Taorureba   taoruru mama no   niwa no kusa.

183   Tomokaku mo   anata makase no   toshi no kure.

185   Jiguruma no   todoro to hibiku   botan kana.
      Uroji yori   muroji e kaeru   hitoyasumi ·
         ame furaba fure   kaze fukaba fuke.
      Inazuma ya   kinô wa higashi   kyô wa nishi.

186   Kite mireba   koko mo kataku no   yado naru wo
         nani sumiyoshi to   hito no yûran.

187   Yoshi ashi to   omou kokoro o   furi-sutete
         tada nani mo naku   sumeba sumiyoshi.

Page

188   Kochi fukaba   nioi okoseyo   ume no hana
        aruji nashi tote   haru wo wasuru na.
      Yama mizu ni   kome wo tsukasete   hirune kana.
      Ôgi nite   shaku wo toraseru   botan kana.

192   Mono iwazu   kya ku to teishu to   shiragiku to.
      Yûbe no ureshisa   ashi arau toki no   futakoto mikoto.

193   Asamashi ya   mushi naku naka ni   ama hitori.
      Tai wa hana wa   minu sato mo ari   kyô no tsuki.

195   Yama no iro   tani no hibiki mo   mina-nagara
        waga shakamuni no   koe no ato kana.

196   Meigetsu ya   kusaki ni otoru   hito no kage.

197   Sate wa ano   tsuki ga naita ka   hototogisu.

199   Ta wo urite   itodo nerarenu   kawazu kana

204   Ganjitsu no   kokoro kotoba ni   amari keri.

205   Inazuma ni   satoranu hito no   tôtosa yo.

209   Medetasa mo   chûgurai nari   ora ga haru.
      Waga haru mo   jôjôkichi zo   ume no hana.

214   Manmaru ni   izuredo nagaki   haruhi kana.
      Tsuki ni e wo   sashitaraba yoki   uchiwa kana.
      Uta ikusa   bunbu nidô no   kawazu kana.

215   Hanaiki no   arashi mo shiroshi   kesa no fuyu.
      Saotome ya   yogorenu mono wa   uta bakari.
      Nete okite   ôakubi shite   neko no koi.
      Hige ni tsuku   meshi sae miezu   neko no koi.
      Osoroshi ya   ishigaki kuzusu   neko no koi.

216   Michi toeba   ichido ni ugoku   tauegasa.

Page

217   Uchiwa uri   sukoshi aoide   dashite mise.
      Kaminari wo   manete haragake   yatto sase.
      Naki monono   yô ni toraeru   tokoroten.

218   Tsuka mo ugoke   waga naku koe wa   aki no kaze.

219   Hiru mireba   kubisuji akaki'   hotaru kana.

220   Hebi nigete   ware wo mishi me no   kusa ni nokoru.
      Shiba no to ya   jô no kawari ni   katatsumuri.
      Kojiki kana   tenchi no kitaru   natsu-goromo.

221   Uguisu ga   ume no koeda ni   fun wo shite.
      Katatsumuri   soro soro nobore   fuji no yama.

222   Miyuki nimo   amigasa nuganu   kakashi kana.

223   Yûgao no   hana de hana kamu   musume kana.

224   Chichi-haha no   kotonomi omô   aki no kure.
      Yaribane ni   makeshi bijin no   ikari kana.

225   Akino yo ya   yume to ibiki to   kirigirisu.
      Sono hito no   ibiki sae nashi   aki no semi.

228   Kasa mo naki   ware wo shigururu   nanto nanto

229   Tada tanome   hana mo hara hara   ano tôri.
      Sabishisa no   ureshiku mo ari   aki no kure.

232   Mutto shite   modoreba niwa ni   yanagi kana.

235   Inu wo utsu   ishi no sate nashi   fuyu no tsuki.

239   Kokoro naki   mi nimo aware wa   shirare keri
      Shigi tatsu sawa no   aki no yûgure.

241   Michi no be no   mokuge wa uma ni   kuware keri.

242   Kimi hi take   yoki mono miseru   yukimaroge.
      Umasôna   yuki ga fûwari   fûwari to.
      Shigure keri   hashiriiri keri   hare ni keri.

Page
243   Sakura chiru   hisae yûbe to   nari ni keri.
Meigetsu ya   tada utsukushiku   sumiwataru.
Mireba kumori   mineba hareyuku   tsukimi kana.
Matsushima ya   aa matsushima ya   matsushima ya.

244   Hatsu-aki ya   umi mo aota no   hito midori.
Ko no atari   me ni miyuru mono wa   mina suzushi.
Kisha sugite   kemuri uzumaku   wakaba kana.

247   Yo wa ureshiku   hiru wa shizuka ya   haru no ame.
Hiyamizu ni   senbei ni-mai   chora ga natsu.

249   Degawari ya   osana-gokoro ni   monoaware.
Degawari ya   karakasa sagete   yû nagame.

250   Degawari ya   tatami e otosu   namida kana.
Kamikuzu ya   degawari no ato no   mono sabishi.

251   Oroshi oku   oi ni naefuru   natsuno kana.
Yûkaze ya   mizu aosagi no   hagi wo utsu.
Hae uchi ni   hana saku kusa mo   utare keri.

254   Rai harete   ichiju no yûhi   semi no koe.

259   Shibui toko   haha ga kui keri   yama no kaki.
Sanmon wo   gii to tozasu ya   aki no kure.
Ware yukeba   tomo ni ayuminu   tôkakashi.

260   Musasabi no   kotori hamiiru   kareno kana.

Section III Haiku and Poetry

270   Inazuma ni   koboruru oto ya   take no tsuyu.
271   Karakasa ni   oshimodosaruru   shigure kana.
272   Fune to kishi to   hanashi shiteiru   hinaga kana.

Page

277 Furuike ya   kawazu tobikomu   mizu no oto.

282 Kumiageru   mizu ni haru tatsu   hikari kana.

284 Ganjitsu ya   nanimo motomenu   yado no sama.
Degawari no   hana to kotaete   bikko nari.
Shiragiku ni   shibashi tayutau   hasami kana.
Kanashisa ya   tsuri no ito fuku   aki no kaze.

285 Hatake wo utsu   okina ga zukin   yugami keri.
Nusundaru   kakashi no kasa ni   ame kyû nari.
Muramura no   nedokoro fukenu   otoshi mizu.

286 Shingiku no   takô miekeri   asaborake.

277 Onozukara   atama ga sagaru nari   kamijiyama.

289 Kusa mura ya   na mo shiranu hana no   shiroku saku.

290 Kawahori no   futameki tobu ya   ume no tsuki.
Ume chiru ya   raden koboruru   taku no ue.

291 Shira-ume ya   kitano no chamise ni   sumai dori.
Ômon no   omoki tobira ya   haru no kure.

292 Sakana-ya ga   haitta mon wa   yanagi kana.
Kumo no mine   shiraho minami ni   muragareri.
Kumo no mine   suzuri ni ari no   nobori keri.
Na-no-hana ya   kujira mo yorazu   umi kurenu.

293 Ushibeya no   ushi no unari ya   oborozuki.
Semi naku ya   tsuku zuku akai   kazaguruma.
Tôyama ga   tsuki ni utsuru   tonbo kana.

294 Kiji tatte   hito odorokasu   kareno kana.
Rokudô no   tsuji ni tachi keri   kareno kana.
Hônen no   koe wo agekeri   kado no hae.
Se no hikuki   uma ni noru hi no   kasumi kana.

Page

Yamadera ya   hiki-zokonai no   kane kasumu.

Hikuki ki ni   uguisu naku ya   hiru sagari.

Fûrin no   naritsutsu negi   soyogi keri.

295   Wara-buki no   hokke no tera ya   keitô-bana.

Ningyô kizamu   komise ya   kiku no hana.

Tera miete   komichi no magaru   nogiku kana.

Iwashi-gumo   ten ni hirogori   hagi sakeri.

Izakaya no   kenka mushidasu   oborozuki.

Machinaka wa   mono no nioi ya   natsu no tsuki.

296   Neko no koi   yamu toki neya no   oborozuki.

Nagedashita   ashi no saki yori   kumo no mine.

Uguisu ya   take no koyabu ni   oi wo naku.

Haikan ni   niwatori asobu   fuyô kana.

Kaminari ni   koya wa yakarete   uri no hana.

313   Nanigoto no   owashi masu ka wa   shirane domo
            katajike nasa ni   namida koboruru.

314   Mi wo wakete   minu kozue naku   tsukusaba ya
            yorozu no yama no   haru ni au beki.

Furusato ya   heso no o ni naku   toshi no kure.

317   Hana ni somu   kokoro no ikade   nokori ken
            sutehateteki to   omou wagami ni.

Ôashita   mukashi fukitashi   matsu no kaze.

322   Imo wo niru   nabe no naka made   tsukiyo kana.

Aki fukaki   tonari wa nani wo   suru hito zo.

Kono michi ya   yuku hito nashi ni   aki no kure.

324   Sazare-nami   tagichite nagaru   tomase-gawa
            yorube naki iso no   saki ga sabushiki.

Kokoro naki   mi nimo aware wa   shirare keri
        shigi tatsu sawa no   aki no yûgure.

Section IV   The Four Great Haiku Poets

Page

330 Fuyu gomori   mata yori-sowan   kono hashira.

331 Meigetsu ya   ike o megurite   yo mo sugara.

Samushiro wo   hatake ni shiite   ume-mi kana.
Haru tatsu ya   aratoshi furuki   kome goshô.

332 Tare yara ka   sugata ni nitari   kesa no haru.
Asagao ni   ware wa meshi kû   otoko kana.

333 Kusa no to ni   ware wa tade kû   hotaru kana.
Tabi-sugata   shigure no tsuru yo   bashôô.
Nozarashi wo   kokoro ni kaze no   shimu mi kana.

334 Toshi no ichi   senkô kai ni   ideba yana.
Hatsu-sigure   saru mo komino wo   hoshige nari.

336 Aki wa kono   hôshi sugata no   yûbe kana.

337 Aki fukaki   tonari wa nani wo   suru hito zo.
Samidare wo   atsume te hayashi   mogami-gawa.
Samidare ya   na mo naki kawa no osoroshiki.

338 Ika uri no   koe magirewashi   hototogisu.
Suzushisa ya   kane wo hanaruru   kane no koe.
Ka no koe su   suikazura no hana   chiru goto ni.

339 Wakaba shite   mizu shiroku mugi   kibami tari.
Yûgao ya   ki ni saitaru mo   aru bekari.
Tsuki ni tôku   oboyuru fuji no   iroka kana.
Tsutsuji saite   katayamasato no   meshi shiroshi.
Kindachi ni   kitsune baketari   yoi no haru.
Kao shiroki   ko no ureshisa ya   makura-gaya.
Kôrô no   hokage ni shizumu   wakaba kana.

Page
340   Botan chitte   uchikasanarinu   futamihira.
Kirigirisu   jizai wo noboru   yosamu kana.
Kinbyô no   usumono wa tare ka   aki no kaze.
Furuike ya   kawazu tobikomu   mizu no oto.
Furuike ni   zôri shizumite   mizore kana.

345   Nomi-domo mo   yonaga darô zo   sabishi karo.

346   Yo no naka wa   ine karu koro ka   kusa no io.

348   Hitotsu-ya ni   yûjo mo netari   hagi to tsuki.
Hototogisu   akatsuki kasa wo   kawase keri.
Wakatake ya   hashimoto no yûjo   ariya nashi.
Kogarashi ya   nijû-yon-mon no   yûjo goya.

349   Funatsuki no   chisaki kuruwa ya   wata no hana.

Section V *The Technique of Haiku*

357   Waga koto to   dojô no nigeshi   nezeri kana.

361   Beta beta to   mono ni tsukitaru   haru no yuki.
Kiri-no-ki ya   tekibaki chitte   tsun to tatsu.

362   Haru no kaze   yanagi ga nakuba   fuku maizo.
Shôjô to   ishi ni hi no iru   kareno kana.

380   Tokoro dokoro   shika no kao dasu   shigemi kana.
Tsuridoko ni   irihi mori kuru   shigemi kana.
Mejirushi no   kyôboku shigeru   komura kana.
Yamabushi no   hora fuki tatsuru   shigeri kana.
Uekiya wa   kitarazu niwa no   shigemi kana.

381   Hashira nimo   narade shigerinu   gohyaku-nen.
Hito sumanu   kochû no shima no   shigeri kana.
Ichimon wa   mina shii goi no   shigeri kana.

Page

Haka no ki wa   shigerinu tamaya   kusaru ran.
Tengu sunde   ono irashimezu   ki no shigeri.

382   Tsuki hana ya   shijûku-nen no   muda aruki.

383   Musashino ya   sawaru mono naki   kimi no kasa.

384   Kokoro sumaseba   hayashi no oku no   shizuku nari.

387   Hi no haru wo   sasuga ni tsuru no   ayumi kana.

388   Tako-tsubo ya   hakanaki yume wo   natsu no tsuki.

389   Sukashi mite   hoshi ni sabishiki   yanagi kana.
Fuki tobasu   ishi wa asama no   nowaki kana.

390   Me ni aoba   yama hototogisu   hatsu-gatsuo.
Ama-gaeru   bashô ni norite   soyogi keri.
Akatsuki ya   u-kago ni nemuru   u no yatsure.

392   Iwa hana ya   koko nimo hitori   tsuki no kyaku.

APPENDIX
III

ORIGINS OF ENGLISH HAIKU

SPRING

1. Wordsworth, *Intimations.*
2. Wordsworth, *Written in Early Spring.*
3. Blake, *Milton.*
4. Milton, *L'Allegro.*
5. Shelley, *The Skylark.*
6. Davenant, *Who look for day.*
7. Shakespeare.
8. Scott, *The Lady of the Lake.*
9. Shelley, *The Skylark.*
10. Chaucer, *The Nun's Priest's Tale.*
11. Herbert, *Cockcrowing.*
12. Milton, *L'Allegro.*
13. Davies, *The Kingfisher.*
14. Aldington, *Images.*
15. Davies, *The Kingfisher.*
16. Housman, *A Shropshire Lad.*
17. Wordsworth.
18. Mitlay, *God's World.*
19. Wordsworth, *The Prelude.*
20. Shelley, *A Dream of the Unknown.*
21. Keats, *Endymion*, Bk. 1, 11. 15, 16.
22. Wordsworth, *The Cock is Crowing.*
23. Abercrombie, *Hymn to Love.*
24. Bridges, *A Passer-by.*

25. *John*, 1, 4.
26. Peacock, *Three Men of Gotham.*
27. Wordsworth, *The Prelude*, 4, 334.

SUMMER

1. E. G. Scott, *The Unnamed Lake.*
2. Shelley, *Written among the Euganean Hills.*
3. Shelley, *The Invitation.*
4. Blunt, *The Old Squire.*
5. *The Prelude.*
6. Wordsworth, *There was a boy.*
7. Robinson, *The Dark Hills.*
8. Arnold, *Bacchanalia.*
9. Thomson, *Hymn.*
10. Henley, *In a Hospital, Vigil.*
11. Arnold. *The Strayed Reveller.*
12. Byron, *The Prisoner of Chillon.*
13. Anon.
14. Marvell, *Thoughts in a Gardon.*
15. Davies, *A Great Time.*
16. Wordsworth.
17. Wordsworth, *Resolution and Independence.*
18. Collins, *Ode to Evening.*
19. *The Ancient Mariner.*
20. Scott, *The Lady of the Lake.*
21. Chaucer, *The Book of the Duchess.*
22. Davies, *The Moon.*
23. Burns, *The Banks of Doon.*
24. Emerson.
25. Shelley, *The Recollection.*

26. Byron, *Childe Harold's Pilgrimage.*
27. Blunt, *The Old Squire.*
28. Thoreau, *A Week.*
29. Whitman.
30. Shakespeare, *They that have power to hurt.*
31. Davies.
32. Keats, *The Realm of Fancy.*
33. Marvell, *Song of the Emigrants.*
34. Wordsworth, *Lucy.*

AUTUMN

1. Wordsworth, *Intimations.*
2. *The Ancient Mariner.*
3. Francis Thompson, *Sister Songs.*
4. Whitman, *Out of the Cradle.*
5. A. Lowell, *Wind and Silver.*
6. Arnold, *Mycerinus.*
7. Tennyson, *Ulysses.*
8. Shelley.
9. Arnold, *In Utrumque Paratus.*
10. Arnold, *Rugby Chapel.*
11. Thoreau, *A Week.*
12. Susan Gaspell, *The Morning is near us.*
13. De La Mare, *Farewell.*
14. Langston Hughes, *Homesick Blues.*
15. Landor, *The Maid's Lament.*
16. Sassoon, *The Dug-out.*
17. *The Excursion.*
18. Morris, *Summer Dawn.*
19. Bryant, *To a Waterfowl.*

WINTER

1. Shelley.
2. *The Prelude.*
3. Wordsworth, *Written iu Early Spring.*
4. *The Prelude.*
5. Wordsworth, *Ode to Duty.*
6. Thoreau, *Walden.*
7. Landor.
8. C. French, *Hidden Sorrow.*
9. C. Bronte, *The Visionary.*
10. *The Excursion,* 409.
11. Odgen Marsh, *Old Man.*
12. Housman, *Eight O'clock.*
13. Thoman Nash, *Litany in Time of Plague.*
14. Masefield, *On Growing Old.*
15. 16. 17. H. Monroe, *Solitude.*
18. Lawrence, *The Man Who Died.*

INDEX OF WRITERS

(excluding Appendix III)

初版発行

再版発行

呉竹の
よゝり
あをゝ
まつ
うる